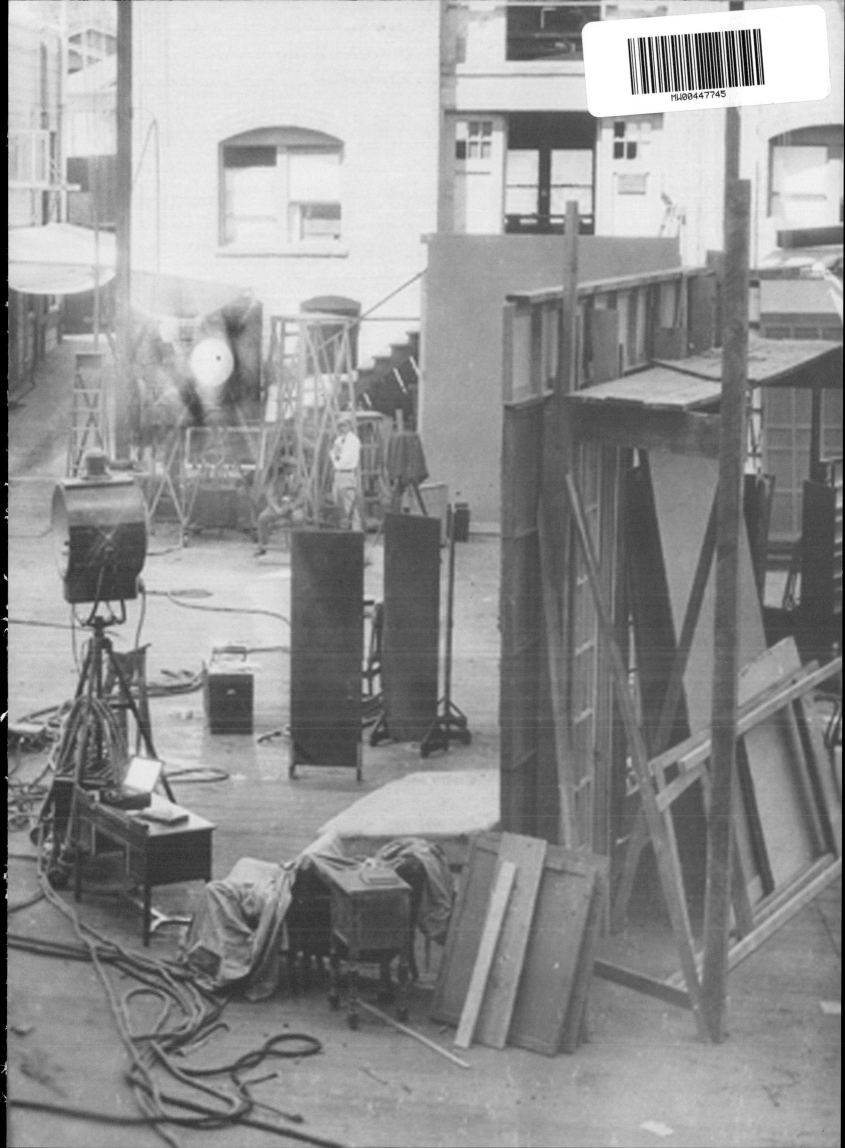

SILENT MOVIES

COMING
ROBERT WARWICK
and DORIS KENYON in
"A Girl's Folly"

SILENT MOVIES

THE BIRTH OF FILM AND THE TRIUMPH OF MOVIE CULTURE

Peter Kobel and the Library of Congress

FOREWORD **by Martin Scorsese** INTRODUCTION **by Kevin Brownlow**

LITTLE, BROWN AND COMPANY
NEW YORK BOSTON LONDON

CONTENTS

Beau Geste, starring Ronald Colman (1926).

To David W. Packard, in recognition of his support of
film preservation at the Library of Congress

"ME FOR NEW YORK NOW."
Morgan Litho Co
3536 CLEVELAND, O.U.S.A.
THE SENSATIONAL FEATURE
THE STREETS OF NEW YORK
IN 3 PARTS
FROM THE WELL KNOWN PLAY BY DION BOUCICAULT.
PILOT FILMS

FOREWORD  Martin Scorsese

The cinema is now more than 110 years old, and everyone is more or less in agreement about its value as an art form. Or so it would seem.

I am still shocked by the fact that 90 percent of the films made during the silent era have disintegrated. That means movies starring Greta Garbo, Clara Bow, and Conrad Veidt, and directed by King Vidor and F. W. Murnau — those films and countless others are now lost to us forever, and there are many others in danger of *being* lost. We can't afford to lose any more. When I look at a picture like *Beyond the Rocks*, the recently unearthed Valentino-Swanson film directed by Sam Wood, I marvel at the sheer beauty and sophistication of silent cinema. Yet, locating old and rare prints and transferring them to safety stock is not the only task of preservationists. More recent works are also in danger, victims of decomposing film stock, color fading, and other forms of deterioration.

We are constantly reminded of the glory of movies, the beauty of movies, and yet we continue to allow them to disintegrate; for every carefully preserved title, there is another that has been rescued from oblivion at the very last minute, ten more that are in danger of disappearing, and twenty more that are already gone. We have made progress, of course. There are many dedicated preservationists out there who have devoted their lives to the cinema's restoration and maintenance; to me, they are heroes. Moreover, we now have what I would call a "film preservation consciousness." But there is still a widespread assumption that movies will just take care of themselves, and nothing could be further from the truth.

As I was reading *Silent Movies*, I was overwhelmed once again by the wonder of cinema, and by the urgent need to preserve it on a systematic basis. I became a sort of time traveler through the lost and forgotten titles of the silent film era. After wandering through these pages of precious images, you may begin to wonder why the passion for film preservation has not grown. Drawing on the extraordinary collection of the Library of Congress, one of the greatest repositories for silent film and memorabilia, *Silent Movies* serves as an introduction to the early days of the film industry, both in the United States and internationally. The lobby cards, stills, and other images — some of them drawn from the Library's collection of paper prints and early titles — provide some of the few existing records of the earliest American films.

Many of the films featured in *Silent Movies* are part of the National Film Registry and provide a sampling of our rich and varied movie history. Saving these and other landmark pictures benefits everyone — the public at large, and the memory of their creators. Ongoing preservation of movies is really a tribute to all of us, for the arts — *all* the arts — are as necessary to us and to our well-being as the food we eat and the air we breathe.

INTRODUCTION  Kevin Brownlow

It used to be the fashion to regard all progress as benevolent and to pity the inhabitants of the past who were denied it. Today we look back nostalgically to a world without pollution and express admiration for old-fashioned craftsmanship. What we would really like, of course, is all of today's advantages and all of yesterday's as well.

As far as silent films are concerned, few would give up wide screens, color, and Dolby sound for the fitful pleasures of the nickelodeon. But thanks to new technology, more and more silents are appearing on DVD, and in the best of them a new generation is discovering a surprising degree of skill, imagination, and sometimes genius. Turner Classic Movies in the United States and Arte in Europe show silents on television. Festivals devoted to silent films are held regularly in Europe and the United States.

When these festivals started, rare prints used to come out of the archives without intertitles, with reels in the wrong order, and with appalling image quality. One wondered what such organizations had been doing all these years. The worst were the so-called paper prints, primitive films so badly printed on 16mm that they suggested a shocking degree of incompetence on the part of the early filmmakers. Had they managed to capture only the sort of jiggling, blurred picture you get with a defective television? Of course not, but who would have believed the original image quality had been first rate and that it was only the copying that had been incompetent? (Ironically, the man responsible received an Oscar for his pains.)

The Library of Congress is gradually recopying these precious early films on 35mm, as had been tentatively done originally. The difference is amazing. Yet far too many silent films still survive in prints that make nonsense of the work the original technicians put into them. They took immense care with the photographic quality in the silent days because it was all they had. A silent film depended on its visuals; as soon as you degrade those, you lose elements that go far beyond the image on the surface. You remove the possibility of enjoyment. A film that seems dull in a poor dupe can leap to life in a first-class print.

This is being understood today as methods of viewing films improve, but ineptly produced videos and DVDs still set back the reputation of silent films. The very word *silent* suggests that something is missing. But if you see a silent film as it was meant to be seen, with live music, you certainly will not feel it is in any way inferior to a talkie. (A crashing chord from a symphony orchestra outdoes even Dolby stereo!)

I was associated with the public presentation of silent films, with David Gill and composer Carl Davis, for twenty years. It was thrilling to discover how the films were transformed when they were put back into their natural environment. And it was equally thrilling to hear unsolicited raves from members of the audience. It all cost a fortune, but we were sponsored by Thames Television and, later, Channel Four, and they got their money back by distributing the films around the world.

As far as modern audiences are concerned, admiration is most easily expressed for the comedies. People inevitably declare a preference for Chaplin or Keaton or Lloyd and imply that by liking one you have to dismiss the others. My late filmmaking partner David Gill used to counter this by saying: "In the eighteenth century, do you think people said 'I love Haydn, but I can't abide Mozart or Beethoven'? Hardly. They were privileged to have so many artists of genius."

Enthusiasm for dramas is more restrained. This is partly because so many silent dramas are unobtainable, shackled by copyright restrictions. The Library of Congress will not thank me for saying it, but the remaining copyright on silent films should be eliminated so that they can be made as easily available as the classics of literature. Otherwise they will perish — just as thousands did years ago at the hands of studios and distributors who had no further use for them.

Ironically, the very studios that destroyed the films invariably renewed their rights, so if you manage to find a print and want to use it in a television documentary, they blithely charge you six thousand dollars a minute.

The silent era was a period of immense creativity, and there seems to be no end to its surprises. But you have to be careful. The period produced just as many bad films as any other. The poverty-row studios churned out films cynically for theaters catering to "transients" — a term covering anyone from railroad passengers to tramps. Some were made with big names — a star would be hired for one day and a series of all-purpose close-ups would be taken and fitted into the plot, no matter how stupid that plot may have been. The object was to fill five or six reels as swiftly and as cheaply as possible. If you spot any of these, produced by companies with names like Aywon or Mastodon or Chesterfield, avoid them like the plague. With 80 percent of silent films lost, these films stubbornly survive. No one wanted them back. They often crop up at silent-film festivals presented with a respect they do not deserve. They are a curse on film history.

I am not talking about routine releases, for in that classification are some of the most beautiful films ever made. My love affair with silent pictures, which has lasted longer than the silent era itself, owes a great deal to a routine release.

I was born too late to see silents when they were new. I first saw them at a boarding school in Sussex just after the war, where the only enjoyable event was the film show given by the headmaster every third Sunday in the winter. He had no sound projector — he showed us the films of our parents' generation.

One evening I was in my usual place, squatting on the floor as close to the machine as I could get, when the projector jammed. In repairing the film, the headmaster tore off a few frames, and they landed next to me. As soon as the show was over, I rushed to the dormitory, picked up my flashlight, and held it against that scrap of film, expecting to see a theater-quality image on the wall. I was dismayed that it remained blurred until I was a few millimeters away. Nevertheless, the fact that you could convert a room into a cinema seemed to me a miracle.

I badgered my parents for a projector, and dutifully, they gave me one the following Christmas — a Pathescope Ace 9.5mm hand-cranked projector and two short films. I ran through these very quickly and set out to find more. By now we had moved to London, and with television just coming in, you could buy old films in junk shops. The first I bought still gives me a frisson of delight whenever I think of it — even though it was heavily abridged for home-movie release and its title changed.

It was called *The First Man*. My parents had been keen filmgoers, and my mother instantly recognized Douglas Fairbanks. Even I had heard of Douglas Fairbanks, and the film was fresh and delightful, although judging by the cars, it had been made a good thirty years before. It combined parody of the nouveau riche with high adventure — gunrunning in the Mexican revolution. Fairbanks played an effete butterfly hunter, a ruse to investigate the gunrunning. The titles were witty — "I am Mrs. Budheiser — you know, Budheiser, the brewers?" "Please! We're distillers!" — and the cinematography was scintillating. Fairbanks used a hydroplane (an early version of a seaplane) and drove a primitive-looking sports car. At one point his hat blew off. To impress the girl (Jewel Carmen), he leaped from the car, raced after the hat, and then sprinted back, jumping behind the wheel with that insouciant Fairbanks grin.

I went to my local library, imagining that I could take a book from the shelf and find out all about my film. There was precisely one film book: *The History of Motion Pictures*, by Brasillach Bardeche. As I took it from the shelf, it fell open at a picture of my Fairbanks film, giving it the correct title: "Fairbanks's biggest success came in 1916, when he made *American Aristocracy*, playing the part of a southerner of good family, who collects butterflies, becomes acquainted with some snobbish Easterners and gets involved with all sorts of melodramatic adventures. A lot of airplane work was entailed and even acrobatics on a hydroplane." My very first film was important enough to appear in a book! This was so remarkable I was compelled to find out more about it.

Someone told me about the British Film Institute, and in its library I found an index to the films of D. W. Griffith, who had nominally supervised the picture. It told me that Anita Loos had written the script, Lloyd Ingraham had directed, and Victor Fleming, the man who would direct *Gone with the Wind*, had photographed it. It also gave me the cast, which I can recite to this day: Charles Stevens, Arturo Ortiega, Lillian Langdon; the villain, Percy Peck, a malted milk manufacturer, was played by Albert S. Parker.

When I first joined the film industry, fifty years ago, I kept hearing of an actors' agency called Al Parker Ltd. Having a one-track mind, I knew this was *my* Albert Parker, and so I rang him up.

"Did you ever act with Douglas Fairbanks?" I asked.

"Act with him? Why, I directed him."

I had no idea that Parker had been responsible for Fairbanks's Technicolor swashbuckler *The Black Pirate* (1926). When I told him of my film, he asked me to bring it to his flat in Mayfair. As I projected it on the wall for Parker, his wife — the actress Margaret Johnston — came in. She was so enchanted by the vision of her husband as a young man, impeccably dressed in white ducks, that she asked me back to run the film at a dinner party.

Parker, now in his seventies, was a tough old bird who had been a close friend of John Barrymore's. He entertained me for hours with stories of Broadway and early Hollywood. When I found a 16mm print of another of his films, *Eyes of Youth* (1919), with Clara Kimball Young and a little-known actor from Italy, he invited his clients, such as James Mason and Trevor Howard, and told us all about discovering Valentino. On another occasion he arranged for me to meet Douglas

Fairbanks Jr., who appeared in his first role, in *American Aristocracy*, as a chubby five-year-old selling newspapers, and who told me marvelous stories about the silent days.

I became a silent-film historian through finding that little film. It struck me that had I been a student of literature and Scott Fitzgerald and Hemingway were still alive, I would have flown to America at the first opportunity. And so I booked a flight in 1964, and in ten days in Hollywood, I tape-recorded twenty-eight interviews with everyone from Buster Keaton to Gloria Swanson.

My excuse for meeting these people was that I was writing a book. I had no intention of writing anything, and a book was far too much like hard work. But one interview, with an associate of D. W. Griffith's, demolished so many myths, and revealed so much that was new, that it forced me to haul out the typewriter. The final result appeared in 1968, and I called it *The Parade's Gone By. . . .* It was dedicated to Abel Gance, a French director who had never been to Hollywood but who had made my favorite silent film, *Napoléon* (1927). He revered D. W. Griffith.

Griffith had been excoriated for the racism in *The Birth of a Nation* (1915). It is a tragedy that the American cinema's first great masterpiece should lionize the Ku Klux Klan. But those who removed Griffith's name a few years ago from the Lifetime Achievement Award of the Director's Guild betray their ignorance of his other films. In *Rose of Kentucky* (1911), the KKK is depicted as a group of villains, and the besieged civilians are saved by a black boy. *Birth* was based on a famous play and a couple of novels; Griffith toned down the racism considerably, although the film is still highly inflammatory. His *Broken Blossoms* (1919) dealt with racial prejudice toward Chinese immigrants and *Intolerance* with religious persecution, brutality toward strikers, and gangsterism. Griffith was a social reformer despite his avowed contempt for reformers.

I found that the veterans still venerated his name. When I pointed out that in film history Griffith's was the one name you heard repeated again and again, and that everything he did was supposed to be "genius," they gently explained how important he had been in leading the industry. The next generation of directors — King Vidor, Henry King — acknowledged all they had learned from Griffith, even as they surpassed him.

These veterans were the most remarkable people I have ever encountered. They were wonderful storytellers and witty conversationalists, and many became lifelong friends. I think they were surprised that an Englishman in his twenties should be so excited about what they had done half a century before. But by now I had progressed from 9.5mm to 16mm, and my respect for their achievements had increased as the range of their work became more apparent. And because I had tried filmmaking myself and had found out how difficult it was, I knew what they had been up against.

I was fascinated to find out that so many of the great figures of the silent era — Griffith, Sennett, Chaplin, Keaton, Garbo — with very little conventional schooling, had been self-taught, intuitive. "Uneducated but intelligent," as Peter Kobel puts it. (How ironic that their work is so often taught in an academic language that would baffle them!)

What excited me was that most of them had retained their enthusiasm for film. Occasionally, someone had been so long out of the business that it took an effort just to get them to remember. I found the best method was to show them their films. Thanks to a collector friend in California, I was able to bring Reginald Denny back together with his comedy *Skinner's Dress Suit* (1926), and I was taken aback at how surprised he was. A myth had built up around silent films that was parroted by my generation — they were jerky, flickery, poorly photographed, badly acted curiosities — and he had come to believe it.

They were jerky because, with the coming of sound, everything had to be projected at twenty-four frames per second. There was no standard silent speed, but early films were projected around sixteen frames per second, and to show these at twenty-four made them look ridiculous. By the late 1910s, many pictures were cranked at twenty to twenty-two and projected slightly faster. According to a senior engineer, when sound arrived, Western Electric took the average of theaters on Broadway — twenty-two to twenty-six frames per second — and decided on twenty-four.

They didn't flicker once it became apparent that three-bladed shutters were required for anything below eighteen frames per second. And as for poor photography, I have been amazed at the high standard of cinematography in silent films — so long as you see a print made from something close to the original negative. It was the endless copying that had produced the dreadful soot and whitewash we all associate with early Chaplin. But look at those films when printed from the original negative, and they are as sharp as a tack, with the full tonal range. This art did not sweep the world by using prints no one could see.

And as for the acting, look for yourself at the skill and subtlety. Yes, there was overacting — players responded to the story, and if it was melodrama, they would act in the style demanded. But in a realistic story — *The Crowd* or *Are Parents People?* — they were as naturalistic as Bogart or Bacall.

The silent era has never ceased to surprise me. Just when I feel I have seen everything, a film comes from left field that upsets all my assumptions. Sometimes the Pordenone Silent Film Festival in Italy will act like an alcoholic's cure, and after a couple of days, you may see so many boring films you feel you never want to look at another frame. But persevere, and you will inevitably see something so extraordinary that your faith will be renewed and your enthusiasm increased.

This book is an ideal introduction to the silent cinema. It takes an incredibly complicated series of events, such as the first few years of cinema, lays them out so we can understand them, and then sails on, keeping our interest through a genuine enthusiasm for the subject.

As my idol Abel Gance told me in 1967, "The cinema is a flame obliterating the shadows. And let me add, it is essential to have enthusiasm. No great work can be achieved without enthusiasm."

Glass slides (or lantern slides, as they were originally called) were used as pauses when reels were being worked on or changed. They were also known as "etiquette" slides because of the lighthearted instructions for patrons' behavior when viewing the show.

From
Magic Lantern to
Moving Pictures

The Technology of Film

ALTHOUGH THE FRENCH, THAT NATION OF CINEPHILES, AND THE AMERICANS, WHO HAVE COME TO DOMINATE THE FILM SCREENS OF THE GLOBE, BOTH LAY CLAIM TO THE INVENTION OF CINEMA, THE BIRTHRIGHT OF FILM CANNOT FAIRLY BE CREDITED TO ANY ONE INDIVIDUAL OR NATION. FILM'S ORIGIN SPRANG FROM A VARIETY OF PURSUITS AND PASSIONS — JUST LIKE THE ART OF THE CINEMA TODAY, IT DEPENDED ON A MIX OF ART AND SCIENCE, BUSINESS AND TECHNOLOGY — AND FROM MYRIAD REMARKABLE PEOPLE WHO, SOMETIMES WORKING TOGETHER, SOMETIMES COMPETING FIERCELY, WERE RESPONSIBLE FOR THE CONCEPTION OF MOVING PICTURES.

Top: French brothers Auguste and Louis Lumière's experimental breakthrough, the Cinématographe, had a mechanism like that in the drive device of a sewing machine. It was lightweight, compact, and versatile for shooting, printing, and projection.

Bottom: The Lumière brothers' short film *Leaving the Lumière Factory* (1895).

Left: Poster of Edison's Greatest Marvel, the Vitascope (1896).

Three things were essential to developing projected motion pictures as we know them today: a camera with a sufficiently high shutter speed to freeze motion, a filmstrip capable of taking multiple exposures swiftly, and a means of projecting the developed images on a screen. The race to achieve that goal reached a fever pitch in the 1890s, and the first to cross the finish line was France.

On March 22, 1895, the brothers Auguste and Louis Lumière gave a historic public showing of a projected film (the instrument did not yet have a name but later became known as the Cinématographe) at the Société d'Encouragement pour l'Industrie Nationale. Louis Lumière showed a number of slides, some of them colored. But the small audience was more interested in the brothers' short film, called *Leaving the Lumière Factory*. The wonder-filled audience demanded that the film, which depicted workers leaving the Lumières' Lyons factory at dinnertime, consisting of some eight hundred photographs and lasting one minute, be shown again.

One month later, on April 21, the first projected movie shown publicly in America was screened in New York City. Using a device originally called the Panoptikon and subsequently the Eidoloscope — the names of many of these early devices seem straight out of science fiction — the brothers Otway and Gray Latham showed a film to guests and reporters at their workshop on Frankfort Street. According to the *New York Sun*, it "portrayed the antics of some boys at play in a park. They wrestled, jumped, fought, and tumbled over one another. Near where the boys were romping a man [played by the Lathams' father, Woodville] sat reading a paper and smoking a pipe. Even the puffs of smoke could be plainly seen."

Thomas Edison, who had developed the Kinetoscope, a movie peep show for individuals, was furious and threatened a lawsuit. It would not be until a year later, on April 23, 1896, that "the wizard of Menlo Park" would publicly present projected films, which he did using the Vitascope projector at Koster and Bial's Music Hall at Thirty-fourth Street and Broadway. Macy's department store is located there now, and the event is memorialized with a plaque.

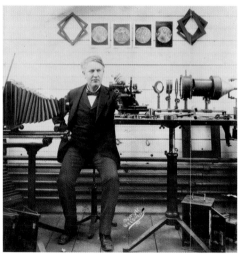

Top: An open Kinetoscope, 1891. Customers could start the machines for a nickel or a dime and watch moving pictures through a peephole.

Bottom: Thomas Edison.

On May 20, 1895, the Lathams beat both Edison and the French when they opened a public exhibition space, at 156 Broadway, where for a few pennies, patrons could watch movies. And what could one see? According to a newspaper account: "You'll sit comfortably and see fighters hammering each other, circuses, suicides, hangings, electrocutions, shipwrecks. . . . Almost anything, in fact, in which there is action, just as if you were on the spot during the actual events."

So if the French were the first to project films publicly, the Americans were the first to create a business to make money from it. (The Lumières debuted their first projection theater on December 28, 1895, in the Grand Café on the Boulevard des Capucines, featuring several films, and all of Paris was soon abuzz; they toured their films in London and New York the following year.) Still, from a broader historical view, these accomplishments seem like the equivalent of a photo finish. The elements that could make cinema a reality were falling into place, and many cinematic alchemists were turning them to gold. The Lumières, as it turned out, were not even the first in Europe to project films for a paying audience. The German Max Skladanowsky, who invented a motion-picture camera and a projector, which he called the Bioskope, inched them out with a film showing at the Berlin Wintergarten, on November 1, 1895.

Something was certainly in the air. The turn of the century was a period of tremendous technological development, firing imaginations with visions of speed. Marconi invented wireless telegraphy in 1895, and the Wright brothers would take flight in 1903 — it's no wonder that even pictures had to move. And it's hardly surprising that early cinema was obsessed with trains and cars, powerful imagery of acceleration.

Still, in the run-up to film projection, no one really seems to have had a sense of the immensity of what was being created — the seventh art form, which would in many ways change the world. In part that was because film projection came about incrementally and would never have been possible without the multiple breakthroughs that preceded it. One such milestone was certainly when Edison first publicly demonstrated the popular and profitable Kinetoscope, which permitted individuals to watch moving pictures through a peephole, in 1891. But before Edison and his younger colleague, William Kennedy-Laurie Dickson, a photographer and inventor who led the team that developed the Kinetoscope, came many others.

Among them was the English photographer Eadweard Muybridge, who in the 1870s developed series photography showing animals in motion, using multiple cameras. In 1882, in France, French physiologist Étienne-Jules Marey, using a camera shaped like a rifle called the Chronophotographic Gun, shot the first series of photos taken by a single camera in order to study the motion of birds and bats in flight.

One could go back further, to the early developments in photography. In 1839, Louis-Jacques-Mandé Daguerre developed the photographic process of the daguerreotype. (Daguerre opened Dioramas in London and Paris, projecting his images on huge screens, sometimes accompanied

Top: Flying ducks captured on paper film by Étienne-Jules Marey.

Bottom: Marey used his Chronophotographic Gun to study animal motion, creating an important body of work on human, bird, and animal movement.

by live music, which could legitimately be considered the ancestors of cinemas.) An Englishman, William Henry Fox Talbot, demonstrated a negative photographic process that allowed multiple reproductions from a negative. Obviously, without photography, there would be no cinema.

The idea of projecting images goes back to the seventeenth century: in 1646, Athanasius Kircher published the first description of the magic lantern in print, in *Ars Magna Lucis et Umbrae*. Using concave glass, the magic lantern was the first apparatus capable of projecting images and was widely used in Europe. In 1665, Samuel Pepys wrote about one in his diary: "Comes by agreement Mr. Reeves bringing me a lanthorn, with pictures in glass, to make strange things on a wall, very pretty."

Perhaps a good place to start, however, is with the basic principle that makes moving pictures possible, called the persistence of vision, which was first described in an 1824 paper by the English polymath Peter Mark Roget. Roget was primarily interested in medicine, but he is best known for his thesaurus, which was first printed in 1852 and has never since been out of print. Because the brain retains images cast on the retina for a fraction of a second after they disappear, Roget asserted that viewing sixteen images per second conveys the impression of motion. While he didn't pursue the notion, he inspired a number of inventors who created toylike machines that produced the illusion of motion. In 1832, the Phenakistoscope, invented simultaneously by the Belgian Joseph Plateau and the Austrian Simon von Stampfer, created motion pictures with phased drawings presented on a revolving disk. Two years later William George Horner developed the Zoetrope, which presented images with a rotating drum.

Ottomar Anschütz used chronophotographs to re-create movement with a device called the Electrotachyscope (1887).

There would be no cinema, however, until photographic processes were sufficiently advanced. The art of photography — portraits, landscapes, cityscapes — improved steadily in the second half of the century, and those improvements came from scientists and artists.

Eadweard Muybridge (born Edward James Muggeridge — he changed his name several times) was the embodiment of both. A skilled landscape photographer, the English émigré was commissioned in 1872 by Leland Stanford, railroad magnate and California governor, to photograph his racehorse Occident at his Palo Alto ranch. Stanford believed that a trotting horse at some point in its stride had all four feet off the ground. A popular story, probably apocryphal, is that the avid horse breeder and racer made a bet for twenty-five thousand dollars to back up his theory. By April 1873 — the exact date is uncertain — Muybridge had produced an image of the horse with all four hooves off the ground. The photograph has since vanished without a trace.

Muybridge's motion studies were interrupted by an unfortunate turn of events. On October 17, 1874, Muybridge shot his wife's lover, Harry Larkyns. Muybridge suspected Larkyns of being the father of his wife's child. Although several people witnessed the incident, Muybridge's lawyers entered an insanity defense, and Muybridge was acquitted of first-degree murder the following year. After the acquittal, he embarked on a photographic expedition in Mexico and Central America.

In 1877, Muybridge resumed his motion studies of horses for Stanford, and over the next two years he perfected his technique. An engineer for Stanford's Central Pacific Railway, John D. Isaacs, designed electromagnetic shutters for Muybridge's cameras, which were triggered by trip wires stretching across the track to create a series of images showing the horse in motion. With shutter speeds of about 1/500th of a second, Muybridge succeeded in definitively proving that a trotting horse does at times have all four hooves off the ground. With Stanford's continued support, he made serial photographs of other animals in motion, such as deer and oxen.

Muybridge traveled and lectured widely, often using his Zoopraxiscope, which allowed him to project moving images by using sixteen-inch disks with photographic or painted images based on his photographs. He made some of his most important motion studies under the auspices of the University of Pennsylvania, from 1884 to 1887, where he produced serial photographs of men and women, clothed and nude. Although his purpose was ostensibly scientific, he was surely not unaware of the erotic frisson of presenting nude women, some of whom were hired prostitutes, in what was then still the Victorian era. At the same time, he didn't hesitate to portray himself walking naked, looking healthful with a purposeful stride, erect military posture, and a long gray beard. In a Darwinian spirit, he published many of these photos of humans and animals in motion together in 1887 under the title *Animal Locomotion, An Electro-Photographic Investigation of Consecutive Phases of Animal Movement*.

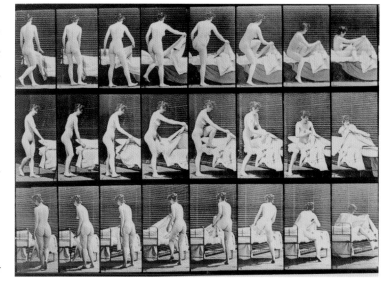

Eadweard Muybridge published many of his research photographs, analyzing the movements of horses, other animals, and humans, in 1887. He also developed the Zoopraxiscope, a device that projected moving images of animals.

Marey's Chronophotographic gun was an advance over Muybridge's technique in that it involved a single camera and a single point of view. (Muybridge's serial photographs of Occident, when shown in cinematic fashion, make the horse look like it is running in place.) Marey's serial photography advanced to the panning shot. Much of Marey's work now looks almost surreal: he would, for instance, dress a person entirely in black, with strips of metal outlining the body, so that the camera would record only the reflective metal.

Like Muybridge, Marey had a scientific purpose. But Muybridge, often called "the father of motion pictures," and Marey were both really more interested in stopping motion than in creating moving pictures.

Although his work was more in the realm of animation than live-action cinema, Frenchman Émile Reynaud developed his Praxinoscope, which used a rotating drum, prismatic mirrors, and projection. Reynaud was a genuine artist, using lithographic strips to create beautiful animations of, for instance, a juggler, a girl skipping rope, and little dogs jumping through a hoop. He first presented his invention to the Société Française de Photographie in 1880.

But film as we know it today needed a photographic process that would make shooting multiple images simpler and faster. That became possible by using celluloid film. In May 1887, Hannibal Goodwin, an Episcopalian minister in Newark, New Jersey, filed a patent for celluloid "photographic film." In April 1889, Harry M. Reichenbach and the Eastman Photographic Materials Co.

Émile Reynaud's Praxinoscope, which used a rotating drum and a prismatic mirror to project lithographic strips of animated images, was a great success at his Optical Theater, as seen in this 1892 engraving from *La Nature*.

filed a new patent, and Eastman began production of filmstrips in Rochester, New York. Celluloid film rolls, strong and flexible, proved an ideal medium for moving pictures. They had, however, a serious drawback, which not only greatly diminished a worldwide treasure but complicated the lives of film historians: celluloid film, composed of methyl alcohol, camphor, nitrocellulose, and acetate, was highly flammable. It also decayed over time, so much of the work of the silent era has been irretrievably lost.

From the late 1880s to the mid 1890s, the race to create moving pictures accelerated after the development of sensitized paper strips. In 1888, Marey used the celluloid strip to create moving pictures shot at twenty images per second. His camera used essentially the same principles movie cameras today use, although his lacked pins and the filmstrips were unperforated. Over the next few years, with his colleague Georges Demenÿ, Marey produced a number of films, including people exercising, naked cyclists, and a menagerie of animals, such as dogs, cats, foxes, birds, insects, and fish.

Louis Aimé Augustin Le Prince, a Frenchman who worked in England and the United States as well as France, developed a camera using a sensitized strip of paper wound onto a wheel. In 1888, he made two films — one showing his mother-in-law in a Leeds garden and the other a view of the traffic on a Leeds bridge. The mystery surrounding Le Prince's disappearance — he boarded a train in Dijon bound for Paris on September 16, 1890, but never arrived and was never seen again — has somewhat eclipsed his professional contributions. In the history of the silent film, in which so much has been lost, this incident remains yet another lacuna.

In England in 1889, William Friese-Greene — with a lanternist, John Arthur Roebuck Rudge, and two photographers, Frederick Varley and Mortimer Evans — developed a camera that could take up to ten photographs on a roll of bromide paper. One preserved series of photos shows a man who appears to be removing his own head. Unfortunately, the pioneering Friese-Greene took out a number of patents but usually left his inventions uncompleted, and he was eventually jailed for bankruptcy. Video versions of his work seem more like a slow-moving series of stills than moving pictures.

In February 1888, Muybridge, who had become a celebrity in his own right and was on a cross-country lecture tour illustrating his motion studies with his Zoopraxiscope, stopped in West Orange, New Jersey, where Edison's laboratories were located. According to the photographer, he and

UNITED STATES PATENT OFFICE.

THOMAS A. EDISON, OF LLEWELLYN PARK, NEW JERSEY.

APPARATUS FOR EXHIBITING PHOTOGRAPHS OF MOVING OBJECTS.

SPECIFICATION forming part of Letters Patent No. 493,426, dated March 14, 1893.

Application filed August 24, 1891. Serial No. 403,536. (No model.)

To all whom it may concern:

Be it known that I, THOMAS A. EDISON, a citizen of the United States, residing at Llewellyn Park, in the county of Essex and State of New Jersey, have invented a certain new and useful Improvement in Apparatus for Exhibiting Photographs of Moving Objects, (Case No. 930,) of which the following is a specification.

The present invention relates to apparatus for using photographs which have been taken in rapid succession of an object in motion, by means of which a single composite picture is seen by the eye, said picture giving the impression that the object photographed is in actual and natural motion.

The object of the invention is to provide an efficient apparatus adapted to pass a large number of pictures rapidly before the eye of the beholder in regular order, and the invention consists in the several combinations forming the apparatus, or definite parts thereof, hereinafter fully described, and set forth in the claims.

In the accompanying drawings, Figure 1 is a plan view of the reproducing apparatus, the top of the inclosing case being removed. Fig. 2 is a rear view of the apparatus, the back of the case and the motor being removed and the frame being broken away to show some of the parts behind it. Fig. 3 is a sectional view showing the arrangement of reflector, light, film, &c. Fig. 4 is a view illustrating the reproduction of stereoscopic pictures; and Fig. 5 shows a modified form of lens and shutter.

The film 3, on which a large number of photographs of a moving object have been taken in such manner that any two successive pictures are almost identical in appearance as set forth in my application, Serial No. 403,534, filed August 24, 1891, is passed back and forth over rollers 36, 37 at the top and bottom of the inclosing case respectively, the ends of the film being connected so that the film forms an endless band or belt. This band is advanced at the proper rapid speed by the reel 38 on the shaft 39 driven through the belt 40 by any suitable motor. The film passes over the pulley 41, under the light spring 42, through the slit 43, and over the reel 38. In order to get a sufficiently long strip or tape—say several hundreds or thousands of feet—the rollers 36, 37 may be multiplied to any desired extent.

44 is a brake-roller, carried by the crank-arm 44', provided with a suitable handle and thrown forward by a spring 44''.

Below the passage through which the film is led is a glass cell 45 containing alum water for the purpose of absorbing heat-rays from the electric or other light 46. This is shown as an incandescent lamp, which, when the apparatus is in use, is continuously lighted, but it is only essential that the light should exist when an opening in the shutter comes over a picture. The cell 45 has a branch 47 terminating in a reservoir or tank 48, which is tightly closed by a rubber diaphragm 49 held in place by the clamping ring 50. On the surface of the alum water is a surface 51 of oil to still further prevent evaporation. Above the cell 45 is a ground-glass plate 52 for still further absorbing the heat-rays and protecting the film. This plate may be tinted to give the picture the appearance of a colored picture, the plate being all of one tint, or partially of one tint and partially of another tint, according to the subject and arrangement of the picture. Above the film are suitable lenses or prisms 53, and a sight opening 54 through which an observer can look to see the reproduced picture.

55 is a reflector below the lamp to throw the light upward to the film.

In the reproducing apparatus a shutter is used for covering and exposing the pictures successively in much the same manner as the sensitive film is exposed in taking the photographs. The position of such a shutter is indicated in dotted lines at 56, Fig. 1. This shutter has one or more openings 57 near its edge, the single opening shown being directly over one of the pictures on the film. This shutter is continuously revolved through the belt 40 with a speed sufficient to bring the opening centrally over a picture at intervals practically equal to the intervals between exposures in taking the pictures. The means for advancing the film and for operating the shutter to expose the pictures may be the same in all particulars as in the apparatus for taking pictures described in my application, Serial No. 403,535, filed August 24, 1891. When the brake 44 is released by means of the han-

(No Model.)   4 Sheets—Sheet 2.

T. A. EDISON.
APPARATUS FOR EXHIBITING PHOTOGRAPHS OF MOVING OBJECTS.

No. 493,426.   Patented Mar. 14, 1893.

Witnesses   Inventor
Norris A. Clark.   T. A. Edison
N. F. Oberly.   By his Attorneys Dyer & Seely.

(No Model.)   4 Sheets—Sheet 4.

T. A. EDISON.
APPARATUS FOR EXHIBITING PHOTOGRAPHS OF MOVING OBJECTS.

No. 493,426.   Patented Mar. 14, 1893.

Witnesses   Inventor
Norris A. Clark.   T. A. Edison
N. F. Oberly.   By his Attorneys Dyer & Seely.

Patent for Edison's Kinetoscope, number 493,426, issued on March 14, 1893.

Top: The first movie studio, "the Black Maria," circa 1882–93. It was constructed of wood and tar paper.
Mounted on a pivot, it revolved, and the roof opened to admit sunlight.

Bottom: A phonograph and Kinetoscope parlor in San Francisco, 1894, one of many that made the new peep-
show entertainment available to the public.

Edison discussed the possibility of reproducing "simultaneously in the presence of an audience, visible actions and audible words." Edison subsequently asked for plates from *Animal Locomotion* for study, but they produced no work together.

In truth, Edison's contributions to the development of moving pictures, while genuine and enormous, have been exaggerated by his hagiographic treatment by the press at the time and by countless biographies lionizing him.

As mentioned previously, Edison, who began by seeking only to augment his phonograph with moving images, developed a private viewing machine, the peep show that he called the Kinetoscope, while strongly resisting the idea of movie projection until competition forced him to develop a projector. Incredibly, he failed to see any financial potential in movie projection. Nevertheless, the invention is a milestone in the development of motion pictures. "Mark you well this Edison peep show Kinetoscope," wrote Terry Ramsaye in his epic 1926 silent-film history, *A Million and One Nights: A History of the Motion Picture*. "Every strand in the thread of motion picture destiny runs through it. It is the inescapable link between the gropings of the past and the attainments of the present."

Ziegfeld star and actress Anna Held is shown peering into and cranking a Mutoscope in an advertisement for the American Mutoscope Company, 1900. Held also appeared in American Mutoscope films.

Writer Gordon Hendricks, in his extensively researched book *The Edison Motion Picture Myth*, argues that Edison's young assistant William Kennedy-Laurie Dickson, who led the effort to develop the Kinetoscope, did most of the actual "inventing." Their relative contributions remain a matter of some debate today. Certainly Edison, in subsidizing and inspiring Dickson's work, made it possible. But it is generally acknowledged that Dickson's practical role in the Kinetoscope's development was crucial.

Dickson, born to English-Scottish parents, wrote to Edison at the age of eighteen asking for a job. Edison wrote back a very discouraging letter, but Dickson immigrated anyway, to Virginia. A few years later, the plucky young man showed up at Edison's office in New York looking for work. According to Dickson's own account, Edison said, "But I told you not to come, didn't I?" Nevertheless, Dickson got a job, working at Edison Electric Works. In 1887, Edison put Dickson, a skilled photographer and inventor, to work on a device, initially called the Kineto-phonograph, that would synchronize motion pictures with his phonograph. Edison instructed Dickson to try putting photographs on cylinders, in imitation of his phonograph. Edison traveled to Europe for the Paris Exposition in August 1889, where he met Marey and was inspired by the Frenchman's use of a filmstrip for serial photography. When he returned and saw that the cylinder concept had not progressed, Edison suggested using photographic film instead.

The Kinetoscope designed by Dickson, along with his colleague William Heise, was a peepshow viewing device that ran a film loop on spools between an incandescent lamp and shutter, with each film lasting about thirty seconds. The Kinetoscope's filmstrip was similar to that still used today — 35mm wide, pulled by sprocket holes, four on each side of a 3/4 inch photograph.

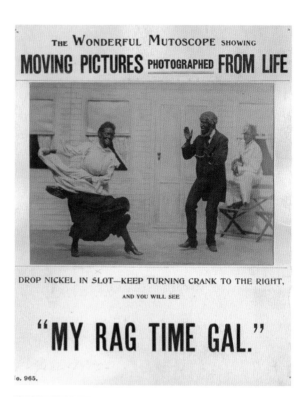

Top: An advertisement for the Wonderful Mutoscope, featuring *My Rag Time Gal* (1899). After dropping a nickel into the slot, a patron saw actors in blackface clapping time for a woman dancing in swirling skirts.

Bottom: *Edison's Wonderful Vitascope*, a pamphlet touting the exhibition of moving pictures, shared a bill with a lecture, a concert of illustrated songs, and views of American and European cities.

Dickson and Edison's lawyers drew up two patent applications — for a motion-picture camera called the Kinetograph and for the peephole viewing device, the Kinetoscope — submitting them on August 24, 1891, to the U.S. Patent Office. The application included the concept of projection, but Edison didn't really believe in it; he was convinced that a mere ten projectors would satisfy the U.S. market.

To sell the Kinetoscope machines, Edison's company also had to supply the films. To produce them, Dickson designed a movie studio that was constructed in West Orange, New Jersey, originally called the Revolving Photograph Building. Workers there soon began calling it the Black Maria, the nickname for the big black patrol wagons favored by the New York City police. Edison wrote in his memoirs, somewhat immodestly: "Our studio was almost as amazing as the pictures we made in it." The building, really little more than a shack about twenty-five feet by thirty feet, could rotate on tracks to follow the sun.

The first Kinetoscope parlor was opened with ten machines by the Holland Brothers at 1155 Broadway, in April 1894. For a twenty-five-cent ticket, a customer could watch films in five Kinetoscopes, and for fifty cents, he could watch all ten films (no discounts, apparently). Edison then began manufacturing coin-operated machines with a nickel slot. By the end of 1899, Edison had sold 973 Kinetoscopes.

Dickson, perhaps because he didn't get along with his supervisor or because he wanted to work on movie projection, began developing a movie projector in secret with former Edison employee and friend Eugene Lauste for the Latham brothers, who ran a Kinetoscope parlor in New York City. Dickson and Lauste's Eidoloscope projector, unlike the Kinetoscope, used a film width of two inches and wound from one spool to another rather than running in a continuous band. Another refinement was that in two places there was a loop of slack film, so that the pull on the filmstrip would not be as stressful — the so-called Latham loop was subsequently used in most movie projectors. Although these changes were at least in part to avoid a lawsuit with Edison, he threatened legal action. The Lathams formed the Lambda Company, in 1894 (later the Eidoloscope Company), of which Dickson was a shareholder, to manufacture the projector and to make movies.

Dickson moonlighted with others outside the Edison laboratories as well. He came up with an idea for a cheaper version of the peep-show Kinetoscope. He proposed a flip-card device, called the Mutoscope, showing in rapid succession a series of photographs attached to a drum, creating the illusion of movement. Dickson worked with a group of colleagues: Herman Casler, who actually designed and built the prototype; Harry Norton Marvin; and Elias Bernard Koopman, who provided the capital. The K.M.C.D. group, as they called themselves, then went on to develop a camera, named the Biograph, to provide films for the Mutoscope. It used a 70mm film roll and a friction feed rather than sprockets to advance the film. In late 1895 (Dickson had quit working for Edison in April), the group developed a Biograph projector, and by the end of the year, the partners incorporated as the American Mutoscope Company, later known as the American Mutoscope & Biograph Company. The new company was to become an important player in the early years of filmmaking.

Once films began to be projected, public interest in peep shows waned, and Edison was forced into the movie-projection business. He bought the rights to a projector developed by Thomas Armat that utilized a Latham loop; in early 1896, Edison began manufacturing and promoting the projector as his own invention (an early example of the power of branding), which he called the Vitascope. After its public debut, in April of 1896, a poster called it "Edison's Greatest Marvel" and quoted the *New York Herald:* "Wonderful is The Vitascope. Pictures life size and full of color. Makes a thrilling show."

Men in a lab drying strips of film.

A new industry was born, with remarkable possibilities. It presaged great wealth but, even more important, a kind of communal waking dream shared in the darkness. The cinema would open new worlds and would reveal our own secrets to ourselves.

One of E. L. Doctorow's novels perfectly conveys the sense of the wonder of the new medium. In *Ragtime,* set during the turn of the century, a Jewish socialist artist named Yateh arrives in New York from Eastern Europe. Yateh begins by creating "flick books," novelty items whose pages, when turned swiftly, make skaters spin and dancers dance, but he eventually transforms himself into a movie director, Baron Ashkenazy. At a dinner party, he explains the importance, the necessity, of films. "In the movie films . . . we only look at what is there already. Life shines on the shadow screen, as from the darkness of one's mind. It is a big business. People want to know what is happening to them. For a few pennies they sit and see their selves in movement, running, racing in motorcars, fighting and, forgive me, embracing one another. This is most important today, in this country, where everybody is new."

The medium would at first attract the lower classes and the immigrants. Gradually, it would become more respectable, middle-class entertainment. Eventually, film would become not only an entertainment medium but an art form. Who knew? Even the wizard of Menlo Park had no idea what was to come.

THE
EARLY YEARS
1893-1914

THE FIRST FLICKERS OF MOVING PICTURES CAUGHT THROUGH THE PEEPHOLES IN THE EDISON KINETOSCOPE WERE EXTREMELY BRIEF — SINGLE SHOTS ON FILMSTRIPS JUST UNDER FIFTY FEET LONG AND LASTING ABOUT TWENTY SECONDS. AT THE KINETOSCOPE'S FIRST FORMAL PUBLIC DEMONSTRATION, AT THE BROOKLYN INSTITUTE OF ARTS AND SCIENCES, ON MAY 9, 1893, THE AUDIENCE STOOD IN LINE TO SEE *BLACKSMITHING SCENE*. FILMED AT THE BLACK MARIA STUDIO, IT FEATURED THREE EDISON EMPLOYEES HAMMERING AT AN ANVIL AND PASSING A BOTTLE OF BEER AROUND FOR REFRESHMENT AS THEY "WORKED."

In January of the following year, Dickson filmed *Edison Kinetoscopic Record of a Sneeze*. The film, produced at the request of *Harper's Weekly* to illustrate an article on the Kinetoscope, showed Fred Ott, another obliging Edison employee, sneezing violently. As a still photographer, Dickson was accustomed to copyrighting his work, and although copyright law did not explicitly cover moving pictures, he submitted a paper print of *Sneeze* to the Library of Congress for copyright, where it was registered on January 9, 1894. (The previous August, Dickson had submitted other films for copyright, but the photographic paper rolls have been lost, so history does not record the first films to be copyrighted.)

Dickson and his colleague William Heise shot more than seventy-five films in 1894. Because the Kinetograph camera was unwieldy, weighing several hundred pounds, nearly all of the films were made in the unprepossessing studio shack the Black Maria. *The Barber Shop*, filmed with a makeshift set for verisimilitude, has a man getting a swift shave while two other customers wait — a matter of seconds.

The Edison Manufacturing Company specialized in vaudeville acts that could be performed indoors. The Austrian bodybuilder Eugene Sandow assumed a variety of poses wearing only a diaper-like loincloth. Other performers included the facial contortionist George Layman, Professor Harry Welton's boxing cats, and Annabelle Whitford doing her butterfly and serpentine dances.

As today, sex and violence held allure. Spanish dancer Carmencita lifted her dress and exposed her legs, and *May Irwin Kiss*, with actors John C. Rice and May Irwin locking lips in close-up, was considered salacious by some. Sandow's bare torso appealed to women (some of whom were known to pay hundreds of dollars to see him perform live).

Other Kinetoscope films included *The Execution of Mary, Queen of Scots* (the beheading was re-created using a dummy and stop-motion), a cockfight with men betting on their respective birds, and terriers killing rats. A few years later, Edison produced *Electrocuting an Elephant* (1903), which sadly depicts just that — the beast's hooves begin to smoke before it collapses on its side.

Above: The first on-screen kiss, between actors May Irwin and John C. Rice, from *May Irwin Kiss* (1896), produced by Edison Manufacturing Company.

Top right: *Edison Kinetoscopic Record of a Sneeze* (1894), photographed by William Kennedy-Laurie Dickson.

Left: *Annabelle Fire Dance* (1896).

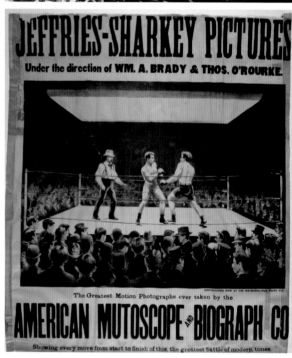

Top: American Mutoscope & Biograph Company cameras and lights set up to film a boxing match between James J. Jeffries and Tom Sharkey in 1899.

Bottom: Poster advertising the film.

Boxing matches were also very popular. In September 1894, "Gentleman Jim" Corbett, the world heavyweight champion, fought six rounds against Peter Courtney at the Black Maria, with Corbett winning and eventually making more than twenty thousand dollars. (Prizefighting was illegal, although showing films of it was not. A grand jury subpoenaed Edison, but the case was dropped.)

The Kinetograph was taken outside, however, to film *Bucking Bronco*, an act from Buffalo Bill's Wild West Show, which also produced *Buffalo Dance* and *Annie Oakley*. There is something intriguingly sexy about the famed sharpshooter, dressed in a fringed buckskin jacket and fit at thirty-five, rapidly firing her rifle and blowing away targets.

The optical and photographic manufacturers Louis and Auguste Lumière used the Kinetoscope as a model to create their Cinématographe projector in 1895 (also spawning the word *cinema*). Their light and portable machine served as camera and printer as well as projector. Like Edison, the brothers were expert at self-marketing, and the Cinématographe quickly became known throughout Europe and the United States. Unlike the early Edison films, the Lumières' films specialized in short, documentary-like works called actualities that purportedly showed events as they would have happened had the camera not been present.

Perhaps their most famous film, *Arrival of a Train at La Ciotat*, a milestone in movie history, premiered at their theater opening in December 1895. It shows the train moving toward the camera and then moving off the left-hand side of the screen; an essential part of film mythology has some terrified audience members hiding under their seats as the train approached.

The Lumières often depicted simple scenes, such as *The Baby's Meal*, in which Louis Lumière shows his brother Auguste feeding his child. Audiences were impressed by the detail of the imagery, such as the leaves moving in the background. With people satisfied by the mere novelty of moving images, narratives weren't yet necessary. Nevertheless, the Lumières did make a story film, *The Sprinkler Sprinkled* (1895). In the one-shot film, cinema's first fully realized fictional moving picture, a man is watering his garden with a hose when a naughty boy steps on it and stops the flow. The man looks down the hose, and when the boy steps away, the water splashes the man's face. He chases the boy and spanks him.

The brothers made films for less than a decade but during that time sent cameramen around the world, producing such actualities as *Leaving Jerusalem by Railway* (1896), with a camera mounted on the back of the train, and *Niagara Falls* (1897). When Edison acquired the more portable Vitascope, his company began traveling as well.

During this early novelty period in the United States, production companies would offer a com-

Top: The Lumière brothers produced what may be the first narrative film — certainly the first sight gag in cinema history — *The Sprinkler Sprinkled* (1895).

Bottom: *Arrival of a Train at La Ciotat* (1895), produced by the Lumière brothers.

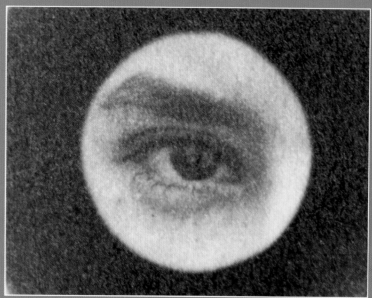

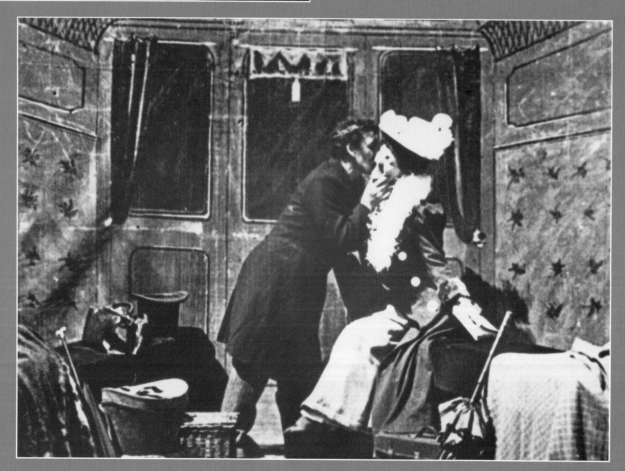

Top left: In the British film *Rescued by Rover* (1905), directed by Lewis Fitzhamon, a dog leads his master to a kidnapped baby.

Top right: *Grandpa's Reading Glass* (1902), made two years after G. A. Smith filmed his similarly conceived *Grandma's Reading Glass*, shows a series of objects magnified by a reading glass.

Bottom: G. A. Smith's *The Kiss in the Tunnel* (1899). This short film, remade later that year by British filmmaking company Bamforth Films, shows two train passengers taking advantage of a moment of darkness when their train enters a tunnel.

plete package to vaudeville markets, providing projector, projectionists, and product. By 1897, however, manufacturers sold projectors and films to exhibitors who traveled extensively, showing their moving pictures in a variety of venues, including vaudeville theaters (where they were only one of many acts), fairs, or circuses. These early exhibitors, who provided narration, sound effects, and music, and chose the order of films, served as de facto directors. Indeed, many projectionists, such as Edwin S. Porter at Edison, went on to become directors themselves. In the United States, theaters did not develop as a regular exhibition space until the rise of nickelodeons in 1905, while in Europe, theaters were used as exhibition spaces earlier.

From the very beginning, European films proved popular in America. Of the six films shown at the Vitascope's public debut at Koster and Bial's Music Hall in April 1896, five were produced by Edison. But one of the best-received films was a British import, *Rough Sea at Dover* (1895), by Birt Acres. During their first six months of operation in the United States, the Lumières had twenty-one cameramen-cum-projectionists touring the country.

Edison's domestic competition came from the American Mutoscope (also known as Biograph) and Vitagraph Company, founded in 1898 by two vaudevillians, J. Stuart Blackton and Albert Smith. Just when Americans were growing weary of the novelty of the new cinema, the Spanish-American War broke out that year, and all three companies capitalized on the fervent patriotism of U.S. audiences.

Dispatched to Cuba were Edison's William F. Paley and Biograph's Billy Bitzer and Arthur Marvin, who collected footage of troops, ships, and "color." Bringing the war home did not necessarily mean going to the front, however. Blackton and Smith shot battle scenes on their New York City rooftop, using cigarette smoke and miniatures. (Sigmund Lubin, another early American producer, also filmed staged war scenes.) Nevertheless, it is not easy to judge today whether audiences at the time were aware that some films were re-creations; it's quite possible that viewers, unfamiliar with the very idea of news films, were not deceived but were merely hungry for images of the war.

Along with France, England was also an important European producer of early films. Edison's Kinetoscope machines were copied by the London scientific-instrument maker Robert W. Paul, who then modified the design with Birt Acres, but they argued over who owned the patent. While Acres disappeared from the scene, Paul went on to make several interesting films, among them *The Countryman and the Cinematograph* (1901), a self-reflexive exercise in which a hayseed is shown watching scenes of a dancer (which delights him), an onrushing train (which frightens him), and of himself courting a dairymaid (which enrages him); he then tears down the screen and manhandles the projectionist. Another noteworthy London filmmaker,

The American Mutoscope & Biograph Company made these re-creations of real-life events that captured national attention. Top: *Landing of U.S. troops near Santiago during the Spanish-American War* (1902).

Bottom: *San Francisco Disaster* (1906).

Cecil Hepworth (*Rescued by Rover*, 1905), built a studio in his back garden in 1900.

Brighton also became a significant area for filmmaking in Britain around the turn of the century. G. A. Smith and James Williamson were both players. Smith, a Royal Astronomical Society fellow, used close-ups as well as superimposition. In his *Grandma's Reading Glass* (1900), for instance, a young boy examines a newspaper, a clock, a bird, Grandma's eye, and a kitten's face through a magnifying glass, the images framed by a circular black mask. Williamson was an exhibitor who began including more of his own works in programs; they have a sense of narrative unusual for the time and prefigure the story films that came to predominate a few years later. In the clever *The Big Swallow* (about 1901), a gentleman tries to shoo away a cameraman. When the man won't leave, the gentleman approaches, until his head and then his mouth fill the screen. The camera and then the cameraman disappear into the mouth of the man, who munches contentedly. The three-shot *Stop Thief!* (1901), a comedy that features a tramp, is a precursor of the chase film.

French films reached a broader audience in the United States than the early British films, although the latter clearly had an impact on American filmmakers. The Lumières' early dominance was superseded by their compatriot Georges Méliès, a magician who owned the Théâtre Robert-Houdin in Paris. Méliès's Star Film Company began production in 1896. While he produced hundreds of films — actualities, dramas, historical films — he specialized in a kind of fantastic work that evoked the mystery of theater magic. Using stop-motion, superimposition, and dissolves and working as a genuine auteur — writing, directing, designing sets, and starring in his own movies — he created a world of fantasy.

The Mermaid (1904) is typical. A man (Méliès) conjures fish, which he places in an aquarium that grows to fill the screen. A mermaid appears, who is turned into a woman by the man, who himself is transformed into Neptune. This male fantasy ends with the god of the sea lording over a bevy of underwater beauties. In *The Black Imp* (1905), a devil harasses a man trying to get ready for bed in a hotel room, moving a chest of drawers around and making chairs reproduce like bunnies or disappear. But certainly Méliès will remain enshrined forever in cinema history for his magnum opus, the thirty-shot *A Trip to the Moon* (1902), a film of nearly infinite charm. It was a huge international success, mainly through piracy, and it contains one of the iconic images of early cinema — the bulletlike spaceship landing in the man in the moon's eye.

Despite his accomplishments, Méliès's works were essentially a series of tableaux, like filmed stage plays (he was unable to go beyond his theater roots). His appeal began to wane in 1908, and competitors forced him into bankruptcy in 1913. He ended up a poor man selling toys in a shop at the Montparnasse train station. But the French poet Guillaume Apollinaire was right when he said

Top: A filmstrip from Georges Méliès's *Fairyland* (1903).

Bottom: Méliès's *Trip to the Moon* (1902).

of Méliès, "You and I are in the same business, since we both lend enchantment to vulgar materials."

The French company that did much to drive Méliès out of business was Pathé-Frères, founded in 1896 by Charles and Emile Pathé. Originally in the phonograph business, they were inspired by the Lumières to enter filmmaking, which they did in 1899. Their studios in Vincennes, outside Paris, began turning out films on a production-line basis under the direction of Ferdinand Zecca, and through aggressive expansion, the firm established sales offices and later production companies in Spain, Russia, Italy, Britain, and the United States. By 1908, Pathé distributed twice as many films in the United States as all the American manufacturers combined.

Pathé made a wide variety of films. It produced a number of short actuality films, leaving important documents of how people lived a century ago. Pathé also made early dramas, such as Zecca's *History of a Crime* (1901) — an eight-shot film depicting a murder, the killer's capture, and his execution by beheading (with a dream interlude in which the imprisoned killer remembers his past life, the scenes staged through a rectangular window in his prison cell) — and documentaries, such as Joseph Mundviller's majestic *Moscow Clad in Snow* (1908), with its panoramas of the Kremlin and onion-domed churches as well as busy market scenes.

Pathé was also noted for its hand-tinted films, put to glorious use in fairy tales like *Ali Baba and the Forty Thieves* (1905), which showcases spectacular sets and dancers from the Paris Opera; and fantasy films such as *The Golden Beetle* (1907), in which a mullah discovers a beetle, which turns into a winged woman who destroys him.

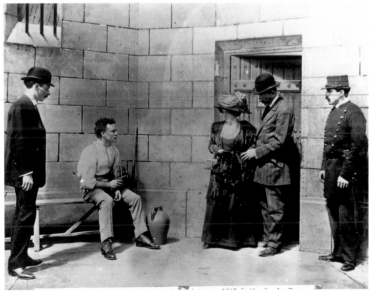

Top: *Execution of Czolgosz with Panorama of Auburn Prison* (1901), directed by Edwin S. Porter, reenacted the historic execution of President McKinley's assassin.

Bottom: Charles Pathé directed Harry Houdini, the Handcuff King and Prison Breaker, in the early 1900s. Mrs. Houdini is in the doorway.

Despite the French competition, American film manufacturers were setting the stage for the United States' eventual domination of world cinema culture. Edison opened a new studio on East Twenty-first Street in New York in early 1901, and Edwin S. Porter, who had worked as a projectionist and engineer, was hired initially to improve the technical facilities. Later he became chief cameraman and then head of studio production. Over the next couple of years, Porter, the most important of early American filmmakers, would move rapidly from single-shot films to multishot narratives, culminating in America's first blockbuster, *The Great Train Robbery*, in 1903.

Porter, in collaboration with actor and set designer George S. Fleming, undertook a four-shot story film, *Execution of Czolgosz with Panorama of Auburn Prison*, in 1901. The first two shots were panoramas taken on the day President McKinley's assassin was to be executed. The last two shots were studio reenactments of the execution: in one, the guards enter Czolgosz's cell and take him away, and in the final shot, he is strapped into the electric chair and, directly facing the audience, executed.

The following year, Porter produced an even more ambitious story film, the ten-shot, six-minute

Jack and the Beanstalk, which took six weeks to make and cost nearly a thousand dollars. Using sets and costumes clearly influenced by Méliès (they have the naive charm of a good high-school production — there are even two people sharing a cow costume), Porter reveals a growing narrative confidence in telling the familiar fairy tale.

Porter's *Life of an American Fireman*, filmed in 1902 and released in early 1903, combined Edison footage on the theme of fire — firehouse scenes and fire engines racing to conflagrations — with staged scenes to create a nine-shot, six-minute drama of a rescue from a burning building. (Edison, in its publicity, cleverly spun the fact that Porter showed different town fire departments: "We were compelled to enlist the services of the fire departments of four different cities. It will be difficult for the exhibitor to conceive the amount of work involved and the number of rehearsals necessary to turn out a film of this kind.")

Life of an American Fireman, probably influenced by the British film *Fire!* by James Williamson, begins with the fire chief dreaming (using a double exposure) of his wife and child in a burning building. Subsequently they are, in fact, rescued from a fire. A medium shot shows the fire alarm being pulled, and the firemen go into action. It ends with the rescue shown in overlapping action, first from the interior of the building and then repeated from the exterior.

Top: *A Morning Alarm* (1896), produced by Edison Manufacturing Company.

Bottom: *Life of an American Fireman* (1903), produced by Edison Manufacturing Company and directed by Edwin S. Porter.

And then came *The Great Train Robbery*, an extraordinary advance for Porter and the most famous American film of the early period. Comprising fourteen shots and clocking in at more than twelve minutes, this compelling crime story is the first real Western. Porter used a variety of techniques — parallel editing, double exposure, camera pans — that advanced his storytelling abilities. But the most significant accomplishment for Porter was his conveying the story without overlapping action — repeating actions when moving from interiors to exteriors, as he'd done in *Life of an American Fireman* — allowing him to build narrative momentum.

The Great Train Robbery was based on a stage play, but there is nothing stagey about it. Without an ounce of narrative fat, it depicts a band of thieves who rob first a train station and then a train's

The twelve-minute-long *The Great Train Robbery* (1903), directed by Edison employee Edwin S. Porter, was the first Western. Some of the scenes were hand colored, and Porter used innovative camera techniques such as crosscutting between scenes to advance the narrative.

Cupid's Pranks (1908), directed by J. Searle Dawley.

passengers, killing one who tries to run away, before making their own getaway by disconnecting the locomotive and riding it to their horses. During a chase in the woods, a shootout occurs (with the gun smoke brilliantly colored), and justice is served. The film ends with the robber chief firing his gun at the audience in medium shot, although the Edison catalog says that the shot — which does nothing to advance the story, but clearly connects with the audience — could come at the beginning or the end. The show was a huge hit and continued to play for years; according to *Moving Picture World*, it had made two million dollars by 1908.

Porter continued to direct films for Edison until 1909. He made socially conscious dramas, such as *The Kleptomaniac* (1905), which reveals the unequal justice meted out to two female thieves, one who steals a loaf of bread for her hungry child, the other a rich woman who shoplifts at Macy's (the former goes to jail, while the latter goes scot-free).

Porter also tried his hand with model animation in the surreal *Dream of a Rarebit Fiend* (1906) and the perhaps more bizarre *The Teddy Bears* (1907). The latter at first appears to be a conventional retelling of the fairy tale "Goldilocks and the Three Bears," with human actors dressed in bear suits, but things get strange when Goldilocks looks into a knothole and sees teddy bears spinning and strutting in stop-action animation. The story becomes stranger still when the bears chase Goldilocks through the snow until Papa Bear and Mama Bear are shot by a hunter, clearly intended to be Teddy Roosevelt, who takes Baby Bear away chained by the neck. Contemporary audiences would have known that Roosevelt was indirectly responsible for the birth of the teddy bear stuffed-animal craze: after having killed a mother bear on one of his many hunting expeditions, he learned that it had a cub, which he took back to camp as a pet.

Porter went on to film such features as *The Count of Monte Cristo* (1914), starring James O'Neill — Eugene O'Neill's father — and *A Good Little Devil* (1914). (Theatrical stars and popular plays were deliberately used by film producers to attract tonier theater audiences.)

Still, film historian William K. Everson argues, convincingly, that Porter failed to evolve. *Monte*

Cristo is a static, lackluster work, even though O'Neill had been performing the starring role for decades. Everson says that Porter never really wanted to be a director but would have been happy to continue as a film technician and inventor. But Porter's place in the silent-film canon is fixed, and he was the most important American director until D. W. Griffith began directing at Biograph in 1908.

Audiences in the United States continued to demand multishot story films in the wake of *The Great Train Robbery*. One compelling way to create narrative momentum is with a chase scene, used by Porter as sequences in *Robbery* and *The Teddy Bears*. Though not widely distributed in the United States, early examples of chase films were produced in England: Walter Haggar's *Desperate Poaching Affray* (1903) and the Sheffield Photo Company's *Daring Daylight Burglary* (1903). Both follow the crime-chase-capture narrative arc with realistically violent captures. French filmmakers also made chase films with flair. That the chase is an extremely compelling form of narrative is evidenced by its endurance to the present day — cars racing through Paris tunnels or speeding the wrong way on L.A. freeways — and the reader may decide how far we've come.

The Edison Moving Picture Theater in Tacoma, Washington (circa 1903), was a typical early movie theater.

Variations on the chase were spun again and again in the first years of the new century. Biograph, for instance, offered several humorous riffs on the chase in 1904, revealing an extraordinary inventiveness within the constrictions of the mini-genre. In *The Lost Child*, a woman puts her toddler outside, and the child disappears into a large doghouse. When the mother comes back and finds her child gone, her suspicions turn to a man with a large picnic basket who runs away, with the mother in pursuit. Soon several others join the chase, including a man in a wheelchair and a one-legged boy with a crutch. When the man is cornered and forced to open the basket, it turns out that he has . . . a guinea pig. The woman returns home to find her child has toddled out of the doghouse.

In *Personal*, directed by Wallace McCutcheon, a rich Frenchman who has advertised for a wife in the newspaper personal section is soon overwhelmed by would-be spouses, who run after him. And in *The Escaped Lunatic*, directed by A. E. Weed, a madman outfitted in a Napoléon costume escapes from an asylum and is chased by guards until he returns to his cell, where the guards find him reading the newspaper. Typically the chase was pursued from background to foreground past the camera, then continued as the camera jumped ahead and the action repeated.

The narratives were getting longer. Having begun as fleeting films ranging from fifteen to sixty seconds, they had grown to mini-epics of twelve minutes (a reel had expanded to accommodate a thousand feet of film, which could run for up to fifteen minutes). In film's infancy, a narrator often helped to explain the action. But as the story films proliferated in 1903–4, intertitles were often needed to make the action clear.

Top: Passion plays, which retold religious stories, were a popular type of narrative film in the early years of motion pictures.

Bottom: The final frame of an Admiral Cigarettes advertisement (1897), directed by Edison.

The new story films, and the growing audience demand for them, called for more permanent exhibition spaces. In Pittsburgh, during the summer of 1905, the first nickelodeon opened. The five-cent storefront theaters, devoted entirely to showing films, spread rapidly. Because nickelodeons were so cheap — compared with vaudeville shows or legitimate theater — they appealed to immigrants and to the working classes. At these films, immigrants could learn American mores, glimpse the latest fashions, and even begin to learn English.

While this book deals primarily with film as entertainment and art, it is important to remember that movies served other purposes as well. More educated audiences attended travel lectures, which originally used magic-lantern shows but quickly began to incorporate actual footage of foreign places. (One offshoot of this was Hale's Tours, a craze that began in 1906, in which railroad cars were turned into small theaters with windowlike projected landscape shots re-creating the travel experience.)

Films could also advance scientific understanding (Edison, for instance, filmed a series of people having epileptic seizures for medical education). Documentary-style films shot in workplaces were used to educate new employees (for example, Britain's *A Visit to Peek Frean & Co.* [1906], about the workings of a biscuit factory). And from the very beginning, it was clear that they could be used as an advertising medium. One of the earliest ad films was Edison's *Dewar's — It's Scotch* (1898), which pictures men in kilts having a grand old time, although no scotch is in evidence, just its effects. And for the new advertising medium, there was a new venue: ads were projected on a building in Times Square. For the religiously minded, Passion plays, depicting the life of Christ and often based on theatrical productions, were popular. As early as 1896, the Lumières' American agent, Charles Smith Hurd, arranged to film a traditional Passion play in the Austrian village of Horitz, where it had been performed since 1816. Other film companies also offered versions. Accompanied by lantern slides, music, and a lecture, the film presentations could last an hour.

But entertainment narrative would become the dominant mode of production. After the summer of 1904, both Edison and Biograph began making large numbers of acted films, and they consistently outsold actualities for both companies. This move from nonfiction to fiction was driven by audience demand (it would have been easier and cheaper to make actualities — just as it is today).

The increased production of fiction films helped make possible the rapid spread of nickelodeons, which in turn increased production pressure on filmmakers. With nickelodeons spreading like mushrooms after an autumn rain, and with the common perception that they appealed to the lower classes, reformers began to be concerned about film content. In 1906, the *Chicago Tribune* warned that nickelodeons "minister to the lowest passions of childhood. They make schools of crime where

Many moviemakers reinterpreted literary classics on film.
Top: Ad for *Jane Eyre* (1915), directed by Travers Vale.

Bottom: The earliest screen version of Sir Walter Scott's classic novel, produced by the Independent Motion Picture Company (IMP) in 1913.

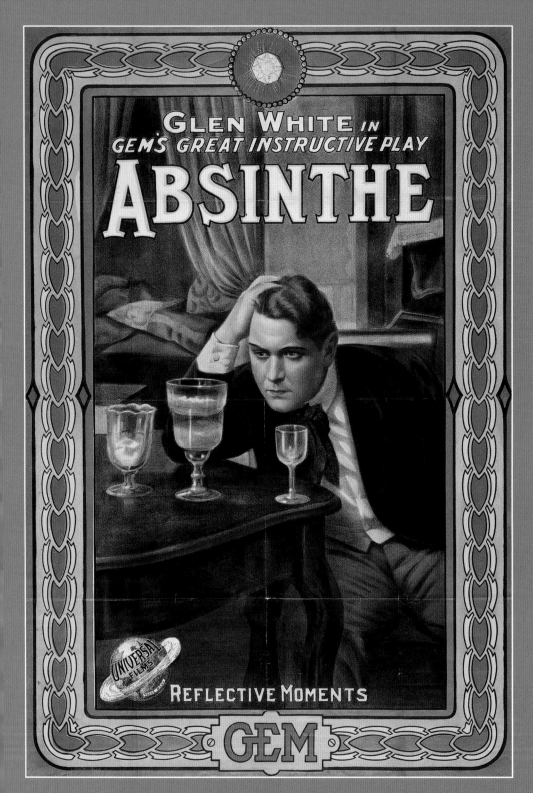

EARLY FILM POSTERS

Large, colorful posters had proven to be a successful marketing ploy for theaters, circuses, and other traveling shows at the turn of the twentieth century. The film industry followed suit, making vaudeville-style posters of various sizes to advertise films in windows and theater lobbies and on sidewalks. At first, studios kept the movies' stars anonymous so that the actors could not demand more money, but in the 1910s, studios realized that certain stars could sell more tickets, and posters began to display actors' names above the studios' billing.

Clockwise, from top left: The U.S. Lithograph Company's poster for Universal Films' *Absinthe* (1913); Jordison & Co., a British printing company, did the artwork for Thanhouser's *Star of Bethlehem* (1912); Edison's *An Unselfish Love* (1910), with poster artwork by ABC Co.

Right: Clockwise, from top left: Posters for Biograph's films *A Barber Cure* and *Three Friends* (1913) and by ABC Co.; Selig Polyscope Co.'s posters for *An Embarrassing Predicament* (1914) by Goes Lithographing Co. and *Arabia the Equine Detective* (1913) by National Pho-Eng. Co.

Clockwise, from top left: Before becoming a director, D. W. Griffith played the lead in *Rescued from an Eagle's Nest* (1908). Narrative films directed by Griffith include *The Informer* (1912); *A Corner in Wheat* (1909); *The Girl and Her Trust* (1912), starring Dorothy Bernard; and *The Lonely Villa* (1909).

murders, robberies and holdups are illustrated. . . . They manufacture criminals to the city streets."

American filmmakers responded to the so-called uplift movement by attempting to present "quality films," drawing from respectable works by the likes of Shakespeare, Dickens, and Tennyson; they were influenced by the *film d'art* movement in France, which produced photoplays based on stage dramas. Vitagraph, for instance, filmed a great number of Shakespeare plays — which may seem a curiosity of the silent era, because it's the Bard's language that makes him great, not his plots. The films would incorporate his words in intertitles. Vitagraph's *Romeo and Juliet* (1908), featuring one of cinema's earliest stars, Florence Lawrence, as Juliet, is typically swift and schematic, with an emphasis on the death scenes.

It was in this cultural milieu that filmmaker D. W. Griffith began directing films, in June 1908 at Biograph, producing more than 450 one- and two-reelers during his five years there. While at Biograph, Griffith made a number of "moral" films, such as *The Drunkard's Reformation* (1909), as well as socially conscious ones, like *A Corner in Wheat* (1909). But his great gift was storytelling, revealed in such movies as *The Battle at Elderbush Gulch* (1913) and *The Girl and Her Trust* (1912). It is hard to think of two more entertaining short films.

Griffith started out as a stage actor and playwright. Apparently he was at best an indifferent actor of the barnstorming variety and poorly paid, and so he made the transition to film in 1907, when many actors looked down on the fledgling medium. He appeared as the lead in Edison's *Rescued from an Eagle's Nest*, then moved to Biograph as an actor and story writer. His acting was wooden, but in June 1908, when director George McCutcheon took ill, Griffith took over direction of the chase film *The Adventures of Dollie*. With the aid of two cameramen, G. W. "Billy" Bitzer (with whom he would work for sixteen years), and Arthur Marvin, who actually shot the film, Griffith produced a solid little story (about a child kidnapped by gypsies), and he was given a directing contract by Biograph.

Griffith effectively used a variety of techniques: crosscutting to show simultaneous actions and to build suspense; combining different perspectives, from close-ups to panoramic shots; moving the camera in panning or tracking shots. Nevertheless, Griffith's innovations have been exaggerated (not least by himself at the time; he was also good at self-promotion). Other filmmakers had used these techniques already.

To give just one example: in Pathé's 1908 *The Physician of the Castle*, a doctor leaves his house to visit a patient, and thieves try to break into his home, causing his wife to barricade herself in with their son. The doctor calls his wife, learns of her plight, and races home to help her. To build suspense and to suggest simultaneity, the film crosscuts among the three lines of action: the doctor racing in his car, the thieves rushing

Henry B. Walthall and Blanche Sweet in D. W. Griffith's *Judith of Bethulia* (1913).

through the house, and the besieged wife trying to hold them off. The film even cuts in closer to show the husband and wife talking on the phone. The following year, Griffith made essentially the same film, *The Lonely Villa*, crosscutting among would-be robbers, besieged wife and daughters, and a racing father who, with a slight twist, must abandon his car for a gypsy cart.

This is not to suggest that Griffith was derivative, just that he didn't invent these techniques. He did, however, exploit them brilliantly to build narrative suspense, to involve audiences emotionally, and even to make an artistic statement. In *The Country Doctor* (1909), for instance, Griffith opens and closes the sad tale with slow panning shots of a rural landscape. The film cuts between the doctor's own sick daughter and his tending to a poor neighbor's sick child; in the end, his own child dies. The slow final panning shot is moving and suggests that nature is larger than man's understanding.

Griffith also revealed an extraordinary ability to work in a variety of genres — from melodramas (*The Adventures of Dollie* or *The Lonely Villa*) to moving, deft dramas (*The Country Doctor*) to Westerns (*The Battle at Elderbush Gulch*) to proto–gangster films (*The Musketeers of Pig Alley*, 1912) to comedies (*Mrs. Jones Entertains*, 1909). He also assembled an outstanding ensemble of actors, especially women, including Mae Marsh, Blanche Sweet, Mary Pickford, and Lillian Gish.

Part of Griffith's fame rests on the fact that so many of his films survive today. While Griffith's genius is undeniable, the works of many other accomplished artists have vanished, and so it is harder to judge their significance. Many of the films that have survived from the silent era did so by sheer serendipity, but there is a reason that so many of Griffith's early works have been preserved — several hundred were deposited with the Library of Congress for copyright purposes.

When the Edison company first started making films for its Kinetoscopes, in 1894, no precedent for copyrighting moving pictures existed. But Edison began depositing paper prints of entire films along with the fifty-cent copyright application fee. Although this really amounted to a string of photographs, each 35mm wide, the Library made a decision to accept them, and other film companies followed suit, until the copyright law was revised in 1912 to cover films. (After that date, film companies tried to submit the actual nitrate films for copyright, but the Library considered them

This poster boasts its copyright information in the lower right corner.

Top: *The Coming of Columbus* (1912), an early large-scale production directed by Colin Campbell.

Bottom: Lobby card for an early production of *Uncle Tom's Cabin*.

too dangerous to store and returned them, keeping synopses instead.)

This remarkable film time capsule, called the Paper Print Collection, preserves many early moving pictures that would otherwise be lost. Although films from a number of companies are included — Vitagraph, Klaw and Erlanger, the Keystone Company, and foreign films from the Great Northern Film Companies — the two motion-picture companies most substantially represented are Edison and Biograph. Why the preponderance of films from those companies? Patrick Loughney — the former head of moving images at the Library's Motion Picture, Broadcasting and Recorded Sound Division — offers an interesting possibility: Dickson, the photographer who developed the Kinetoscope for Edison, was already familiar with the copyrighting process and probably encouraged depositing paper prints with the library. When Dickson moved to Biograph, he may have pushed that company to do the same.

So the films in the Paper Print Collection, while a genuine treasure trove of preserved early films, do not really proportionately reflect the films produced during that period. One simply has to be glad that these films have been saved. (They have all been rephotographed, new negatives have been produced, and then they've been developed as film positives.)

Among the hundreds of Griffith's Biograph films preserved in the Paper Print Collection and elsewhere (the Museum of Modern Art has a strong Griffith collection as well), one can see an evolving maturity in his work. As his works grew longer in such two-reelers as *Man's Genesis* (1912) and *The Mothering Heart* (1913), they can barely contain his vision. Biograph, however, was opposed to the idea of lengthier films. Finally, Griffith secretly filmed the biblical-themed, four-reel *Judith of Bethulia*, in 1913. Biograph was appalled by the expense and tried to rein in Griffith by promoting him to a less creative position, studio production chief. Griffith quit instead.

There were already precedents for longer, so-called features. (Initially the term *feature* was ambiguous, with the word coming from vaudeville, where it meant the main attraction. Until 1909, a feature film was about a thousand feet long; but for about five years after that, a feature could be any film from two to eight reels. Eventually, a feature would refer to a film an hour in length or longer.) These multireel features could be distributed outside the usual nickelodeons, in larger theaters, and exhibitors could charge more. They cost more to make, more to buy, and more to rent. But, potentially, there was more money to be made.

Vitagraph's five-reel biblical blockbuster *The Life of Moses* (1909), a series of tableau-like scenes depicting the story of the Hebrew prophet, helped to lead the way. But it was a number of European imports that established feature films as the norm in the United States. Among the first was Henri Desfontaines and Louis Mercanton's historical film *Queen Elizabeth* (1912), starring Sarah Bernhardt. Brought to America by Adolph Zukor and Edwin S. Porter, it played in legitimate theaters and was a box-office hit.

A series of lavishly produced Italian superspectacles, many based on Roman history, proved successful in the United States as well. Ernesto Pasquale's ten-reel *The Last Days of Pompeii* (1913) and the Cines company's ten-reel *Quo Vadis* (1913) — with its huge sets of ancient Rome, five thousand extras, and real lions — were huge hits for their importer, George Kleine, who distributed them to legitimate theaters. The *New York Dramatic Mirror*'s reporter described *Quo Vadis* this way: "The scenes have depth, and the massive furnishings appear so genuine that the spectator feels as if he might walk down the orchestra aisle and enter Nero's banquet hall."

Even more extravagant was Giovanni Pastrone's twelve-reel *Cabiria* (1914), a stunning evocation of the Second Punic War,

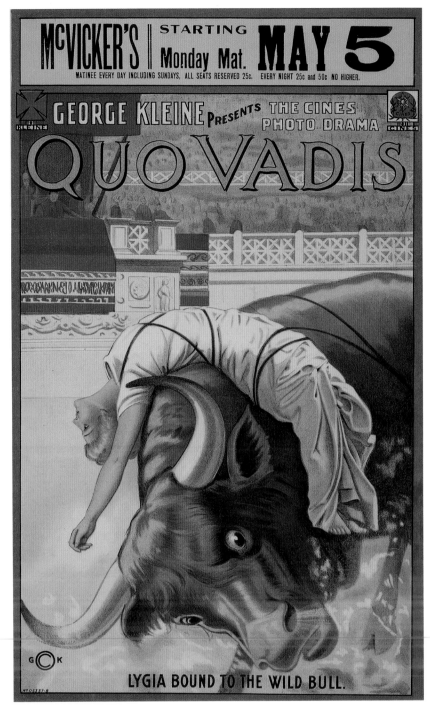

Quo Vadis (1913), directed by Enrico Guazzoni and distributed by George Kleine.

featuring the burning of the Roman fleet at Syracuse and Hannibal's famous crossing of the Alps, complete with elephants. The majesty of the spectacle was heightened by Pastrone's use of glacially slow tracking shots, which came to be known as the *Cabiria* movement. Lionel Barrymore saw *Cabiria* with Griffith, who said, "I wonder how they do that goddamn thing." It inspired Griffith to make his own epic, *Intolerance*.

Other features during this transitional period were the Danish film *Atlantis* (1913) and the American motion pictures *Traffic in Souls* (1913) and *The Italian* (1915), all of which have an almost astonishing degree of naturalism. In the second decade of the twentieth century, Scandinavia had a thriving film industry. Among the most important directors was the Dane August Blom, who produced *Atlantis*, based on a novel (written before the *Titanic* disaster) in which an ocean liner collides with an iceberg. With its big budget (in the shipwreck sequence, a real ship is used) and great length, *Atlantis* played a role in legitimizing cinema as an art form.

Traffic in Souls, directed by George Loane Tucker, is an exposé of white slavery (it is also based

ITALIAN CINEMA Many early Italian films were multireel epic spectacles that ambitiously tackled historical and mythological subjects. Crowd scenes were often shot on location and typically showed a theatrical depth of staging, while many smaller scenes were reminiscent of classical Italian paintings. With its large casts, lavish sets, and elaborate costumes, early Italian cinema boasted expensive production values and set a high standard for filmmakers.

Top: A crowd scene from *Quo Vadis* (1913), produced by CINES and directed by Enrico Guazzoni.
Bottom: Italia Almirante-Manzini starred in Guiseppe de Liguoro's *La Statua di Carne* (1912).

The martyrdom of Saint Sebastian from Enrico Guazzoni's *Fabiola* (1917).

Bartolomeo Pagano as Maciste in Giovanni Pastrone's *Cabiria* (1914).

on a couple of earlier Danish films). Although the film has a melodramatic plot full of coincidences, it transcends the sensationalism of its subject through the naturalism of the acting, the realism of its setting (much of it was filmed on location in New York City), and the careful foreshadowing of the plot twists. In revealing the head of the white slavery gang to be a respectable citizen whose wife is a leader in the uplift movement, the film takes a stab at social hypocrisy.

With its powerfully moving story and beautiful crisp photography, Thomas Ince's *The Italian*, directed by Reginald Barker, prefigures Italian neorealism. A gondolier (George Beban) is compelled to immigrate to America, where he must succeed within a year or his lover will be forced to marry a much older man. Arriving in New York, he shines shoes until he saves enough to bring his girlfriend to America, where they marry and have a child. After the child becomes sick, the father rushes to buy milk, but he is robbed of all his money. Later, he is unfairly jailed, and after his release he learns that his child has died.

The story's tragedy is never overplayed or sentimentalized, adding to its poignancy. The canals of Venice, California, stand in for Italy's, and the streets of San Francisco for New York's

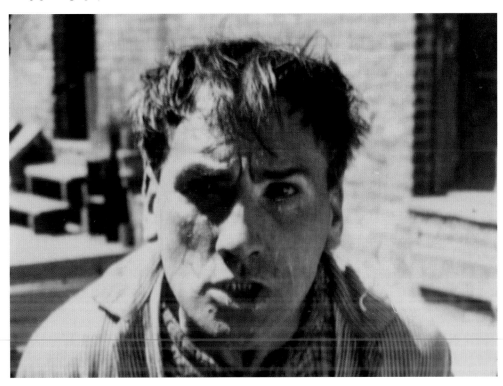

The Italian (1915), directed by Reginald Barker and produced by the New York Motion Picture Corporation, follows the story of an Italian gondolier who moves to New York and hits hard times.

Little Italy. Nevertheless, *The Italian* is remarkably realistic, so much so that Francis Ford Coppola studied it in preparing to film *The Godfather*.

These films — along with others such as Sidney Olcott's feature *From the Manger to the Cross*, a life of Christ filmed at several Middle Eastern locations — moved the movie industry closer to making features the standard (although one- and two-reelers would continue to be released).

The European film industries still dominated the world market (60 to 70 percent of film imports in Europe and the United States were French). But in August 1914, with the outbreak of World War I, everything would change. By the war's end, Hollywood would be the capital of the film world.

THE BUSINESS OF FILM

THE FILM INDUSTRY HAS ALWAYS BEEN A BUSINESS. OF COURSE, THERE WERE, FROM THE VERY BEGINNING, FILMMAKERS WITH AN ARTISTIC SENSIBILITY. BUT AT THE TURN OF THE CENTURY ARTISTS WERE MOSTLY DOING OTHER THINGS. CONSIDER, FOR INSTANCE, THAT IN 1895, THE YEAR THE LUMIÈRES FIRST PROJECTED FILMS TO A PAYING PARISIAN AUDIENCE, THE IMPRESSIONIST PAINTER CLAUDE MONET SHOWED HIS SERIES OF PAINTINGS OF THE ROUEN CATHEDRAL AT DURAND-RUEL GALLERY IN THE SAME CITY, OSCAR WILDE'S *SALOMÉ* PREMIERED IN PARIS THE FOLLOWING YEAR, AND ERIK SATIE HAD JUST FINISHED WRITING HIS *SIX GNOSSIENNES*.

The fin de siècle in Paris was a time of artistic and intellectual ferment, but the idea that moving pictures, works that literally lasted only seconds, could be an art form was hard to imagine. It was, however, possible to imagine their making money (despite Lumière père's famous remark to Méliès, when he inquired about buying a moving-picture camera, that there was no future in the business).

The United States had its own artists, of course, but at the time it was better known for its scientific, technological, and financial prowess. And epitomizing that skill set was Thomas Edison. In 1894, Edison's peep-show Kinetoscope was a moneymaker; he marketed the machines through the Raff and Gammon company for $250 to $300 each, and they were placed in penny arcades and amusement parks. The firm Maguire and Baucus bought the rights to sell the peep-show machines in Europe, but because Edison hadn't patented either the Kinetoscope or the Kinetograph camera in Europe, they were legally copied and often improved on there. Sales of the devices slowed in the United States in

Above: A Kleine Optical Company express wagon hauls a large motion-picture projector in Chicago, circa 1910.

————————————

Top right: Before the advent of movie palaces, any barn or shed big enough to hold a screen, a projector, and a dozen or so people could earn the title of movie theater.

————————————

Left: Director Thomas H. Ince.

1895, and Edison was forced to acquire projection technology.

In 1896, as noted earlier, Edison debuted the Vitascope projector, which competed in the United States with the Lumières' Cinématographe and the American Mutoscope and Biograph Company's Biograph projectors. Production companies began selling projectors and films to itinerant exhibitors, who traveled to vaudeville theaters, fairgrounds, carnivals, or other sites to show their films. These traveling showmen put together their own programs, which often used narration and music, and acted as de facto "directors." A similar system of independent traveling projectionists developed in Europe as well.

Because the producers sold their films rather than renting them, the showmen had to keep moving, as audiences tired of their limited repertoire; this system delayed the development of permanent venues for exhibiting films. But after the turn of the century, a new system began to evolve that separated the industry into a triad of production, distribution, and exhibition, set in motion by the

rise of film exchanges, essentially middlemen between producers and exhibitors. Exchanges bought prints from producers and leased them to exhibitors at a profit. In 1903, Harry J. Herbert Miles opened the first film exchange, in San Francisco.

This arrangement made permanent exhibition spaces possible, and in 1905 the first nickelodeon opened, in Pittsburgh. Nickelodeons — usually converted storefront theaters that charged five or ten cents for admission — spread rapidly: by 1908, between eight and ten thousand of them had sprung up, and this "nickel madness" spawned a voracious appetite for new product. In 1905, programs changed twice a week; the following year, programs usually changed thrice weekly; and by 1907, most nickelodeons were changing their programs every day but Sunday. This, in turn, caused American producers to increase their film output, which was supplemented by European film companies.

In addition to being a genius at inventing, Edison was also gifted at litigation. He was constantly charging other film producers with patent infringement and taking them to court. To end the expensive war over patent rights and business practices, Edison joined in 1908 with several competitors — Biograph, Vitagraph, Lubin, Essanay, Kalem, Selig Polyscope, the American branches of French Star Film and Pathé-Frères, and Kleine Optical, the largest distributor of foreign films in the United States — to form the Motion Picture Patents Company. The MPPC, known as the Trust, pooled sixteen patents and signed an exclusive deal with Eastman Kodak for celluloid stock. It set out to control every aspect of the nascent film industry, establishing licensing fees to manufacturers, film producers, distributors, and exhibitors that used the Trust's patented equipment and product.

The Trust was a blatant monopoly: Trust films could be sold only to licensed distributors, which in turn could lease them only to licensed exhibitors. Only licensed exhibitors could use Trust projectors. The licenses produced millions of dollars in fees, the lion's share of which went to the Edison and Biograph companies. This arrangement began to freeze foreign films out of the American market — by the end of 1909, fewer than half of the films released in the United States were foreign.

Top: The Bijou Dream, a silent-era nickelodeon in Camden, New Jersey.

Bottom: A poster for *Love's Stratagem* (1909), one of the first films produced by Carl Laemmle's Independent Motion Picture Company (IMP).

Not surprisingly, many in the American film industry resented and resisted the Trust. Carl Laemmle, a diminutive but tenacious businessman, led a group of independent film producers. In late 1909, he established the Independent Motion Picture Company, appropriately known as IMP, which eventually became Universal. He joined with several others, including the Nestor Company, the New York Motion Picture Corporation, and the Centaur Film Manufacturing Company, to form their own trade association, the Independent Film Protective Association, and in 1910, a stronger anti-Trust group, the Motion Picture Distributing and Sales Company, was created. The

Hitherto unpublished anti-trust cartoon, designed by **Mr. George Kleine**, before he became poet laureate for the trust.

A cartoon chronicling the flurry of litigation that came to be known as the patents war.

U.S. Department of Justice filed suit against the MPPC in 1912 for "restraint of trade," but the MPPC was not officially dissolved until 1918, although it was dead as a functioning entity long before then.

American filmmaking was originally based in New York and New Jersey, with some film companies working in Philadelphia and Chicago. With most producers still using available light to shoot (either outdoors or in glassed-in studios), they began to move to sunnier climes in winter to keep up production. For a while, it looked as though Jacksonville, Florida, might become a major film center, but more and more production companies settled on Southern California.

It has often been said by film historians that the move to California was inspired not only because of the weather but because of its distance from Trust enforcers. Silent film historian Kevin Brownlow has recorded many instances of the Trust's violent tactics. He quotes Allan Dwan recollecting his days as an independent director: "They began to hire hoodlums to put us out of business — either by destroying the camera, if they could get a hold of it, or by burning down our studios, if we happened to have one. That's one of the reasons most of us went to California, and to distant places, to get away from the packed areas where hoodlums could hide, appear with a gun suddenly and take away the camera. They found that by shooting holes through the camera, they could stop their use and that became their favorite method."

California offered a warm climate, open spaces in which to build sets, and separation from the controlling power of the Trust. By the 1920s, most U.S. films were made there.
Left top: Warner Brothers; left bottom: Universal studios, showing the future location of the famous Hollywood sign.

Top: Mack Sennett studios; bottom: filming at Majestic studio.

Still, California attracted not just independents but Trust companies as well. Certainly, if the Trust's henchmen showed up, independent producers could hightail it down to Mexico. But MPPC companies such as Selig, Kalem, Essanay, and Biograph had set up facilities in Southern California by 1911. The area offered myriad attractions: sunshine, a huge variety of natural settings, and cheap real estate and labor. By 1915, 60 percent of American films were produced there. While the production companies were scattered, many settled in the L.A. suburb of Hollywood, and the town became a metaphor for the industry if not always a studio's exact location.

From 1910 to 1913, the longer feature film emerged, and many proved hugely successful and profitable. The average nickelodeon, however, couldn't accommodate longer films, so features were usually shown in more traditional theaters or opera halls. Features also appealed to middle-class audiences, which demanded better venues and more amenities. Huge, elegant theaters

THE SPIRIT OF 1915

NEW YORK MOTION PICTURE CORPORATION
LONGACRE BUILDING, 42ᵈ STR. ᴬᴺᴰ BROADWAY.   NEW YORK.   KESSEL & BAUMANN, EXECUTIVES.
THOS. H. INCE & MACK SENNETT, DIRECTOR-GENERALS

Constructive analysis of
"Head Winds"

1. Introduction of Rosslyn on schooner. (Action introduction).

2. Retrospect. Rosslyn almost proposes to Pat. Character of Pat established — head-strong girl. Deliberately defies Rosslyn and rides dangerous horse. (Action — rescue.)

3. From retrospect to schooner. Rosslyn heads for San Francisco. (Objective established. Drama.)

4. In San Francisco. Rosslyn with Pat's brothers. Rotter's character established. Pat's determination. (Conflict established. with comedy-drama values.)

5. The Van Pelt home. Rosslyn and Pat meet again. Established that Pat would have married Rosslyn; indications that she still loves him. Rosslyns decision that she will marry him and not the rotter. (Comedy: conflict: romance: second objective [to marry Pat] established).

6. On the schooner — the plot. (Drama — comedy).

7. Pat learns of the "accident". (Drama — comedy).

8. The marriage. (Definite drama — comedy relief. Dramatic conflict between Pat and Rosslyn.)

9. The first dinner on the schooner. (Comedy-drama conflict.)

10. Pat escapes. (Definite drama in Pat's determination)

11. Peter's nightmare. (Melodrama)

12. Pat captured and brought back. (Drama. in Pat's fear of Chinamen. Drama. between Pat and Rosslyn.)

13. Pat's delirium. (Drama.)

14. Rosslyn suffers as he believes Pat is lost. (Very definite dramatic values.)

15. Pat well, discovers Rosslyn is her husband. (Romantic conflict. with drama.)

16. The storm. (Spectacular values with romantic conflict and drama.)

Top: An advertisement promoting films made in 1915 by the New York Motion Picture Corporation, a member of the Independent Film Protective Association.

Bottom: A constructive analysis of *Head Winds* (1925).

were built to attract them, and the so-called dream palaces were born — one of the first was Broadway's Strand theater, which opened in 1914 and seated more than three thousand.

The well-staffed new theaters included restrooms and lobbies and were often beautifully appointed with marble and mirrors. They frequently had exotic architectural designs as well: Chinese pagodas and Egyptian or Aztec temples. The better movie palaces had two projectors, to avoid breaks between reels, and an orchestra pit and organ. They were a far cry from the crowded, dank nickelodeons of yore (although those didn't disappear overnight; they served the poorer classes, who couldn't afford the higher ticket prices of the splendid new theaters). By 1916, there were more than twenty thousand picture palaces in the United States.

The members of the MPPC lacked a weatherman to tell them which way the wind was blowing and resisted the concept of longer features — which would become the dominant movie format — while the independents embraced them. Many of the more conservative Trust members believed audiences wanted the variety of shorter films. (It's important not to generalize too much; one of the first longer features, 1909's *The Life of Moses*, was produced by MPPC member Vitagraph.) Trust members also resisted the star system, that is, the idea of promoting films on the basis of their popular stars. Many independents, however, aggressively marketed their stars. In a way, the Trust members became the dinosaurs of their era, and the independent film producers were the quick, small mammals that would eventually take over the industry and establish the big studios. Still, many independents had by this time adopted some of the same business tactics used by the MPPC. Just as in Darwinian evolution, there are no heroes and villains.

It is remarkable that by 1910, twenty-six million Americans went to the movies when the population of the United States was ninety-two million. The incredible demand for more product and longer, more complicated features spurred an increasing need for job specialization and greater central organization, which evolved into what became known as the studio system. Directors were assisted by an array of writers, camera crews, set and costume designers, artists and carpenters, makeup artists, and film editors. As studios began to employ several directors, a new job was called for — the producer, who oversaw the entire filmmaking process. It was cheaper and faster to film scenes out of sequence, with an editor piecing the scenes together following the script. This called for a shooting script, which not only helped to organize production but also proved a reliable guide in predicting film costs.

Movie palaces reflect the evolution of silent film from a cheap attraction consumed mostly by the lower classes into a highly artistic, big-budget enterprise. Clockwise, from top left: Boyd Theater, Philadelphia (built in 1928); Tampa Theater, Tampa (built in 1927); Aztec Theater, San Antonio (built in 1926).

No single person invented this production system; it emerged as the most effective means of regularly producing films on time and on budget. As early as 1907, Vitagraph developed a producer system, with three directors working under company cofounder J. Stuart Blackton as producer. But Thomas Ince, a director and producer, is often cited by film historians as having helped to firmly establish the studio system. At the New York Motion Picture Corporation, several directors worked under him, shooting from scripts that detailed not just action but camera shots. Ince enforced budgets and had the final cut. If Ince did not develop the prototype, at least he represented a paradigm.

From left: D. W. Griffith, Mary Pickford, Albert Banzhaf, Charlie Chaplin, Dennis O'Brien, and Douglas Fairbanks at the signing of the contract that created United Artists, 1919.

During the silent era, however, the apotheosis of the production supervisor — the man who under the new system made the trains run on time — was Irving Thalberg, who worked first for Carl Laemmle at Universal and then for Louis B. Mayer at MGM. Charming, handsome, intelligent, and incredibly young (he was just twenty-one when he ran Universal), he wrangled with difficult directors and invariably won. When the notoriously free-spending Erich von Stroheim went over budget on *Merry-Go-Round* at Universal, for instance, Thalberg simply replaced him with another director and finished the film, which turned out to be a hit.

The "independent" producers triumphed in the patents war (although the MPPC was formed to hold down the costs of litigation, battling the independents in court proved hugely expensive as well). Many of the independents evolved into major Hollywood players, following the studio production system: they included IMP (later Universal); Famous Players-Lasky Corporation (later Paramount); Goldwyn Picture Corporation, Metro Picture Corporation, and Louis B. Mayer Pictures (later MGM); First National Pictures; Warner Bros.; Columbia Pictures; and RKO.

The major Hollywood studios were largely established by first- and second-generation Jewish European immigrants who had worked as independent exhibitors and distributors and who viewed the movie industry as a sort of retail business. Their backgrounds were remarkably similar. Laemmle, for instance, was born in a village in Germany and immigrated to America alone after his mother died, when he was thirteen; he would eventually found Universal. Adolph Zukor hailed from a small Hungarian village. His parents died when he was quite young, and he was packed off to live with his uncle, a rabbinical scholar. He arrived on American shores at sixteen, worked in the fur trade, and went on to create Paramount. William Fox, also a Hungarian, would start Fox Film Corporation; Louis B. Mayer, born in Russia, would run MGM; Benjamin Warner was a Polish immigrant whose four sons — Harry, Sam, Albert, and Jack — gave birth to Warner Bros.

Neal Gabler in *An Empire of Their Own* explains the appeal of the film industry to the Hollywood Jews this way: "There were no social barriers in a business as new and faintly disreputable as the movies were in the early years of this century." He also delineates the shared experience that made them so successful: "Having come primarily from fashion and retail, they understood public taste and were masters at gauging market swings, at merchandising, at pirating away customers and beating the competition. As immigrants themselves, they had a peculiar sensitivity to the dreams and aspirations of other immigrants and working-class families that made up a significant portion of the early moviegoing audience."

United Artists — founded in 1919 by Griffith, Chaplin, Douglas Fairbanks, and Mary Pickford — was an anomaly in that it was started by the talent side of the industry, not by businessmen (although businessmen certainly were involved in its formation). But the early history of UA was bumpy. Griffith, Chaplin, and Pickford still owed films under contract to First National, so Fairbanks was the only partner who was immediately free. Although the company produced some major hits (1920's *Way Down East*, 1925's *The Gold Rush*), the partners encountered distribution difficulties, highlighting another important part of the Hollywood studio system — vertical integration.

Vertical integration refers to a single company controlling the means of film production, distribution, and exhibition. Laemmle, for instance, refused to get a license from the Trust for his exchange and theaters, hoping to show European films rather than Trust-produced ones. When he couldn't get enough films from Europe, Laemmle reluctantly went into film production himself. Marcus Loew, owner of a huge national theater chain, began buying film production companies, eventually creating MGM. Zukor, an early partner of Loew's, established the movie studio Famous Players-Lasky, then took over the distributor Paramount, and finally began buying up theaters in major American cities. This formula of production-distribution-exhibition made possible extraordinary profits.

European producers attempted to emulate Hollywood's studio system, and they visited Southern California to study its secrets. But by the mid 1920s, American films dominated screens around the world — with the notable exceptions of Japan, Russia, and Germany. Europeans tried protection-

A magazine advertisement for *The Woman God Changed* (1921), produced by Famous Players-Lasky.

Left: Will Hays, head of the Motion Picture Producers and Distributors of America (MPPDA), depicted on the cover of the film magazine *Screenland*.

Right: A cartoon published in *Motion Picture Magazine* in 1914 pondered whether the movie industry could weather the storm of criticism being leveled at it by morality groups across the country.

ist measures to stop the tidal wave of American cinema, through tariffs and quotas, but they met with little success. In 1927, a Motion Picture Department was created by the Department of Commerce to facilitate the worldwide spread of American films.

But while the film companies were consolidating and growing into one of the major industries in America, a series of scandals rocked Hollywood in the early twenties. On Labor Day weekend in 1921, while film comedian Roscoe "Fatty" Arbuckle was reveling in grand style at a wild party at San Francisco's St. Francis Hotel, a young actress, Virginia Rappe, became violently ill and died soon after at a local hospital. Arbuckle was charged with the rape and manslaughter of the twenty-five-year-old woman, and an ambitious DA, Mathew Brady, eagerly pursued the case.

The press had a field day with rumors, although the evidence was suspect — many of those present at the party had been too drunk to be credible witnesses. Arbuckle was tried three times: the first two trials resulted in hung juries, but by the time the third trial ended, on August 12, 1922, with an acquittal and an apology from the jury, the comedian's career was over. His films were banned from the screen. A scapegoat for the industry, he died a broken alcoholic in New York, in 1933.

Style maven Elinor Glyn was unforgiving, if a bit blind to the goings-on. "If they are flagrantly immoral, hang them, do not show their pictures; suppress them; but do not make them suffer for a few. This Arbuckle party was a beastly, disgusting thing and things like it should be stamped out. But I didn't see any such things in Hollywood, and if there are dope parties there, they must be very small."

While Arbuckle's trials dragged on, the prominent director William Desmond Taylor was found shot to death in his Los Angeles home on February 2, 1922. Sex and drugs quickly became part of the story in the press, and the case was never solved. But actresses Mary Miles Minter and Mabel Normand were implicated — both had been romantically linked with him — and they were forced into retirement.

Then matinee idol Wallace Reid, one of Famous Players-Lasky's biggest stars, collapsed on the set. A morphine addict, Reid went into rehab in March 1922, and he died in the sanatorium nearly a year later. The studio was complicit in his addiction, for after he was injured on location, a studio physician gave him morphine so that he could keep working. And Reid worked at a ferocious pace — while actors of his caliber might appear in a couple of films a year, he would make nine or ten. The grueling pace no doubt contributed to his problems.

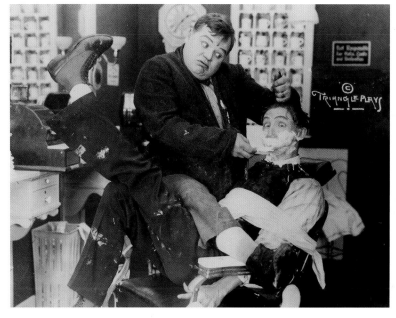

Fatty Arbuckle, at work and in court. Top: *His Wife's Mistake* (1916), also starring Minta Durfee; bottom: at his trial for the rape and murder of Virginia Rappe, 1921, for which he was later acquitted.

"I PRESUME YOU WILL EXCUSE ME WHILE I---DRESS?"

WALLACE REID
IN
"TOO MANY MILLIONS"

Wallace Reid's death in 1923 from morphine addiction helped motivate Hollywood executives to spend more money on censorship and public relations campaigns in order to minimize scandal.

The Hollywood industry panicked. To head off boycotts and government censorship, the studio chiefs in 1922 formed the Motion Picture Producers and Distributors of America (MPPDA), a self-regulating trade group. They chose postmaster general Will H. Hays to run it. The unprepossessing Hays, variously described as "bat-eared" and having "the face of a frightened mouse," had run Warren G. Harding's presidential campaign, so he knew his way around politics. He was a Presbyterian church elder, an appropriate choice for what was to become essentially a well-paid PR job. Hays got out of the Harding administration, one of the most corrupt in U.S. history, before his reputation was tarnished.

But he was soon tested in his new position. He accepted the MPPDA job in mid-January. Two weeks later, William Desmond Taylor was found dead, and the following day, February 3, the second Arbuckle trial ended in another hung jury. In August, six days after Arbuckle was finally acquitted, Hays banned the funny fat man from the screen, making Arbuckle a scapegoat and giving himself and his office some credibility as an arbiter of morality. Hays used his lobbying skills to fend off any new censorship legislation.

Hays established thirteen points as guidelines for filmmakers intended to improve the morality of movies, discouraging scenes that dealt improperly with sex, made vice attractive, or undermined the authority of public officials. Complying with these guidelines was entirely voluntary, however. Reformers remained unsatisfied, and in 1927, the formula was further refined into a list of "Don'ts" and "Be Carefuls." MPPDA members agreed to avoid eleven subjects and to deal with twenty-six others with care. Still, the so-called Hays Office lacked any authority to enforce the guidelines. The Hays Office also offered a way of bending the rules, called "compensating values." All kinds of vice could be portrayed on-screen, as long as in the end its practitioners were "punished." Cecil B. DeMille proved a genius at the art of compensating values, producing such films as *The Ten Commandments*, which was full of sex and violence under the banner of religion.

The specter of film censorship did not begin in the 1920s but was an issue from very early on.

The shot that wounds Tori.

MORALITY

was the subject of choice for filmmakers and audiences alike. Clockwise, from top left: Bessie Love stars as the morphine-addicted Mary Finnegan in the lost feature *Human Wreckage* (1923). The film was released nearly six months after the death of Wallace Reid and starred his wife, Dorothy Davenport. • Bootleggers, blackmail, infidelity, and suicide are some of the sins dramatized in *Morals for Men* (1925). • Babs Van Buren (Viola Dana) tries to save her boyfriend from the electric chair in *The Social Code* (1923). • After being blackmailed, manhandled, and branded, Edith Hardy (Fannie Ward) aims a gun at her tormentor in *The Cheat* (1915). • Roxie Hart (Phyllis Haver) gives a little "razzle-dazzle" to a corrections officer while behind bars for the murder of her lover in *Chicago* (1927). • Viola Dana stars as a fallen woman who rises to success in the 1924 version of *Revelation*. The fallen woman was a popular character in silent cinema. • An artist played by Thomas Holding is angered when he learns his wife (Pauline Frederick) posed semi-nude for a painter to repay his debt to a corrupt art dealer (Russell Barrett) in *Sold* (1915).

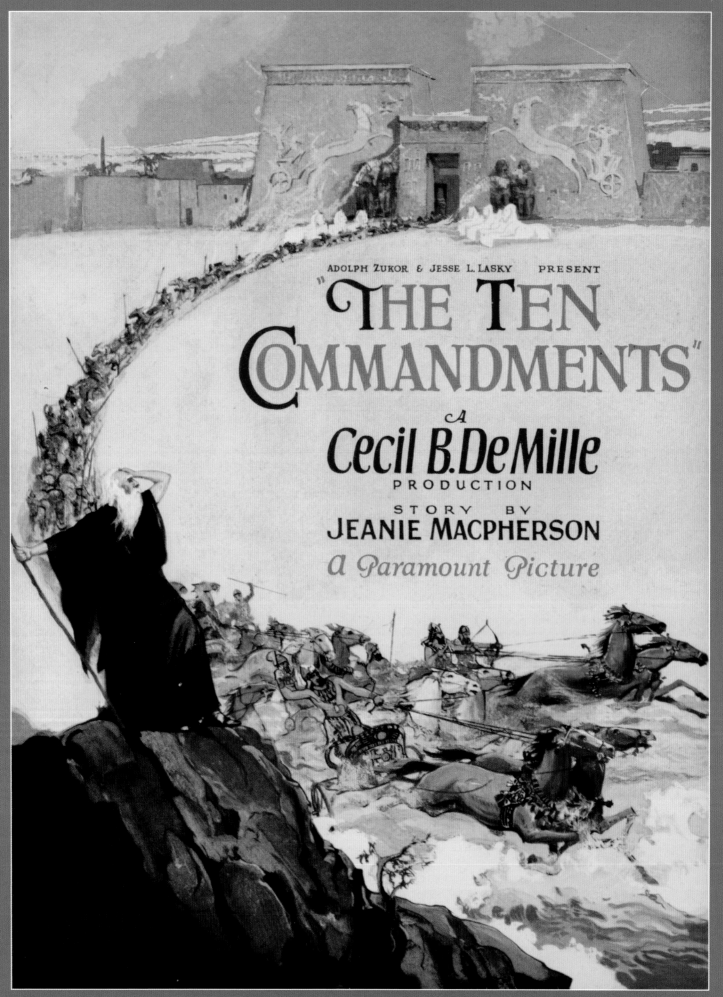

The film contained plenty of sex and violence, but a magazine advertisement for Cecil B. DeMille's *The Ten Commandments* (1923) was able to escape censorship because of its ostensibly religious subject matter.

Many saw the nickelodeons, with their working-class audiences full of women and children, as a threat that needed to be closely controlled. On Christmas Eve of 1908, for instance, New York City mayor George B. McLellan closed every movie theater in the city, ostensibly for safety reasons, but the move was motivated by moral concerns as well. The closure was overturned in court, but it caused alarm among movie producers.

In the wake of the theater closings, film producers realized that they would have to offer some form of self-regulation to avoid outright government censorship, and they were instrumental in creating the National Board of Censorship, in 1909. The board reviewed films and suggested cuts, and the producers agreed to follow its recommendations. (The board began as a New York City organization but soon became national in scope.) Several state and city censorship boards were formed (Chicago established a licensing board in 1907, for instance; Pennsylvania in 1911; and Ohio in 1913) that had the clout of government regulation. Each demanded different cuts and changes, so that several different versions of a film might circulate. Legislation was introduced in Congress in 1914 to establish a federal film-censorship commission, which was opposed by the National Board and filmmakers on First Amendment grounds. But the following year, a landmark Supreme Court decision, *Mutual Film Corporation v. Ohio Industrial Commission*, took the steam out of the movement for federal regulation and undercut the First Amendment arguments. The unanimous decision affirmed the state of Ohio's prior restraint of screenings of Griffith's *The Birth of a Nation*. The Court argued: "The exhibition of motion pictures is a business pure and simple, organized and conducted for profit, . . . not to be regarded, nor intended to be regarded by the Ohio Constitution, we think, as part of the press of the country or as organs of public opinion."

The same year, the National Board of Censorship changed its official name to the National Board of Review and its mandate to improving film quality rather than censoring films. Still, many in the industry welcomed some acceptable national standards rather than those of a hodgepodge of local and state boards, which led to the creation of the MPDDA. The Hays Office was established more in response to the behavior of actors than to the content of films, but it would have an influence on both. Still, the Hays Office would remain in Hollywood's pocket, doing damage control for the industry while appearing to assuage demands for decency on-screen and in private lives.

Hollywood survived its scandals and continued to party on through the twenties, while producing some of the best films of all time. The actors worked hard, and they played hard in a lavish landscape of excess. As Gloria Swanson said, "Oh, the parties we used to have. In those days the public wanted us to live like kings and queens. So we did — and why not?"

Nearly every major film shown in the United States through the 1950s was subject to scrutiny by the National Board of Review. Those that were cleared for public consumption bore its official stamp of decency.

GENRES

Nearly every major film genre was codified during the silent period, and much of what we see on screens today was shaped by the evolution of form during the silent era. Tastes and times change, of course: Westerns, enormously successful for a time in the silent era, are nearly moribund now, and the popular serials and series films have become sequels and television-network dramas. Still, an understanding of silent-era genres reveals a lot about film art now as well as then.

COMEDY

Some of the most iconic images from silent cinema come from comedy (Charlie Chaplin's poignant Tramp, Harold Lloyd hanging from a clock outside a department store window), and in many ways, comedy was the single most successful style adapted to non-dialogue drama.

Paul Auster, in his novel *The Book of Illusions*, about a writer researching a fictional silent-film comedian, explains why the medium of silent film was so perfectly suited to comedy:

> It struck me that I was witnessing a dead art, a wholly defunct genre that would never be practiced again. And yet, for all the changes that had occurred since then, their work was as fresh and invigorating as it had been when it was first shown. That was because they had understood the language they were speaking. They had invented a syntax of the eye, a grammar of pure kinesis, and except for the costumes and the cars and the quaint furniture in the background, none of it could possibly grow old. It was thought translated into action, human will expressing itself through the human body, and therefore it was for all time. Most silent comedies hardly even bothered to tell stories. They were like poems, like the renderings of dreams, like some intricate choreography of the spirit.

Among the earliest comedians to gain a worldwide reputation was the French actor Max Linder, an entertainer of extraordinary charm and finesse. Dapper and suave, humor emerged from the contradiction of Linder's elegance and the chaos that followed him everywhere. In *Troubles of a Grass Widower* (1908), for instance, he plays a middle-class husband whose wife walks out on him because he refuses to look up from the newspaper. His initial joy over an end to his wife's nagging disappears when he finds the simplest domestic chores, such as washing dishes, shopping, and cooking dinner, so beyond him that he ends up destroying their house. Linder was an important influence on Chaplin, who in the early twenties inscribed a photograph to Linder, calling him "the Professor, to whom I owe everything."

Another significant French comic was Onésime (Ernest Bourbon), who starred in some eighty often bizarre comedies, much admired by the Surrealists. In *Onésime, Clock-Maker* (1912), he

Above: Max Linder, an early French film comedian, in *Le Roi du Cirque* (1924).

Left: Buster Keaton in *The General* (1927).

Top: Mack Sennett created the Keystone Kops, an incompetent group of policemen, who appeared in numerous shorts and features beginning in 1912.

Bottom: *War Feathers* (1926), an Our Gang (aka The Little Rascals) short produced by Hal Roach.

speeds up time in order to get his inheritance more quickly, and in *Onésime Against Onésime* (1912), he battles his evil alter ego, played by himself, whom he ends up devouring.

In the United States, Mack Sennett and Hal Roach helped create the shape of comedy and nurtured many of the great performers of the era. Sennett, who ran Keystone, specialized in frenetic action that never allowed the viewer a moment of reflection. Chaplin, Roscoe "Fatty" Arbuckle, Ben Turpin, Harry Langdon, and Frank Capra all emerged from Keystone. On the other hand, Roach — who had Lloyd, Laurel and Hardy, and Charlie Chase in his stable — crafted more sophisticated and solidly constructed comedies. The humor of Lloyd and Laurel and Hardy under Roach is grounded in real life, and their struggles are more recognizably human.

Sennett, uneducated but intelligent, learned movie craft at Biograph under Griffith and clearly had an instinct for comedy. But Keystone's anarchic slapstick, while hugely popular at the time, wasn't universally admired. An anonymous *New York Times* critic opined that Sennett's "alleged" comedies were utterly dull, and it's true that Keystone Kops chase scenes do grow repetitive after a while. Sennett struck comedic gold in 1914, when his greatest star, Charlie Chaplin, became world famous over the course of a few months. When Chaplin's contract was up after a year, however, Sennett declined to give him the big raise he asked for, and Chaplin moved on, first to Essanay Studios, then to Mutual and First National. He then cofounded United Artists in 1919 with Fairbanks, Pickford, and Griffith.

Poster for Chaplin's 1916 comedy.

Chaplin's London youth was Dickensian. His alcoholic father deserted the family when Chaplin was still a baby. His mother, a music-hall performer, became unhinged and was put in a mental hospital, and Chaplin was placed in an orphanage. It was not always thus: his family was once well to do enough to have had a maid. At the age of ten, Chaplin joined a clog-dance act and then played comic stage roles. He was hired by London impresario Fred Karno, who trained him further in comedy, and it was during Karno's tour of the United States that Sennett signed Chaplin to Keystone. It was after only one film that Chaplin, rummaging through the Keystone wardrobe room, put together the costume and persona of the Tramp. He was first seen in full Tramp regalia in 1914's *Kid Auto Races at Venice*.

Certainly Chaplin's early encounters with drunkenness, abandonment, madness, and squalor influenced and inspired his art. He was capable of sentimentality and cruelty, and some of his early

Mack Swain and Charlie Chaplin fight in a teetering cabin in *The Gold Rush* (1925).

work was mean spirited. But by the time of his Mutual films (1916–17), including short masterpieces such as *The Immigrant* and *Easy Street*, he was doing some of his best work.

In the Mutual two-reeler *The Vagabond* (1916), for instance, the Tramp is an itinerant violinist who finds himself in the country after trying to compete for change with a brass band in a bar. There he meets a beautiful girl (Edna Purviance) who was kidnapped by gypsies as a child and is forced to work as a drudge. (Child-snatching gypsies were a popular plot device in the silent era: they figure in Cecil Hepworth's *Rescued by Rover* and Griffith's directorial debut at Biograph, *The Adventures of Dollie*.) The Tramp charms her, and they escape together in the gypsy wagon. The Tramp prepares a meal for her, but as she goes to collect water, she meets an artist who paints her. The artist enters his portrait of the girl in a competition, where she is recognized by her wealthy mother, who races in a limousine to retrieve her long-lost daughter. As the limousine pulls away, the girl demands that they return to pick up the Tramp. The happy ending is leavened with ambiguity; one wonders what kind of future they could ever have together.

The Kid (1920), an early Chaplin feature with his typical mix of pathos and humor, has a similarly ambiguous ending. Clearly drawing on the pain of his own childhood, the down-and-out Tramp reluctantly adopts a baby abandoned by his unwed mother (Edna Purviance). He tries getting rid of the child — he even looks down a sewer grate, then shrugs off the idea — but raises the boy (played with scruffy charm by Jackie Coogan Jr.) as best he can. The Tramp makes a living as a glazier, and the Kid assists by smashing windows. When the police and social workers take the boy away to an orphanage, where he will presumably live a better life than with the socially marginalized but responsible and loving Tramp, the scene, almost Victorian in its sentimentality, is nevertheless still heartbreaking. The film ends with the Kid being reunited with his birth mother, who has become a star on the stage. She invites the Tramp into her splendid home, but once again one wonders how the situation could ever be happily resolved.

The Kid was a huge critical and box-office success. Chaplin made only a handful of silent features. He starred in the first feature-length American comedy, *Tillie's Punctured Romance* (1914) — although not in his Tramp persona — with Marie Dressler and Mabel Normand. In *The Gold Rush* (1925), Chaplin's most critically acclaimed film, he joins the Klondike lemming race and, famously, eats his shoe. In his last silent masterpiece, *City Lights* (1931), he falls in love with a blind flower seller (Virginia Cherrill), whom he convinces he is a millionaire. Through a set of wonderfully implausible accidents, he acquires the money for a sight-restoring operation. The film was released after talkies had triumphed; he added only a score and sound effects.

Within the Tramp costume, Chaplin's range of characters was extraordinary: he could be a waiter, a down-and-outer turned cop, a hapless immigrant, a vagrant violinist, a soldier — all with equal conviction. Walter Kerr, in *The Silent Clowns*, offers this insight into Chaplin's chameleon-like gift: "The secret of Chaplin is that he can be anyone. That is his problem. The secret is a devastating one. For the man who, with a flick of a finger or the blink of an eyelash, instantly transforms himself into absolutely anyone is a man who must, in his heart, remain no one." Jorge Luis Borges, in a story titled "Everything and Nothing," describes Shakespeare in the same way.

Because we love such arguments, people will debate till the end of time who was better: Chaplin or Keaton. In Bernardo Bertolucci's *The Dreamers*, which is set during the tumultuous events in Paris in 1968, two young men, an American and a Parisian, argue their merits, while other kids head to the barricades. Woody Allen, in an interview with Penelope Gilliatt in the *New Yorker*, gives them equal weight: "*City Lights* and *The Gold Rush* and *The Navigator* and *The General* are the four great comedies, aren't they?" By citing two masterworks by Chaplin and two by Keaton, Allen acknowledges them as a kind of double star in comedy's firmament.

Glass slide advertising the Buster Keaton short *My Wife's Relations* (1922).

If Chaplin appeals to the audience's emotions, Buster Keaton, with his stone face, remains a blank slate. One is drawn into his films by his stoic persistence in the face of an often ridiculously, hilariously hostile universe. There is a Zen-like quality in Keaton films like *The Navigator* (1924), *The General* (1927), and *Steamboat Bill, Jr.* (1928). He faces obstacles with a sense of acceptance, and he has a Buddhist present-mindedness to deal with every catastrophe he encounters and to walk away unscathed.

While one risks investing a single incident in a life with too much importance, a strange occurrence related in Rudi Blesh's biography *Keaton* does explain something about the comedian's equanimity in the face of calamity. When Keaton was just three, his parents left him with their housekeeper as they performed their vaudeville act. While they were away, a cyclone came and tore

Top left: Magazine advertisement for Buster Keaton's *Sherlock, Jr.* (1924), in *Motion Picture News*.

Top right: Harry Langdon, with Priscilla Bonner (left) and Alma Bennett in *Long Pants* (1927).

Bottom: Lobby card for *Haunted Spooks* (1920), starring Harold Lloyd and his future wife, Mildred Davis.

the roof off the house and sucked Keaton out the window. Keaton flew over houses and trees, landing gently in an empty street four blocks away. Of course, a cyclone figures in one of his films.

Of all the best silent comedians, Keaton was the most interested in the medium itself. Others were essentially filming stage bits polished for the film, with the camera a few rows back. But when Keaton apprenticed himself to Arbuckle at Comique Film Company, in 1917, and made a string of shorts, he wanted to know everything. Keaton recalls in his autobiography, *My Wonderful World of Slapstick*: "Roscoe . . . took the camera apart for me so I would understand how it worked and what it could do. He showed me how film was developed, cut, and then spliced together."

In the twenties, Keaton wrote, produced, directed, and acted in ten features. Like Chaplin, Keaton had a huge range as an actor — he played a railroad engineer, a projectionist, a cowboy, and a young and spoiled rich man. Unlike Chaplin, who became the darling of critics and intellectuals, Keaton was among the least appreciated comedians of his day (that has changed over the years, and now the intelligentsia has switched its allegiance to the more "cerebral" comedy of Keaton).

Certainly part of the appeal of Keaton's films is their realism and drama. In his masterpiece *The General*, Keaton plays a dogged Confederate soldier who single-handedly retrieves the titular train from the Yanks. But Keaton's not just funny — he convincingly evokes the South. As film writer David Thompson notes, "*The General* has the topographical vividness of an Anthony Mann film."

Harold Lloyd is probably underrated today, although in the twenties he was one of the most popular — and richest — screen comics. His optimism and aggressive pursuit of success epitomize the decade, but they are really timeless American values. Lloyd's gags, in features such as *Grandma's Boy* (1922) and *Safety Last* (1923), have the clockwork precision of a fine Swiss watch.

No other silent comedians achieved the celebrity of Chaplin, Keaton, or Lloyd. Harry Langdon's on-screen persona, however, was close to Chaplin's; he played a fragile, waiflike, almost infantile

Top: Dorothy Coburn, Stan Laurel, and Oliver Hardy in *The Second Hundred Years* (1927).

Bottom: Although much of his work has been irretrievably lost, film historians consider Raymond Griffith's surviving pictures as some of the best comedies of the silent era.

Many female comedians dominated the screen during the silent era. Two of the biggest stars: Mabel Normand (below), in *Mickey* (1918), and Marie Dressler (bottom).

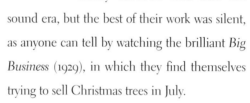

character. Frank Capra directed him in *The Strong Man* (1926) and *Long Pants* (1927). Arbuckle's career was famously cut short by scandal, and he was not as talented as the foregoing silent clowns. Still, the fat man could move with an unexpected grace, as when he dresses up in "drag" and dances like an Egyptian in *The Cook* (1918), in which he teamed with Keaton. Laurel and Hardy survived well into the sound era, but the best of their work was silent, as anyone can tell by watching the brilliant *Big Business* (1929), in which they find themselves trying to sell Christmas trees in July.

The world of silent comedy was dominated by men (indeed, much of it was misogynistic), but some women reached the pinnacles of comedic fame comparable to those attained by Chaplin or Keaton or Lloyd. Accomplished actresses such as Mabel Normand, Constance Talmadge, Marion Davies, and Dorothy Gish all made short and feature-length comedies. In Sennett's *Tillie's Punctured Romance* (1914), for instance, Marie Dressler and Mabel Normand have genuinely funny turns that rival Chaplin's (Dressler as the country girl whom Chaplin and Normand, his partner in crime, try to gull).

Normand was as close to a major film comedienne as any woman in the silent era came. At Keystone with Sennett and Chaplin, she proved herself up to any bit of slapstick — tied to railroad tracks or getting dragged through the mud. She made nearly two hundred shorts and several features, but her connection to the William Desmond Taylor scandal proved her undoing.

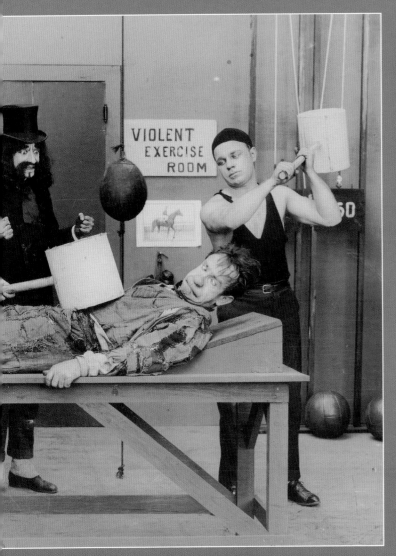

COMEDY was an audience favorite, and many comedians delivered laugh-worthy performances. Clockwise, from top left: Harry Watson in *Keep Moving* (1915); glass slide advertising *His Wooden Wedding* (1925), starring Charley Chase; lobby card for Syd Chaplin's 1925 comedy *Charley's Aunt*; Billy West in *Adventures of Hairbreadth Harry* (1920); *Flaming Fathers* (1927), starring Max Davidson; glass slide advertising Ben Turpin's comedy *Cupid's Day Off* (1919); and Lupino Lane in *Summer Saps* (1929).

Crime disrupts life in the back city of Boley, Oklahoma, in this 1922 Western filmed on location with an all-black cast.

Westerns

Because of their fast action, elemental conflicts, and eventually, scenic landscapes, Westerns had a natural appeal, in the United States and in Europe. The Wild West was passing into history, even as vestiges still existed during the silent era. In fact, many Westerns were given contemporary settings — featuring automobiles, for instance — rather than distant historical ones. After all, Arizona didn't become a state until 1912.

The earliest Westerns included three 1894 Edison films of Buffalo Bill's Wild West Show (*Annie Oakley*, *Buffalo Dance*, and *Bucking Bronco*) and the company's *Cripple Creek Bar-Room Scene* (1899), which suggests the West at least in costumes. Then in 1903 came Edwin Porter's blockbuster *The Great Train Robbery*, also from Edison, which set the bar high for the genre.

G. M. "Broncho Billy" Anderson was the earliest Western hero. Of Jewish descent, he was born Max Aaronson in Arkansas and later became a New York actor and model. He played several small roles in *The Great Train Robbery* (including the "dude" who is made to dance when men start shooting at his feet, the train passenger who is shot and killed by the bandits, and one of the outlaws). His beginning as a screen cowboy was inauspicious, however. *The Great Train Robbery* was shot in four days in New Jersey, but on the very first day, Anderson was thrown from his horse after trying to mount it the wrong way. He caught the train back to New York and missed the whole first day of shooting.

Poster for *Adventures of Buffalo Bill* (1917).

After joining the Chicago-based Essanay Company, Anderson began developing his Broncho Billy character in a series of one-reelers. Not particularly good looking and a bit stout, he made hundreds of short Westerns — such as *Broncho Billy and the Baby* (1908) and *Broncho Billy and the Schoolmistress* (1912) — with credible costumes and geographic plausibility. They were shot in California, not in New Jersey, which helped; audiences had grown tired of the monotony of the scenery in "Eastern Westerns."

William S. Hart brought a heightened realism and astonishing intensity to the Western. Hart grew up in the West and learned to ride well before becoming a stage actor. He performed in a couple of two-reelers for director-producer Thomas H. Ince, then starred in Ince's five-reel *The Bargain* (1914), which Hart cowrote with C. Gardner Sullivan. It was the first of his famous good badman roles. In movies such as *The Return of Draw Egan* (1917) and *Hell's Hinges* (1916), he often plays an outlaw who is redeemed by the love of a woman. Hart, who directed many of his own films, was a stickler for realism, and his films are often full of dust and grit.

The strange, extreme *Hell's Hinges* is perhaps Hart's best film. In a town so evil it is known as Hell's Hinges, Hart plays gunslinger Blaze Tracy, who falls in love with the new preacher's sister,

Popular cowboy Tom Mix in *Hands Off* (1921).

Top: Hoot Gibson, who starred in *Let 'er Buck* (1925), was a popular cowboy actor of the time.

Bottom: Cowboy star William S. Hart, featured here on the cover of *Screenland* magazine (1922).

Faith. Silk Miller, owner of the saloon, is annoyed by the minister's presence and conspires to get him drunk and in bed with the barmaid Dolly. Then while drunk, the preacher is persuaded to burn down his own church. Blaze, by now transformed into a kind of destroying angel, burns the entire town and escapes with Faith and its few good citizens. The movie inspired Clint Eastwood's *High Plains Drifter*.

Tom Mix and Hart overlapped in performance, but Mix would supersede him. Mix, a consummate entertainer, had no interest in realism; he was the Western equivalent of Douglas Fairbanks. Mix's films, such as *Sky High* (1921) and *The Great K and A Train Robbery* (1926), combine remarkable stunts, humor, and picturesque locations. In *The Great K and A Train Robbery*, for example, he slides down an impossibly long rope from a cliff top into a deep canyon, landing square in the saddle of his horse, Tony, before racing off. He later rides Tony up the stairs of the K and A owner's splendid hacienda and then off a balcony into a pool. Such stunts and his screen charisma endeared Mix to huge audiences.

In the twenties, two epic Westerns were released that helped to reinvigorate the genre: John Cruze's 1923 *The Covered Wagon*, about a cross-country wagon train, and John Ford's 1924 *The Iron Horse*, about the building of the first transcontinental railroad. *The Covered Wagon*, with its big wagon train snaking its way across the country, is remembered today mainly for its epic scope and panoramic scenes provided by Karl Brown's superb camera work. The story itself is rather plodding, and its hero, J. Warren Kerrigan, is too good to be interesting. The film, however, gave the genre a big boost and paved the way for Ford's extraordinary *Iron Horse*, which came out the following year. Like *The Covered Wagon*, *The Iron Horse*, which takes as its huge canvas the building of the Union Pacific railroad, was shot almost entirely on location, offering both a sense of the immensity of America and of the promise and perils of its ethnic melting pot. A bit slow off the mark, Ford then packs the film with romance, comedy, and drama, especially in the climactic race to save the railroad workers from an Indian attack.

Films about Native Americans were a subgenre of the Western. In the early years, Indians were often romanticized by displaying a Rousseauistic nobility in the midst of unspoiled landscapes; but in later Westerns, they often served merely as convenient stereotypical villains. Some filmmakers showed sensitivity, however. For example, *The Invaders* (1912), scripted by C. Gardner Sullivan and directed by either Thomas Ince or Francis Ford (it is still not known for certain), gives Native

"THE VANISHING AMERICAN"

with RICHARD DIX and WALLACE BEERY

The final epic romance of the American Indian.

Red Wing
(Copyright 1911, Pathé Freres)

AMERICAN INDIAN FILMS were a popular genre in the early years of the movie industry. Several directors, including D. W. Griffith, Thomas Ince, and Allan Dwan, filmed stories that depicted the complex issues surrounding American Indians — prejudice, assimilation, and miscegenation — with depth and sensitivity. The American Indian was routinely portrayed as a tragic hero largely misunderstood by the white man.

Although American Indians were usually portrayed by white actors, there were some American Indians working in the film industry at the time, including actor and director James Young Deer and his wife, actress Red Wing. Young Deer began his film career in New York working for the Lubin, Vitagraph, and Pathé companies and moved to Los Angeles in 1910 when Pathé hired him to set up its West Coast branch. Red Wing, whose real name was Lillian St. Cyr, made her acting debut in *The White Squaw* (1908) and was much in demand through the early teens. Red Wing performed her own stunts and appeared in at least three feature films, including a lead role in Cecil B. DeMille's *The Squaw Man* (1914).

Audience interest in American Indian stories began to wane in the early teens, but Westerns, where American Indians usually appeared in more stereotypical roles, were increasing in popularity. The American Indian genre merged with Westerns, and as film historian Eileen Bowers writes, "it became common to use Indian treachery and warfare as a plot motive in action Westerns, with scriptwriters feeling no need to explain Indian actions on the basis of the white man's mistreatment. . . . People were interested in action, thrills, mystery, and happy endings, not tragic heroes."

Above: American Indian actress Red Wing in *Motion Picture Story Magazine*, October 1912.

Top left: Advertisement for *The Vanishing American* (1925) in *Motion Picture News*.

Top right: Richard Dix in *Redskin* (1929).

Bottom left: Scene from *White Fawn's Devotion* (1910).

Americans motivation for attacking the cavalry because it's the *white men* who are the invaders, breaking a treaty to build a railroad on Indian land. By using parallel plots set in the cavalry fort and the Sioux village (real Native Americans were used as actors), *The Invaders* gives the natives an equality with the whites. Other films that portray Indians as round, convincing characters include George B. Seitz's *The Vanishing American* (1925) and Victor Schertzinger's *Redskin* (1929), both set in Navajo country in the Southwest.

Native Americans were also realistically represented by James Young Deer. He wrote scenarios for Lubin, Kalem, and other film companies and directed more than a hundred films for Pathé in America (because he was never given on-screen credit, it is impossible to say exactly how many he wrote or directed). His *White Fawn's Devotion* (1910), preserved by the Library of Congress, may be the earliest surviving film by a Native American (James Young Deer was purportedly a Winnebago from Nebraska, but recent research suggests that he may not have been an Indian after all). *White Fawn's Devotion* features an interracial couple: a British white man and his Indian wife, White Fawn, who live together in a Dakota cabin. From 1908 till 1912, Native Americans appeared on screen more than in any other period in film history.

HORROR AND SCIENCE FICTION

Horror was the more developed genre during the silent era, perhaps because there were so many literary antecedents ripe for adaptation (Robert Louis Stevenson's *The Strange Case of Dr. Jekyll and Mr. Hyde*, the first version of which was made as early as 1908 by Selig Polyscope; and Bram Stoker's *Dracula*), but there were certainly a number of science fiction features as well.

Horror adaptations came early, as in Edison's fourteen-minute *Frankenstein*, made in 1910, preceding James Whale's classic version of Mary Shelley's novel by some twenty years. *Dr. Jekyll and Mr. Hyde* (1920), starring John Barrymore in a virtuoso dual role and directed by John S. Robertson, is often considered America's first great horror film.

Nosferatu: A Symphony of Horror (1922), F. W. Murnau's eerie adaptation of Bram Stoker's *Dracula*, is part of the canon for its indelibly disturbing imagery and Max Schreck's performance as the cadaverous vampire Count Orlok. The title and names were changed to avoid copyright issues (unsuccessfully), but scriptwriter Henrik Galeen interpolated the film with fresh ideas. Count Orlok is not only the bloodsucker of legend but an avatar of plague: wherever he goes, Orlok is accompanied by swarms of rats, and people drop dead. And the images still haunt: the white trees of Carpathia against a grim sky, the death ship carrying its terrible cargo of coffins to Bremen. The film still resonates today. In *Shadow of the Vampire*, John Malkovich played Murnau filming the horror classic. Murnau's fellow countryman Werner Herzog offered a tribute to the silent film in his remake *Nosferatu the Vampyre*, with Klaus Kinski in the Schreck role.

Frankenstein, Edison Manufacturing Company (1910).

Top: Max Schreck in F. W. Murnau's *Nosferatu* (1922), one of the earliest screen adaptations based on Bram Stoker's *Dracula*.

Bottom: Scene from *Häxan: Witchcraft Through the Ages* (1922), directed by Benjamin Christensen.

The Germans produced a number of noteworthy horror films. Borrowing from the Faust legend, E. T. A. Hoffmann, and Edgar Allan Poe, *The Student of Prague* (1913) is a variation on the doppelgänger theme. Directed by Stellan Rye, it stars Paul Wegener as the student Baldwin, who exchanges his mirror reflection for riches and power in a deal with a strange mountebank named Scapinelli. The reflection, also played by Wegener, steps out of the mirror and assumes a life of its

Der Golem (1915), directed by Henrik Galeen and Paul Wegener.

own. Of course, things turn out badly, and when Baldwin shoots his reflection, he himself falls dead. The film was remade in 1926 by Henrik Galeen. Galeen and Wegener codirected *The Golem* (1915), based on the Jewish legend in which a clay statue of a giant man created by Rabbi Loew of Prague comes to life. The Golem, played by Wegener, falls in love with his master's daughter, but when she flees in terror, he is driven mad with rage and is eventually destroyed. The same team remade the film in 1920.

Perhaps unclassifiable, but genuinely horrifying and even still shocking today, is Danish director Benjamin Christensen's bizarre cult classic *Häxan: Witchcraft Through the Ages* (1922), which purports to be a kind of documentary arguing that witches suffered from a psychological state akin to "hysteria." In fact, the film is a witches' brew of fact and fiction, documentary and acted scenes, with the director himself playing the devil.

In the United States, Lon Chaney, still known today as "the man of a thousand faces," specialized in a kind of psychological horror that depended on physical and mental deformity. In *The Penalty* (1920), a surgeon mistakenly amputates Chaney's legs, and he is twisted by his desire for revenge; and in Tod Browning's bizarre *The Unknown* (1927), Chaney deliberately has his arms amputated in his hopeless pursuit of Joan Crawford, who can't stand the touch of men. In *The Phantom of the Opera* (1925), probably his best film, he sums up his screen persona neatly: "If I am a Phantom it is because man's hatred has made me so." Writer Ray Bradbury described Chaney as "someone who acted out our psyche. He somehow got inside the shadows inside our bodies. He was able to nail some of our secret fears and put them on the screen."

There also developed a subgenre of the haunted-house film, including Roland West's *The Bat* (1926) and Paul Leni's *The Cat and the Canary* (1927), the latter greatly admired by James Whale, whose talkie *The Old Dark House* (1932) is the apotheosis of the formula.

Although Méliès's *A Trip to the Moon* has the trappings of science fiction and was inspired by the works of Jules Verne and H. G. Wells, it really is more in the realm of science fantasy. True science fiction, because its sets are expensive to produce convincingly, really emerged during the feature era.

Lon Chaney, the Man of a Thousand Faces, in three of his most notorious films.

Top left: Chaney as the legless Blizzard in *The Penalty* (1920).

Top right: Chaney as the vampire fiend in *London After Midnight* (1927).

Bottom: Chaney as Alonzo the Armless in *The Unknown* (1927).

Lon Chaney (center) as Quasimodo
and Patsy Ruth Miller as Esmerelda
in *The Hunchback of Notre Dame*
(1923), directed by Wallace Worsley.

Top: Still from *20,000 Leagues Under the Sea* (1916).

Bottom left: Shooting diagram for the Williamson photosphere, used to film *20,000 Leagues Under the Sea*. A camera and cameraman were placed in the photosphere under sea and connected to the surface via a watertight tube.

Bottom right: *The Lost World* (1925) was special-effects pioneer Willis O'Brien's first Hollywood feature. He used cutting-edge stop-motion techniques to combine animated dinosaurs with live-action humans in the same shots. O'Brien later worked on *King Kong*.

Many early science fiction features were also adaptations. Jules Verne's *20,000 Leagues Under the Sea*, released as a film in 1916, is notable today for the extraordinary underwater photography of George and Ernest Williamson. Another adaptation, from Sir Arthur Conan Doyle's *The Lost World*, directed by Harry O. Hoyt and released in 1925, has an expedition finding dinosaurs on a Brazilian plateau. Willis O'Brien's model-animation dinosaurs move with remarkable lifelike fluidity.

Interestingly, the first big-budget Soviet film was science fiction: Russian director Yakov Protazanov's *Aelita: The Queen of Mars* (1924). It is as compelling for its picture of contemporary Soviet life as for its dazzling scenes of Mars, with their Constructivist sets. There is even a revolutionary uprising to create a Martian Union of Soviet Socialist Republics!

In Germany, Fritz Lang produced two science fiction films, *Metropolis* (1927) and *Woman in the Moon* (1929). *Metropolis* pictures a dystopian world in which the ruling elite lives in skyscraper pleasure palaces, while the workers are banished to subterranean dens. Some writers have criticized *Metropolis* — especially for its pat ending — but it remains an awesome cinematic spectacle. Even as a flawed masterpiece, it ranks with some of the greatest science fiction films of all time, such as Stanley Kubrick's *2001: A Space Odyssey*, Andrei Tarkovsky's *Solaris*, and Ridley Scott's *Blade Runner*.

Whereas *Metropolis* mixes medievalism with futurism, *Woman in the Moon* attempts to bring a greater realism to its science fiction imagining. Lang hired missile experts as technical advisers in building his rocket, among them rocketry expert and science writer Willy Ley, who said that the launch countdown — in films and in space science — was used for the first time in *Woman in the Moon*. The actual voyage to the moon and landing involves a lot of genre clichés — an eccentric scientist, a boy stowaway, a love triangle, a battle for gold — but it remains entertaining today and pointed the way toward filmmaking that incorporates real science with its fiction.

DOCUMENTARIES

The actualities of the first years of film served as a kind of documentary and were often combined with slides in a lecture format. A collection of short films on such subjects as Queen Victoria's Jubilee (1897) and the Spanish-American War (1897–98) could produce an extended narrative. The "news value" of such nonfiction cinema dated quickly, but that problem was resolved with more regular programming. Pathé-Frères began distributing a

Top: Yakov Protazanov directed the Russian sci-fi film *Aelita: Queen of Mars* (1924).

Bottom: Advertisement in *Motion Picture News* for the sci-fi spoof *A Message from Mars* (1921).

Trade advertisement for a 1920 documentary on Shackleton's expedition to Antarctica aboard the *Endurance*.

weekly newsreel in Paris in 1908 and, subsequently, throughout France, Germany, and England. A version was introduced in the United States in 1911 that was quickly imitated by domestic producers.

Robert Flaherty is the best-known silent-era documentarian, and his first feature, *Nanook of the North* (1922), about the Inuit of northern Canada, remains one of the most popular silent films of all time. Centered on Nanook and his family's daily struggle to survive in their harsh environment, it makes a compelling and personal drama. (Nanook died of starvation two years after the film was made, and obituaries ran in newspapers around the world.) Flaherty spent years among the Inuit, and much about *Nanook* is authentic. "I was an explorer first, and a filmmaker a long way after," he said. But Flaherty has been criticized for turning back the cultural clock at times: the filmmaker dresses the Eskimos in traditional garb, for instance, when they already favored Western-style clothes. In his next film, *Moana* (1926), about the Samoans, Flaherty similarly asked the natives to resurrect the male puberty rite of tattooing. But Flaherty, like an anthropologist, spent *time* with his subjects. (The word *documentary* was used for the first time by British critic and filmmaker John Grierson to describe *Moana*.)

Other documentarians who explored exotic locales and cultures were Merian C. Cooper and Ernest B. Schoedsack. Their film *Grass* (1925) focuses on the seasonal migration of the Bakhtiari people shepherding their animals across snowy mountains and icy rivers in Persia. Beautifully filmed, *Grass* powerfully evokes the hardships of the journey and the indomitability of the human spirit. The team's next outing, *Chang* (1927), focuses more on individuals, depicting a family in Siam. While some scenes are staged — a herd of elephants destroys a village — the filmmakers spent a year in the jungle doing research to give the film authenticity. They made a highly successful conversion to fiction with 1933's *King Kong*.

Among documentaries there is a subgenre of "city symphony" films depicting modern urban life, often set during a single day. Urban Paris, for instance, is the subject of Alberto Calvalcanti's 1926 *Only the Hours*. The two most famous examples of the city film, and deservedly so, are Walter Ruttmann's *Berlin: Symphony of a City* (1927) and Dziga Vertov's *The Man with a Movie Camera* (1929), which actually uses footage of several cities — Moscow, Kiev, Odessa, and areas of Ukraine.

Just as today, film was used to make explicitly political statements. A classic example in American filmmaking is *The Passaic Textile Strike* (1926), which dramatized an immigrant family's struggle against a local mill. Finally, in 1927, the textile workers won their demands.

Top: Advertisement for Fox newsreels in *Motion Picture News* (1925).

Bottom left: This advertisement in *Motion Picture News* (1925) promoted a documentary by Robert Flaherty about life in western Samoa.

Bottom right: Another Flaherty production, advertised here in *Motion Picture News* (1922), documented a year in the life of an Inuit family in the Canadian Arctic.

SERIALS AND SERIES FILMS

The series genre was inaugurated in France with Éclair's *Nick Carter: King of Detectives*, in 1908. In the United States, Edison launched *What Happened to Mary?* in 1912, which numbered twelve one-reel episodes released in monthly installments, in tandem with stories published simultaneously in the women's magazine *Ladies World*. This successful synergy between film and print was widely copied: for instance, the film company Selig and the *Chicago Tribune* cross-promoted *The Adventures of Kathlyn* (1913–14). A distinction is often made between serial and series films; *What Happened to Mary?* is considered a series because each episode is self-contained — although overall it has a unified story line. *The Adventures of Kathlyn*, on the other hand, continued its plot directly across weekly episodes, so it is considered a true serial.

Poster for the ninth episode of the Fox serial *Bride 13* (1920). A total of fifteen chapters of two reels each tells the story of brides kidnapped at the altar and threatened with being put in a harem if the villain does not collect a ransom.

Serial or series stories became so popular in the teens that nearly every important studio made them: for example, Kalem produced the longest-running "chapter play," *The Hazards of Helen* (1914–17), starring Helen Holmes in most of its first forty-seven episodes, and Pathé made the famous Pearl White series *The Perils of Pauline* (1914).

Because they developed longer narratives, serials bridged the transition from one- and two-reel films to features, which attracted more sophisticated audiences. At the same time, however, because of their sensationalist melodrama, serials were stigmatized as low-brow. "I am the serial," read an article in the *New York Dramatic Mirror*, in 1916. "I am the black sheep of the picture family and the reviled of critics. I am the soulless one with no moral, no character, no uplift. . . . Ah me, if I could only be respectable. If only the hair of the great critic would not rise whenever I pass by and if only he would not cry, 'Shame! Child of commerce! Bastard of art!' "

Still, the serial in America in the teens featured strong, independent, and athletic heroines, and serial queens represented what the media heralded as the "new woman," casting off the passivity of Victorian mores and invading traditionally male realms. To give just one example: in episode twenty-six of *The Hazards of Helen*, "The Wild Engine" (1915), Helen must, absurdly, prove her mettle once again merely because of her sex. She works as a railroad telegraph operator in remote areas, and the railroad superintendent is reluctant to employ her. He tells the man who wants to hire her, "Women cannot use their heads in case of emergency, and if you employ her, I shall hold you entirely responsible." Of course, Helen proves herself up to the task, which here involves saving not one, but three separate trains during the course of one reel, and then only after riding a motorcycle over a rising drawbridge and diving into the water.

The serial queens were adored by their fans. The American serials themselves, however, were profoundly formulaic: typically a villain repeatedly tried to kill or kidnap the heroine, while also trying to obtain some important object — a blueprint, a will, a secret formula — which Pearl White, with *le mot juste*, called the *weenie*. Film historian Shelley Stamp points out that the serial queens

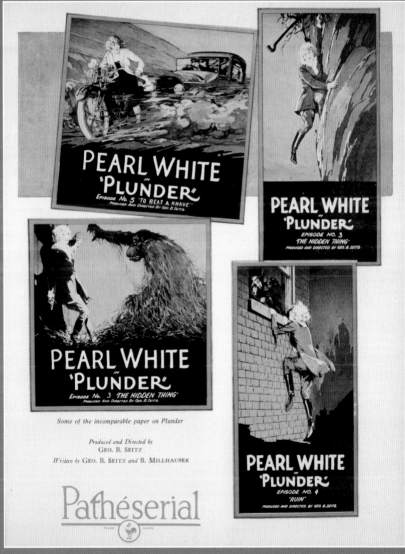

Some of the incomparable paper on Plunder

Produced and Directed by
GEO. B. SEITZ
Written by GEO. B. SEITZ and B. MILLHAUSER

Pathéserial

Top: Pearl White, the most popular of the plucky heroines, on the Palisades in Fort Lee, New Jersey for a Pathé serial, *The Perils of Pauline* (1914). With her is cameraman Arthur Miller and the fearless director George Seitz.

Bottom: Posters offered in the pressbook for Pearl White's last serial, *Plunder*, with episodes such as "To Beat a Knave," "Ruin," and "The Hidden Thing."

Above: Louis Feuillade's *Tih Minh* (1918).

Top left: Helen Holmes on top of a train, in one of the forty-eight episodes of her railroad serial *The Hazards of Helen* (1914). Almost as popular as Pearl White at her peak, she braves everything to save the train, a child, and a hurt engineer, doing her own stunts in titles such as "The Car of Death," "From Peril to Peril," and the "Demon of the Rails" (1914).

Bottom left: *Les Vampires* (1915–16). The prolific director of hundreds of French serials and short films, Louis Feuillade was inventive, imaginative, and daring.

Bottom right: The Gaumont serial *Fantômas Under the Shadow of the Guillotine* (1913).

often offered "a double-edged pleasure" by having it both ways; they were adventurous, single women who saved the day but then ended up getting married, receiving big inheritances, or being rescued by men. Although serials continued to be made in the United States, in the twenties men took over the leading roles.

Serials also continued to be produced in France, even during World War I. In 1913, Louis Feuillade made the first of a crime series called *Fantômas*. Incredibly, in Paris in 1915–16, even while the battle of Verdun raged, Feuillade produced the cult classic, seven-hour series *Les Vampires*, which features a reporter-hero (Éduard Mathé) battling the distaff crime figure Irma Vep (Musidora, who in one scene wears a black bodysuit). Irma Vep's gang, the Vampires (her name is an anagram for *vampire*), steals jewels and banknotes, but its real motives remain larger and more mysterious. The bourgeois order is constantly in danger, as the Vampires race across the rooftops of Paris or plot mayhem in low dives. Olivier Assayas created an homage to Feuillade with his 1996 film *Irma Vep*, about a director remaking *Les Vampires* (as a silent!) starring Hong Kong actress Maggie Cheung.

In Germany just after the war, films set in exotic locales were extremely popular (the Germans no doubt craved escapism in the wake of their defeat and the Great War's devastation). Fritz Lang's series films, *The Spiders* (1919), offer Indiana Jones–style entertainment in the most far-flung places. The two feature-length episodes of a planned series of four (two were never made) follow the adventures of millionaire Kai Hoog (Carl de Vogt): in *The Golden Sea*, he travels to Peru, where he discovers the treasures of the survivors of Incan civilization; and *The Diamond Ship*, whose plot revolves around the search for the "Buddha Head" diamond, has scenes set in India and the Falkland Islands. (Shooting *The Spiders*, Lang's earliest surviving films, kept him from directing *The Cabinet of Dr. Caligari*. Producer Erich Pommer, who had originally picked Lang, assigned the film to Robert Wiene instead.)

Top: *Humorous Phases of Funny Faces* (1906), J. Stuart Blackton. A hand (Blackton's) sketches caricatures of a man's and woman's face on a blackboard. The faces roll their eyes; the man's cigar blows smoke and covers the woman; an outline of a man with a bowler and umbrella draws itself, and the man tips his hat.

Center: *Modeling* (*Out of the Inkwell*; 1911), Max Fleischer, animator. Fleischer appeared as "the artist" with Koko the Clown (later called Ko-ko) in these films and became a celebrity in his own right.

Bottom: *There It Is* (1928), a two-reel comedy by Charles Bowers.

ANIMATION

Stop-motion, which made the trick films of Méliès and others possible, was used to create animated cartoons: expose a single drawing for a frame or two, make changes or substitute a new drawing, expose it briefly, and voila, the illusion of movement.

Perhaps the first true animated cartoon was J. Stuart Blackton's *Humorous Phases of Funny Faces* (1906), which showed an artist's hand drawing faces that subsequently appeared to move their eyes and mouths of their own accord. Émile Cohl, a French caricaturist, was the first great artist to enter the animation field. His *Fantasmagorie* (1908) also showed a hand drawing figures. His films eschewed narrative for a bizarre series of metamorphoses. Eventually he was brought to the United States, where he adapted a comic strip series, "The Newlyweds and Their Baby," to film, which became a common tactic.

In 1911, Winsor McKay, a brilliant American comic strip illustrator, made a short film based on his "Little Nemo in Slumberland" strip, which he drew on thousands of cards. The cartoon, filmed by Vitagraph, has a live-action introduction with McKay showing off his work, and the giant stacks of drawings required for the short film are indeed impressive (the drawings are hand colored as well). In his second film, *How a Mosquito Operates* (1911), McKay imbues his bug with personality, a feat he also manages in 1914's *Gertie the Dinosaur*. He gives Gertie the persona of a little girl who doesn't always do what she's asked. McKay's 1918 masterpiece, *The Sinking of the Lusitania*, is a serious dramatic work, more akin to the graphic novels of today.

The labor-intensive work of animating early films required time and obsessiveness, and John Randolph Bray and Earl Hurd developed a patented technique that used transparent overlays of celluloid, allowing static backgrounds to be employed several times while the artist concentrated on the moving figures. Their work set the stage for the division of labor in animation.

Other important American animators included the brothers Max and Dave Fleischer, who began their innovative series *Out of the Inkwell* in 1920. Again a hand is seen drawing a character, an obstreperous clown who is forced back into the inkwell at the end of each film. Otto Messmer and Pat Sullivan created, in 1919, an animal character with a strong personality that became Felix the Cat. In the mid to late 1920s, Walter Elias Disney made a series of comedies with a live-action character named Alice who romped in an animated world. He also produced two Mickey Mouse cartoons in 1928, but distributors were not interested. Little did they know . . .

Top: Modeled on the brontosaurus in the American Museum of Natural History, *Gertie the Dinosaur* (1914) was among the first American animated films. New York newspaper cartoonist Winsor McKay collaborated with John A. Fitzsimmons to make the hungry Gertie's adventure, which required 10,000 drawings on rice paper and took two years to complete.

Bottom left: Felix the Cat in *Uncle Tom's Crabbin'* (1927), in which Felix escapes from an evil slave owner and his whip. Pat Sullivan produced and directed this film, animated by Otto M. Messmer.

Bottom right: *Aesop's Fables Modernized* by cartoonist Paul Terry. The president of Fables Pictures, Inc., decided to produce *Aesop's Fables* every week. Keith-Albee, which would become one of the most proficient and profitable theater chains of the decade, underwrote the studio's expenses and guaranteed bookings.

Cecil B. DeMille's *The King of Kings* (1927). DeMille was the complete director-as-auteur, using chiaroscuro and diffused light so that the picture moves with a measured dignity perfectly in tune with his reverential style. As Derek Elley writes in *The Epic Film* (1985), "By not using a modern story to parallel the biblical one, DeMille advanced the historical epic from adolescence to adulthood."

EPICS

Before the digital age, when it would become possible to create virtual ships and armies with a few computer keystrokes, epic films required real ships and real extras. Labor was relatively cheap in the silent era, which made epic spectacles tempting, and silent directors yielded to that temptation frequently. Jorge Luis Borges once noted the irony that the form perfected by Homer would be continued by Hollywood. But it was the Italians who first brought the epic form to the screen with works like *Cabiria*. Hollywood soon took up the torch with such epics as Griffith's *The Birth of a Nation* (1915), Cecil B. DeMille's *The Ten Commandments* (1923), and Fred Niblo's *Ben-Hur* (1925).

Ben-Hur is a perfect example of the crowd-pleasing possibilities of cinematic spectacle. Combining the life of Christ with a conflict between friends turned bitter enemies — Messala, a Roman soldier played by Francis X. Bushman, and Ben-Hur, played by Ramon Novarro — the film's highlights include a violent sea battle and a breathtaking chariot race between the antagonists. The latter scene was filmed in a gargantuan re-creation of the Circus Maximus. Forty-two cameramen shot a total of 200,000 feet of film for the one sequence, which in the final film ran 750 feet. Several scenes were shot in two-strip Technicolor. The film's negative cost was about four million dollars, and even though it was a box-office smash, it lost a million dollars because of the expense of distribution and rights. Still, it was a hugely prestigious project for MGM.

The coliseum set for the chariot race in director Fred Niblo's *Ben-Hur: A Tale of the Christ* (1925). The set in Italy was abandoned because of vast cost overruns, and a new one was built in Culver City, California.

Noah's Ark: The Story of the Deluge tells a tale of idolatry, extravagance, and enslavement versus simplicity and freedom in mid-third millennium northern Mesopotamia, paralleled with a story of soldiers in World War I. Narrated by a minister played by Paul McAllister (who also plays Noah), the movie stars Dolores Costello as Mary/Miriam and George O'Brien as Travis/Japheth. A transitional film with a musical score and sound effects, as well as a few talking sequences, director Michael Curtiz's spectacle is noted as one of the most impressive ever put on film: the destruction of the temple of Akkad, the coming of the rains, the arrival of the animals, and a relentless flood overwhelm the World War I story.

EXPERIMENTAL FILMS

In a sense, experimental films represent an antigenre, in that they rarely follow "the rules" of commercial cinema, while mainstream films generally follow certain conventions. But in the 1920s, artists appropriated film as a working medium, using cameras and celluloid rather than paint and canvas. They created an art cinema, producing avant-garde works that might use purely abstract imagery or actors but generally eschewed narrative or conventional storytelling.

France, already a hotbed of modern art, was a cauldron of avant-garde filmmaking. In Cubist painter Fernand Léger's *Mechanical Ballet* (1924), photographed by Man Ray and Dudley Murphy, and with a score by American composer George Antheil, inanimate objects "dance" with animation, while the humans depicted seem drained of life. René Clair's Surrealist *Entr'acte* (1924) was screened between acts of Erik Satie's ballet *Relâche* (also scored by Satie), with cameos by such luminaries as Marcel Duchamp and Man Ray (playing chess), Francis Picabia, and Satie himself. The film features an outrageous funeral procession, ending with the "corpse" rising from the dead and causing everyone at the funeral to disappear.

Russian émigré director Dimitri Kirsanoff, working in Paris, made one of the most powerful experimental films of the time, *Ménilmontant* (1926). Beautifully filmed, it also has a strong narrative: it begins with two sisters murdering their parents with an axe, then heading for Paris. There, a man seduces and impregnates the younger girl, then abandons her for her sister. It ends with his murder. *New Yorker* movie critic Pauline Kael told an interviewer that it was one of her favorite films.

Surely the most famous silent art film of all time is Luis Buñuel's *An Andalusian Dog* (1928). The Spaniards Salvador Dalí and Buñuel collaborated on the script, and Buñuel shot the film in two weeks for a pittance (borrowed from his mother). A surreal montage of striking images — an eye being sliced by a razor, ants emerging from a hole in a hand — it haunts one's imagination even today. Generations of film critics and writers have speculated about its "meaning." Let's let Buñuel have the last word. "Our only rule was very simple: No idea or image that might lend itself to a rational explanation of any kind would be accepted. We had to open all doors to the irrational and keep only those images that surprised us, without trying to explain why," he wrote in his memoir, *My Last Breath*.

France may have created myriad art films, but it certainly didn't have a monopoly on experimental imagination. Americans also produced avant-garde works. An early example is *Manhatta* (1921), by photographer Paul Strand and painter and photographer Charles Sheeler. It depicts contemporary Manhattan as a cold forbidding place, using verses from the poetry of Walt Whitman as intertitles, sometimes ironically. Much of it is shot looking down from atop skyscrapers, their

Top: Robert Florey's *The Life and Death of 9413, a Hollywood Extra* (1928), the story of the short and unhappy life of an extra in Hollywood who wears a number on his forehead for casting calls that never come. Only in heaven is he numberless.

Bottom: In Hans Richter's *Ghosts Before Breakfast* (*Vormittagsspuk*, 1928), hats dance in an antic Dada experience.

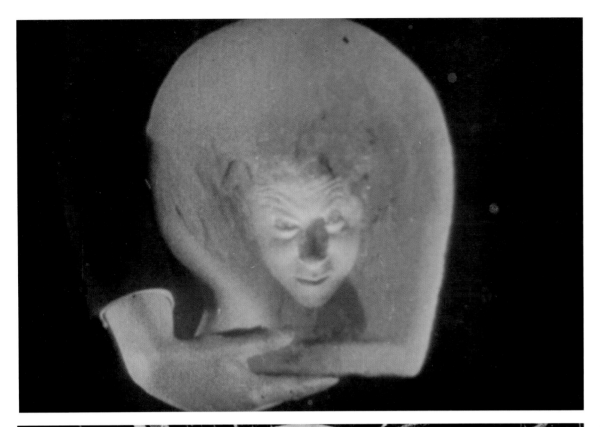

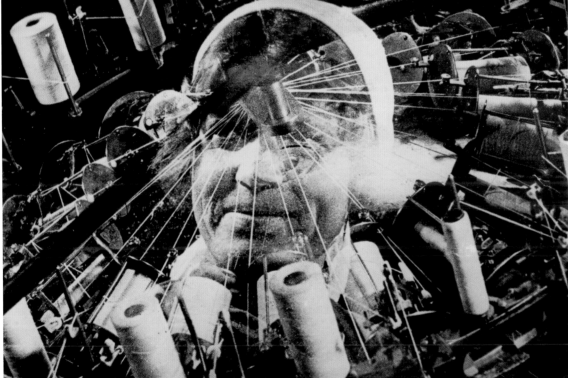

Top: *The Seashell and the Clergyman* (*La coquille et le clergyman*, 1927), directed by Germaine Dulac and written by Antonin Artaud, contains a montage of a priest's struggle to suppress his sexual desires.

Center: In Dziga Vertov's *The Man with a Movie Camera* (*Chelovek's kino-apparatom*, 1929), a cameraman travels around a city, documenting urban life from many angles and at dizzying speed.

Bottom: Fernand Léger's *Mechanical Ballet* (*Charlot présent le ballet méchanique*, France, 1924), photographed by Man Ray and Dudley Murphy, mixed inanimate objects with humans.

towering, abstract architecture giving its denizens and workers the likenesses of insects in a hive.

The Life and Death of 9413, a Hollywood Extra (1928) is a ninety-nine-dollar satire of the star system. Directed by Robert Florey and Slavko Vorkapich and photographed by Gregg Toland, it tells the story of an actor wannabe who is so dehumanized by the system of "auditions" that he has the number 9413 emblazoned on his forehead. In a parody of Hollywood happy endings, he eventually dies and goes to heaven. The film was made on a table, using cardboard, paper cutouts, kitchen utensils, and some live footage. Chaplin was enamored of it and it got some distribution in commercial theaters. Florey went on to direct more than sixty features, while Toland shot a little film called *Citizen Kane*.

THE
ART of FILM

THE VERY EARLIEST FILMMAKERS, LIKE HOME-MOVIE ENTHUSIASTS, MADE MOVIES ALL BY THEMSELVES — DOCUMENTING SIMPLE DOMESTIC LIFE OR PARADES OR A VAUDEVILLE ACT. BUT ONCE THEY BEGAN TELLING STORIES, TO USE A BIOLOGICAL METAPHOR, THE EMBRYO BEGAN TO GROW AND THE CELLS TO DIFFERENTIATE: DIRECTORS NEEDED ACTORS (WHO IN TURN REQUIRED COSTUMES AND SETS TO PERFORM IN FRONT OF), EXPERIENCED CAMERAMEN TO FILM THE PERFORMANCE, AND OF COURSE, A NARRATIVE TO TIE IT ALL TOGETHER. AS MOVIE PRODUCTION INCREASED, MORE PEOPLE WERE NEEDED TO KEEP PACE WITH THEATER DEMAND — SCENARIO AND TITLE WRITERS, ART DIRECTORS, PRODUCTION DESIGNERS, CARPENTERS, PAINTERS, COSTUME DESIGNERS, LIGHTING TECHNICIANS, MAKEUP ARTISTS. AND AS MOVIEGOING BECAME A MORE RESPECTABLE, MIDDLE-CLASS PASTIME, PRODUCTION VALUES GREW INCREASINGLY IMPORTANT IN SATISFYING A MORE DISCRIMINATING AUDIENCE. DIRECTORS PUT THEIR STAMPS ON FILMS, AND MANY HAD DISTINCTIVE STYLES, BUT THEY RELIED MORE AND MORE ON A TEAM OF SPECIALISTS. BY 1915, HOLLYWOOD SUPPORTED SOME FIFTEEN THOUSAND WORKERS.

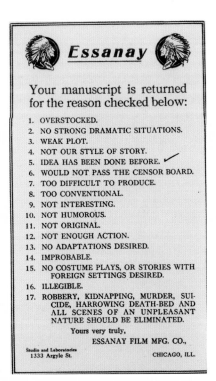

Above: A sample rejection slip used by the Essanay Film Manufacturing Company.

Left: Set painting for Georges Méliès's *Palace of Arabian Nights* (*Le Palais des milles et une nuits*, 1905), tableau 14 (*Descente dans la grotte de cristal*).

WRITING

Screenwriters often complain about their invisibility. Sure, they get some largely token acknowledgment during the award season, but by and large audiences, and even movie reviewers, pay far more attention to actors, directors, even special effects. But in the beginning, at least as far as screen storytelling goes, is the word.

In early photoplays, filmmakers often relied on literary works — well-loved stories, novels, plays, or even poems in the public domain were ripe for the picking because they were free. That helps to explain the large number of silent Shakespeare productions. Still, someone had to write a scene-by-scene synopsis, and so the scenario (known today as the screenplay) was born.

A scenario for a two-reeler might run one or two pages. As feature-length films emerged in the early teens, scripts grew longer. Anita Loos, one of the most successful scenarists of the silent era, said that by the middle of the decade, her scenarios were running forty pages. These were not detailed continuity scripts; only after a scenario was acquired were the details worked out for camera positions and lighting in the shooting script.

Scenarists might write the intertitles or not. Often, doing so was a separate task. But in the teens, there was a thriving freelance market for original scenarios. (Another strategy would be to acquire the rights to a successful contemporary stage play, but that could prove costly. Frances Marion, another very successful screenwriter, estimated in 1924 that the average cost of the rights

Advertisements for screenwriting schools flooded the pages of early movie magazines.

to a successful play was $20,000. The rights to the play *Way Down East*, filmed by Griffith, cost $175,000.)

But in 1914, *Photoplay Author* magazine reported that scenarios usually sold for fifty dollars or less per reel. The paltry sums paid to scenario writers were not especially discouraging. Everyone seemed to think that he could write a photoplay scenario, and the studios were overwhelmed with submissions. Schools and agencies, often scams, cashed in. One ad that appeared in the January 1915 issue of *Motion Picture Magazine* promised, "YOU can earn BIG MONEY WRITING PHOTO-PLAYS. Great demand. We teach only sure method of writing or selling photoplays. No experience or literary ability required." "Millions of People Can Write Stories and Photoplays and Don't Know It!" enthused an ad for the Irving System. All one needed, apparently, was a typewriter.

Several books on scenario writing appeared as well, such as A. Van Buren Powell's *The Photoplay Synthesis* (1919). Elinor Glyn (of *It* fame) published a book on writing scenarios, the third volume of her series *The Elinor Glyn System of Writing* ("Keep Your Hero Smiling!" she opined).

The studios also developed their own scenario departments — with writers working on contract — and by the early twenties, the freelance market had dried up. Frequently writers were connected with stars — Loos often wrote for Douglas Fairbanks, and C. Gardner Sullivan frequently worked with William S. Hart. Many of the writers were women: in addition to Loos, they included Frances Marion (*Stella Maris, The Wind*), Jeanie MacPherson (*The Cheat, Male and Female*), and June Mathis (*The Four Horsemen of the Apocalypse, Ben-Hur*). Goldwyn took writers seriously and recruited a number of noted print authors, including Somerset Maugham and Rupert Hughes, with decidedly mixed results.

The story of Anita Loos has a fairy-tale quality. She was raised in California, and her father ran a theater that showed films between acts; she grew up watching them from behind the screen. "It occurred to me that they must need stories," she said. "So I wrote one. . . . I mailed it in and it was accepted immediately. The title was *The New York Hat*; Mary Pickford played the lead and D. W. Griffith directed. I got twenty-five dollars. I was twelve years old."

She wrote so many stories for Biograph that she was put on the payroll. When she arrived at the studio, Griffith mistook her mother, who accompanied her, for the scenarist. No, it was the gamine in pigtails who was the writer. She worked with Griffith — writing the intertitles for *Intolerance* a few years later — Douglas Fairbanks, and the Talmadge sisters. Loos wrote hundreds of scripts for silent movies, often with her husband, John Emerson, but is probably most famous for her novel *Gentlemen Prefer Blondes*, which was first released as a film in 1928, directed by Malcolm St. Clair from a scenario by Loos and Emerson.

Another scenarist, June Mathis, became one of the most powerful women in Hollywood. Hired by Metro as a writer, she adapted Vicente Blasco Ibáñez's novel *The Four Horsemen of the Apocalypse* and convinced the studio to hire Rex Ingram as director and the virtually unknown Rudolph Valentino to star in the lavish production. At Famous Players-Lasky, she adapted another Blasco Ibáñez novel, *Blood and Sand*, for Valentino, which was also a huge commercial success.

Mathis then became editorial director at Goldwyn Pictures. Most of her time there was spent on *Ben-Hur*, which she insisted be shot in Italy. The production proved an enormous debacle, and after Goldwyn merged into MGM, Mathis, her handpicked director, Charles Braban, and George Walsh, whom she chose to play Ben-Hur, were all fired, and *Ben-Hur* was moved to Hollywood. Mathis, however, landed on her feet, moving to First National, where she wrote for stars like Colleen Moore.

Another important role for writers was the crafting of intertitles: well-written titles could greatly enhance films, and bad titles could kill them. While scenarists might also write titles, some wordsmiths specialized in intertitle writing. In the early days of film, intertitles were often crucial, needed purely for information or to explain confusing action. As longer features developed, titles became an even more significant part of the entire film (dialogue titles were first used around 1907).

Screenwriter C. Gardner Sullivan contributed greatly to the success of the Western as a genre, penning the screenplays for William S. Hart vehicles like *Tumbleweeds* (1925) and *Hell's Hinges* (1916).

Intertitles could be wide-ranging in style and lent photoplays much of their individual feel. Fairbanks's intertitles were often chatty and witty, fitting the devil-may-care character he played. Hart's intertitles mixed "authentic" Western argot with purple prose. In *Hell's Hinges*, for example, Hart's character says to the preacher's sister, "I reckon God ain't wantin' me much, Ma'am, but when I look at you I feel I've been ridin' the wrong trail." At the extreme edge of the purple part of the spectrum, the final title reads, "And then from the mothering sky came the baby dawn, singing as it wreathed the gray horns of the mountains with ribbons of rose and gold."

D. W. Griffith's film intertitles careened from poetic to careless, but they are truly absorbing in *Intolerance*. Written by Loos, they are even footnoted to give the film the sense that it is based in historical fact, when in truth, it often veers far from it. But it has at least one immortal line: "Women who cease to attract men often turn to reform as a second choice."

As filmmakers developed their craft in the twenties, however, titles became less necessary. Acting, photography, and editing had sufficiently evolved so that directors could tell their stories with a minimum of words. In F. W. Murnau's *The Last Laugh*, for example, he dispenses with intertitles altogether except for one at the film's very end, which explains the film's parodic happy ending.

The Four Horsemen of the Apocalypse (1921), screenplay by June Mathis.

"Drink, my beauties, drink to your master."

Many women made significant inroads into the movie business by writing screenplays. With nearly three hundred films to their credit, Frances Marion, Elinor Glyn, and June Mathis showed they could be successful and move millions with their tales.

Top: Frances Marion, *Stella Dallas* (1925); bottom: Elinor Glyn, *Three Weeks* (1924).

ART DIRECTION and SET DESIGN

The earliest films, actualities, required no sets. Audiences were content, indeed amazed, to see a train coming into a station or waves lapping against the shore or a policemen's parade. Later, film sets grew quite naturally out of the stage tradition. In 1896, Méliès, a pioneer in art direction, began making films using scenery techniques derived from theater. He sometimes used a single painted backdrop,

Robin Hood (1922), art direction by Wilfred Buckland. The set for *Robin Hood* was the largest ever built in the silent era.

but more often employed a large canvas frame flanked by two smaller ones to suggest depth. On these "walls," he painted pictures or cabinets, while a canvas floor was illustrated to resemble a rug or tiles. Inside this stage were placed furniture and various props. His palaces, underwater caverns, and moonscapes with mushrooms are still charming and poetic; they are convincing because they create a self-contained world in which the viewer can suspend disbelief.

This theatrical style of set design was widespread. But once the camera moved outside, such stage scenery became what it obviously was — stage scenery. If an exterior scene, clearly "real," clashed with an indoor stage set, the viewer noticed the disconnect, and paradoxically, the illusion of reality was broken. As filmmakers sought to spin narratives with outdoor actions, the sets needed a sturdier authenticity.

Gradually, between about 1908 and 1912, filmmaking moved from stage scenery to constructed sets. The Italians set the bar very high in the early teens, with the three-dimensional sets of *Quo Vadis* and *Cabiria*, in which the camera glides through the faux marble halls, giving the films their sense of depth and space. Set design had emerged from the realm of the stage into the landscape of architecture.

D. W. Griffith was then inspired to create four worlds for four separate stories in 1916's monumental *Intolerance*. The film's look was researched by one of his actors, Joseph Henabery, for historical accuracy (with room for Griffith's artistic license — elephants were not a known motif in Babylon, but he was probably inspired by Hannibal's elephants in *Cabiria*). The sets were built by Frank "Huck" Wortman, based on designs by Walter L. Hall. Despite demands from the Los Angeles Fire Department that it be torn down, Babylon towered over the intersection of Sunset and Hollywood boulevards for a year after the film was finished. It seems somehow appropriate.

There was no turning back. Art directors, who sketched out scenes in detail, became a permanent part of film production, giving films their overall look and atmosphere as well as a sense of authenticity.

Erich von Stroheim's obsession with realism led to full-scale reproductions of Monte Carlo's Casino, Hotel de France, and Café de Paris for *Foolish Wives*. In writing his scripts, Stroheim

Top: The massive Wall of Babylon set for D. W. Griffith's *Intolerance* (1916) and, bottom: its construction. This set
holds the distinction of being the first exterior set ever built in Hollywood.

included drawings of sets, props, and costumes, but because of the enormity of the Monte Carlo sets, he collaborated with designer Richard Day.

The huge castle in 1922's *Robin Hood*, starring Douglas Fairbanks and directed by Allan Dwan, was the largest set built to date in Hollywood. *Robin Hood*, a masterpiece of set design, was overseen by supervising art director Wilfred Buckland. Fairbanks, at his first glimpse of the completed structure, exclaimed, "My gosh! It's astounding." But after touring the ninety-foot-high castle, he had second thoughts. "I can't compete with that," he said to Dwan. "I can't work in a great vast thing like that. What would I do in there?" He was eventually persuaded by Dwan and others that the film could be done without turning the star into a dwarf.

We tend to remember the monumental architecture of silent films, but in truth art direction is sometimes at its best when we notice it least. Buckland, a stage designer who worked for David Belasco, was one of Hollywood's first important art directors; he was hired by Famous Players-Lasky in 1914. He worked on many Cecil B. DeMille films, including *The Cheat, Joan the Woman*, and *Male and Female*, as well as Douglas Fairbanks's *Wild and Woolly*. Other early art directors included Day, who worked with Stroheim on *Foolish Wives, Greed*, and *The Wedding March*; Joseph Urban, a Viennese architect, who served as art director on several Marion Davies films, such as the medieval pageant *Yolanda*; and Ben Carré, a scenery painter for the Paris Opera, who worked for Maurice Tourneur (*Prunella*) and on the historically important *Don Juan*.

Two of the most influential art directors of the 1920s were William Cameron Menzies and Cedric Gibbons, who both had long careers that lasted into the 1950s. Menzies created the magnificent sets for *The Thief of Bagdad* but also worked on such significant late-twenties films as *The Son of the Sheik* and *Sadie Thompson*. At the first Academy Awards ceremony, Menzies won for Best Interior Decoration for *Tempest* and *The Dove* (both 1928).

Gibbons worked for Edison and Goldwyn before joining MGM, where he resided from its inception in 1924 till 1956. His contract stated that he be credited as art director on every film MGM released in the United States, which during his tenure numbered well over a thousand. However, his role was mostly supervisory, and the actual work on most of those productions was done by others. Still, he must be credited for giving the studio its distinctive, polished style. Gibbons also exploited stylistic trends; for instance, he inspired interior decorators around the

Above: Art director Richard Day worked on Erich von Stroheim's *The Wedding March* (1928).

Top left: An aerial view of the set for *The Thief of Bagdad* with the *Robin Hood* set in the background.

Bottom left: George Kleine commissioned the construction of this set for a film version of Boito's opera *Mefistófeles*, but the film was never completed due to the outbreak of World War I.

Top: *Male and Female* (1919), directed by Cecil B. DeMille, with art direction by Wilfred Buckland.

Bottom: *The Rustle of Silk* (1923), directed by Herbert Brenon, featured elaborate set designs but gave no credit to its art director.

globe with the Art Deco sets of *Our Dancing Daughters*, starring Joan Crawford. Gibbons also designed the Oscar statuette, based on the original model by Los Angeles sculptor George Stanley.

Hollywood strove for realism, even in films that involved fantasy, such as Fairbanks's *The Thief of Bagdad*, but Europeans were more tolerant of avant-garde techniques. When French director Tourneur, working in the United States, collaborated with art director Carré on *The Blue Bird* (1918), they used whimsical, highly artificial sets. American audiences rejected the film. But when Robert Wiene's Expressionist *The Cabinet of Dr. Caligari* (1920) — art directed by Hermann Warm, Walter Reimann, and Walter Röhrig — was seen in the United States a few years later, it was widely acclaimed.

Erich von Stroheim's *Queen Kelly* (1929) is seen by many as art director Richard Day's finest achievement.

In the era of over-the-top design, some art directors achieved fame while others worked in obscurity. From top left, clockwise: *Cobra* (1925), art direction by W. C. Menzies; *Paying the Piper* (1921), art director unknown; *Broadway Jones* (1917), art director unknown; *Her Reputation* (1923), art director unknown; *Annie Laurie* (1927), art direction by Gibbons; *Our Dancing Daughters* (1928), art direction by Gibbons.

The Pioneer Scout (1928), cinematography by Mack Stengler.

CINEMATOGRAPHY

Like screenwriting, the art of the camera is often unheralded: the director frequently gets credit for the beauty and subtlety of the film's visuals, even though directors rarely look through the camera. But everything in making a film depends on just this one thing: getting images onto film. As in all trades, some cinematographers are better than others, but some are extraordinarily gifted artists. Not for nothing was the brilliant 1992 documentary on cinematographers called *Visions of Light*.

Camera technology evolved swiftly. Motion-picture production companies made their own cameras (Edison, Vitagraph, and Biograph each had its own cameras, and film shot on cameras of different makes could not be intercut without having the footage go out of frame). The Pathé camera became immensely popular, for it was rugged, light, and dependable, made of wood encased in leather with a hand crank positioned in the rear. Before 1918, some 60 percent of all films — in the United States and Europe — were shot using a Pathé.

The Pathé's first real competition was the Bell & Howell 2709, introduced at market in 1911–12, not really popular until 1915, and produced until 1958. It was a precision, all-metal device. In 1920 George Mitchell, a cameraman himself, developed a camera that would supersede the Bell & Howell at the studios.

In the silent era, cameras were hand cranked by choice rather than necessity (the Bell & Howell had a motorized crank, but few chose to use it). Hand cranking allowed cameramen to slow down or speed up the action. They came to know instinctively whether audiences would, for instance, be bored because the action was moving too slowly or not take a scene seriously if it moved too fast. With the advent of sound synchronization, however, motorized film became necessary in order to standardize shooting speed.

Many cameramen were on contract with studios on a per-week or per-film basis. Others freelanced, hustling for jobs. But the best cinematographers worked regularly with specific directors or stars. The most famous team in silent-film history was director Griffith and his cameraman G. W. "Billy" Bitzer, who worked together from 1908 to 1928. Bitzer shot hundreds of films for Griffith, including the features *Judith of Bethulia*, *The Birth of a Nation*, *Intolerance*, *Broken Blossoms*, and *Way Down East*.

Bitzer used a variety of innovative techniques: he would shoot scenes entirely with artificial light at a time when studios were usually built like greenhouses to use available daylight; he made frequent use of fade-outs, in which a scene would dissolve, and irises, beginning a scene with a small circle in a black-out frame that opened up to reveal the full

THIS IS THE NEW FALL STYLE IN CAMERA "MEN"

Meaning, the style you could fall for. Nor is this a masquerade get-up. Margery Ordway, regular, professional, licensed, union crank-turner at Camp Morosco, has gone into camera work as nonchalantly as other girls take up stenography, nursing, husband-stalking.

Top: Billy Bitzer, favorite cameraman of D. W. Griffith, films from the front of a moving train.

Bottom: Margery Ordway, one of the few camerawomen of the silent era.

Cameraman James Wong Howe.

picture; and he developed a soft-focus photography using screens.

Often innovations were the result of pure serendipity. During a break in work at Biograph, Mary Pickford and Owen Moore were walking on a gravel path. Bitzer noticed that the gravel reflected a soft light on their faces and eliminated shadows. He quickly improvised the use of reflected light, a technique that has become standard in filming to this day.

James Wong Howe, who emigrated from Canton at the age of five and rose from Beverly Hills Hotel busboy to one of the most famous cameramen in Hollywood, hit upon another important technique quite by accident. He was asked to do some stills of actress Mary Miles Minter, which turned out splendidly. She had lovely blue eyes, but unfortunately the film in use at the time made blue-eyed actors look fish-eyed and expressionless. His photographs made her eyes look dark. Howe figured out that it was the reflection off black velvet in the room that had darkened her eyes and started shooting light-eyed actors through a scrim of black velvet. Howe went on to film Minter in *The Trail of the Lonesome Pine*. Howe also filmed Victor Fleming's *Mantrap*, with Clara Bow, and Herbert Brenon's *Laugh, Clown, Laugh*, with Lon Chaney. He made films into the seventies and was nothing if not versatile. "I have a basic approach that goes on from film to film," he told Charles Higham, "to make all the sources of light absolutely realistic."

Charles Rosher was one of Hollywood's first cameramen, at Nestor Films. In those early days, the early teens, everyone wore several different hats. Wallace Reid, who was not yet a superstar and was playing small parts, would sometimes take over the camera from Rosher, who in turn would put on makeup and act. Rosher worked with Sessue Hayakawa and DeMille. But he made his mark, and became the highest paid cinematographer in Hollywood, when he became Mary Pickford's cameraman and filmed more than fifteen features with her. He filmed *Little Lord Fauntleroy*, in which he used double exposures to have Pickford, playing a dual role, kiss herself. Rosher also shot *Rosita* and collaborated with Karl Struss on *Sparrows*.

Rosher and Struss followed up *Sparrows*, a film heavily influenced by German Expressionism, with F. W. Murnau's *Sunrise*. It was an enormous undertaking. "That was a very difficult film," he recalled. "For some scenes, such as the swamp sequence, the camera went in a complete circle. This created enormous lighting problems. We built a railway line in the roof, [and] suspended a little platform from it, which could be raised or lowered by motors."

In Struss's work on *Ben-Hur*, he used panchromatic film and filters to create Christ's miraculous healing of the lepers. The lepers' sores were painted red — to show them he used a green filter and to make them disappear, he put on a red filter. That's how cameramen worked miracles in the days before digital special effects.

F. W. Murnau's *Sunrise: A Song of Two Humans* (1927) was filmed entirely indoors on
an enormous soundstage built specifically for the movie.

THE STARS

FILM GAVE BIRTH TO A NEW PHENOMENON: CELEBRITY. OF COURSE, THERE HAD BEEN FAMOUS STAGE AND OPERA PERFORMERS AND SPORTS STARS WITH STRONG FOLLOWINGS, BUT FILM PUT THE ACTORS BEFORE MUCH LARGER AUDIENCES — A FEW THOUSAND MIGHT SEE A PERFORMER ON STAGE DURING A PLAY'S RUN, BUT MILLIONS COULD VIEW THEIR FAVORITE ACTORS IN A FILM. A KIND OF PERFECT STORM OF PUBLICITY BLEW UP IN THE POSTWAR ERA: MASS-CIRCULATION TABLOID NEWSPAPERS AND GOSSIP COLUMNISTS SUCH AS WALTER WINCHELL AND LOUELLA PARSONS COMBINED TO EXPLOIT THE STARS' GLAMOUR AND HIGH JINKS, AND FAN MAGAZINES FED THE VORACIOUS APPETITE FOR MOVIE NEWS. STUDIO FLACKS DID A HIGH-WIRE ACT, TRYING TO KEEP THEIR ACTORS' NAMES IN FRONT OF THE PUBLIC WHILE GIVING THE STORIES A POSITIVE SPIN.

Above: Mary Pickford (1917).

Left: Lillian Gish, Richard Barthelmess, and Dorothy Gish.

Too, the lack of dialogue in the darkened theaters allowed for a more intense identification with the figures on the screen, almost dreamlike in intensity. It was a heady experience for the actors, many of whom came from poor or middle-class backgrounds, and the successful ones found themselves awash in money and adulation. Just as in the Hollywood of today, some couldn't deal with sudden fame and fortune and turned to drugs and alcohol. Others donned the cloak of celebrity quite naturally. Norma Talmadge, a poor Jersey girl, could find herself in Hollywood slipping into furs and limousines, free of angst.

Their lifestyles were frequently incredibly opulent. Douglas Fairbanks and Mary Pickford were the equivalent of American royalty. When they traveled, Doug and Mary were greeted by huge throngs — in New York, London, or Moscow. The hysteria reached a crescendo at Valentino's funeral, when tens of thousands crowded the streets for a glimpse of his coffin. It was a kind of madness, like the outpouring of grief for Princess Diana or Beatlemania.

But even with the rise of mass-media coverage, silent-era stars in the 1920s were more remote than the stars of today — they remained Olympian creatures who inhabited a mystical realm. There were not yet paparazzi photos of actors going grocery shopping without makeup, bringing them down to earth, or ritualized televised confessions, like those with Barbara Walters.

Many of them found a persona and stuck with it: Mary Pickford played the spunky adolescent, Clara Bow the fun-loving flapper, John Gilbert "the Great Lover." Others, like Blanche Sweet, took on a greater variety of roles.

Some were part of the zeitgeist — Clara Bow was a twenties phenomenon, as was Norma Talmadge — while others, like Greta Garbo, transcended their period and became stars for all time. Some are remembered and still revered, while others have all but disappeared. The following twenty-four actors represent a necessarily partial list of the many talents who moved millions and made audiences laugh, cry, or gasp in the teens and twenties.

BABY PEGGY (1918–)

In the early twenties, Baby Peggy, nee Margaret Montgomery, was, with Jackie Coogan, one of silent film's great child stars. She started young — at a mere twenty months of age — and by the age of six, when her film career crashed, she had made some 150 shorts and a handful of features. During her silent heyday, she was enormously popular, reportedly making at least two million dollars.

She was an adorable and unself-conscious actor. Baby Peggy was also an excellent mimic, and in her comedies, she often imitated famous contemporary stars, such as Rudolph Valentino, Mary Pickford, and Pola Negri. In a bit of business, she would often chastise pets or adults, revealing the ideal sense of justice only children can hold. In *The Family Secret*, she berates a cop for stealing an apple. And in her best-known feature, *Captain January*, in which she plays a shipwrecked orphan adopted by a crusty but kind lighthouse keeper, she shakes her finger at her pet pelican and dog when they fight, wondering why we can't just all get along.

Her parents' free spending and bad management left her in poverty. She tried an unsuccessful comeback in films in the thirties, but eventually reinvented herself as a writer, under the name Diana Serra Cary. She has said that she often wondered about the appeal of Baby Peggy, usually a foundling, orphan, or daughter of divorced parents. Her answer is insightful: "I think it's to a great extent that we're an immigrant nation, very unsure of our identities. Maybe we really do want to be taken in and told that we really are home."

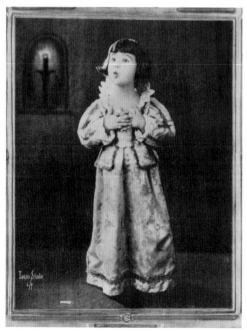

Top: *Darling of New York* (1923).

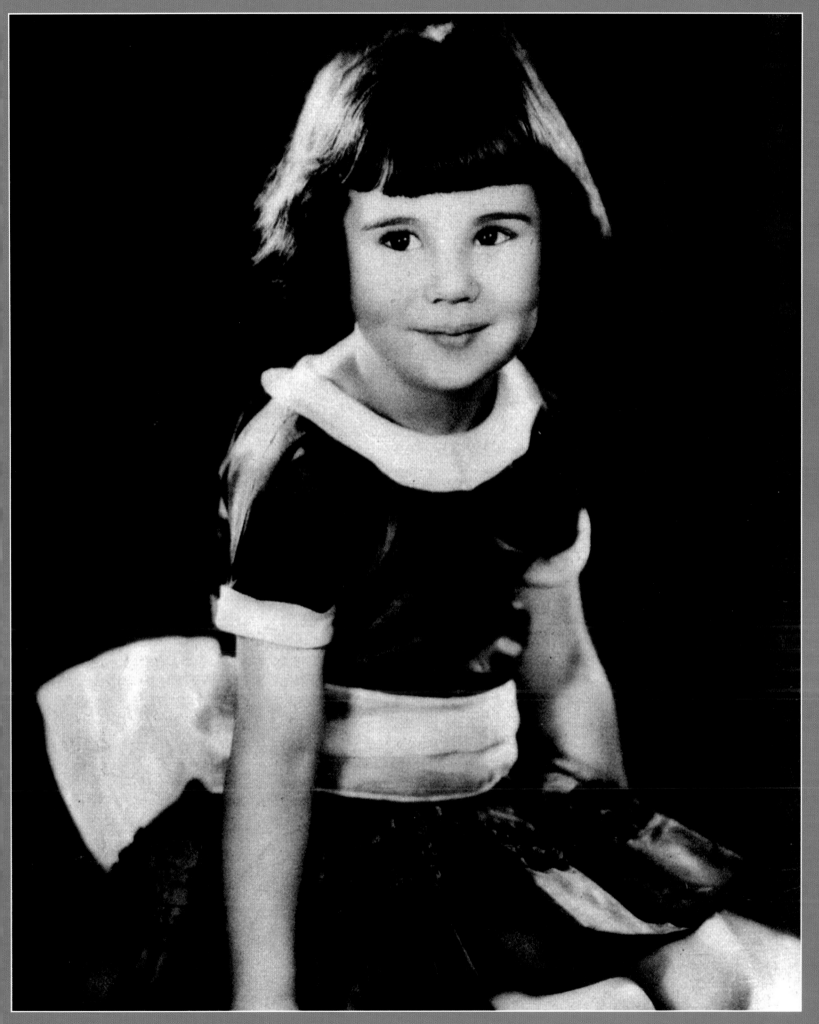

BABY PEGGY

DR. JEKYLL

Philanthropist
Humanitarian
Good Samaritan

Beloved by
all mankind

No admittance to Mr Hyde

How did Mr. Hyde get in ?

Above: Trade magazine ad for Barrymore in *Dr. Jekyll and Mr. Hyde* (1920).

Right: Barrymore's penultimate silent film, *Tempest* (1928).

JOHN BARRYMORE (1882–1942)

John Barrymore was perhaps the most celebrated actor in the most famous theatrical family in America, but something in him caused him to treat his great gift with disdain. His stage performances as Richard III and Hamlet were widely acclaimed. But unlike so many thespians, he felt no qualms about slumming in "the flickers," making his film debut in 1914, in *An American Citizen*.

Barrymore, nicknamed "the Great Profile," translated his stage training and extraordinary good looks to swashbuckling roles and romantic leads. In *Raffles, the Amateur Cracksman*, he plays a gentleman crook, and in *The Beloved Rogue*, he is the adventurer-poet François Villon. In 1926,

JOSEPH M. SCHENCK presents John Barrymore in "TEMPEST" with CAMILLA HORN & LOUIS WOLHEIM

A SAM TAYLOR Production

SUPERVISED BY JOHN W. CONSIDINE, Jr.

United Artists Picture

Barrymore played the title role in *Don Juan*, the first feature-length film to have a recorded soundtrack and the perfect assignment for the hedonistic actor. Colleen Moore played opposite him in the exotic romance *The Lotus Eaters* and wrote later, "He was almost unbearably handsome. In my first love scene with him . . . I was so overwhelmed, I froze."

His most famous film role was in *Dr. Jekyll and Mr. Hyde* (1920), directed by John S. Robertson. Barrymore is utterly credible in the dual role, although he shines more in the libidinous and physically repulsive persona of Mr. Hyde. He also starred as Ahab in the first screen adaptation of Melville's *Moby Dick*, 1926's *The Sea Beast*. In classic Hollywood fashion, it interpolates a love story into the all-male whaling world, with Barrymore's future wife, Dolores Costello, as the love interest.

Barrymore's stage training smoothed the transition to talkies, but by then his lifestyle was catching up with him. A lifetime of heavy drinking took its toll, and many saw him as a joke, a mere parody of himself.

JOHN BARRYMORE

RICHARD BARTHELMESS

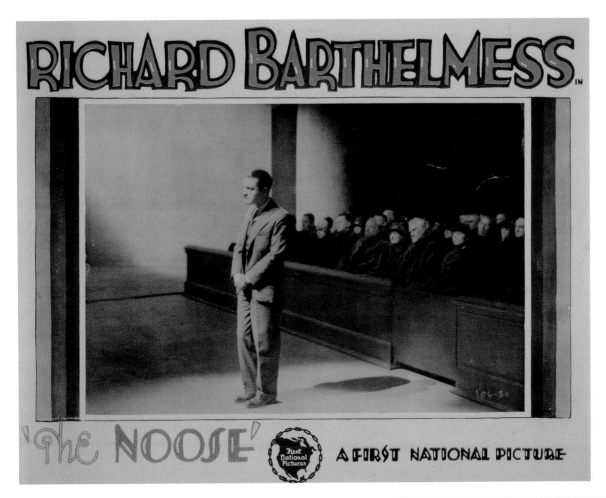

RICHARD BARTHELMESS IN

'THE NOOSE' A FIRST NATIONAL PICTURE

First National Pictures

RICHARD BARTHELMESS (1895–1963)

Although he had the good fortune to star in two of Griffith's best works (*Broken Blossoms*, *Way Down East*), and he worked with great directors (Howard Hawks, Michael Curtiz, William Wellman) in the sound era, Richard Barthelmess is not necessarily a name that leaps to the tongue when film fans are asked to rank the silent greats. People remember his films, but they tend not to remember his name.

After graduating from Trinity College in Hartford, Connecticut, Barthelmess made his film debut in 1916. A few years later, he went to work for Griffith. In *Broken Blossoms*, he played "the Yellow Man" with subtlety and grace, and in *Way Down East*, the earnest young man who saves Lillian Gish from an icy death. Gish once said he had "the most beautiful face of any man who ever went before the camera."

He formed his own production company, Inspiration, to film 1921's *Tol'able David*, directed by Henry King. In this delightful rite-of-passage film, which transcends its rural-melodrama clichés, Barthelmess plays country boy David, who proves himself a man after the brutish Hatburns kill his dog and cripple his brother Allen, the local mailman. David delivers the mail, dispatches the villains, and gets the girl (all with less fuss and more fun than Kevin Costner in the ridiculous post-apocalyptic *The Postman*).

He was nominated for an Oscar for *The Patent Leather Kid* and *The Noose*. Barthelmess outgrew his boyish innocence, and during the early talkie period, he often starred in films dealing with social issues.

Louise Huff (left) and Anne Cornwell join Barthelmess in *The Seventh Day* (1922).

CLARA BOW (1905–65)

"More than any other woman entertainer of her time," the *New York Times* wrote in a front-page obituary, "Clara Bow perhaps best personified the giddier aspects of an unreal era, the 'Roaring Twenties.'" Along with Colleen Moore, Bow was a quintessential flapper. Jeanine Basinger, in her book *Silent Stars*, contrasts them: "Clara Bow and Colleen Moore offered audiences two different kinds of flapper: one that was sexy (Bow) and one that was wholesome (Moore). . . . Colleen Moore has an Art Deco look. She's trim, slim, and sleek, with the boyish figure of the 1920s silhouette . . . Bow has a mass of tangled, sleepy-time hair, thick and lush, and her breasts are not only generous but frequently spilling out of her blouse." There were other flappers — Joan Crawford, for example, flaps like crazy in *Our Dancing Daughters* (1928), but she was on the cusp of stardom and wouldn't be as closely associated with the twenties as Bow and Moore.

Bow grew up poor in Brooklyn, daughter of an abusive father and a schizophrenic mother, and got her break when she won a movie-magazine beauty contest. Her first films were made in 1922, when she was still a teen, and she stands out in a small role in *Down to the Sea in Ships*, Elmer Clifton's almost documentary-like portrait of whaling in old New England. Bow shines as a spunky kid, full of light and bringing life to the dour seafarers.

Bow worked hard and was cast in dozens of films. *The Plastic Age*, critically and commercially successful, features her in a typically frisky, footloose role. Promoted as "the hottest jazz baby in films," Bow plays a reckless, fun-loving college girl who bewitches an athlete (Donald Keith), but then unselfishly gives him up so that he can play football (they get together in the end, of course). But with Clarence Badger's *It* (1927), she attained film immortality. As a department-store salesgirl who gets her man, the store's rich boss (Antonio Moreno), she became the embodiment of "It," a term coined by Elinor Glyn, which means something like "animal magnetism." Asked later what "It" meant exactly, Bow gave an honest answer: "I ain't real sure."

Top: Glass slide advertising *It* (1927).

Bottom: Clara Bow and William Powell in *The Runaway* (1926).

Right: Clara Bow and Clive Brook in *Hula* (1927).

Bow's last big hit was 1927's *Wings*, William Wellman's spectacular war movie in which she plays the love interest; it won an Oscar for Best Film. But scandals spawned by the It Girl's real-life sexual escapades and gambling damaged her career, and she had a terrible fear of the microphone (although she made some talkies). Bow made her last film in 1933 and grew reclusive and melancholy, suffering numerous breakdowns.

CLARA BOW
'HULA'
A Paramount Picture

Clara Bow

LOUISE BROOKS

LOUISE BROOKS (1906–85)

During the 1920s, when Europeans were flocking to Hollywood, Louise Brooks went the other way, from California to Germany. It is in some ways symbolic of what film historian Lotte Eisner called "the miracle of Louise Brooks."

Brooks started out as a dancer, working as a showgirl on Broadway in "George White's Scandals" and "Ziegfeld Follies" before becoming a film actress in the late twenties. She had roles in the comedies *Love 'Em and Leave 'Em* (Frank Tuttle) and *A Girl in Every Port* (Howard Hawks), but in William Wellman's underclass drama *Beggars of Life*, there was a real sense of Brooks's complexity and skill as an actress.

With her classic bob, Brooks was one of the most beautiful actresses of the decade. She also lived by her own rules and turned her back on Hollywood to star in two extraordinary films by German director G. W. Pabst — *Pandora's Box* and *Diary of a Lost Girl* (both 1929) — on which her reputation rests today. In *Pandora's Box*, Brooks, incarnated as the amoral Lulu, embodies a sexual allure that is simultaneously innocent and dangerous. Its American release was ludicrously bowdlerized by the censors, who changed her fatal encounter with Jack the Ripper to a moral ending, in which she joins the Salvation Army.

It just proves that even in the Jazz Age, America didn't know what to do with such a free spirit. Returning to Hollywood, she found herself ostracized. Brooks even made a two-reeler with the forlorn Arbuckle and, subsequently, managed only a handful of supporting roles. She worked for an escort service for a while.

Brooks was rediscovered in the fifties, and film writers journeyed to Rochester, New York, where she lived in seclusion, to hear the extravagant, highly intelligent actress offering the unvarnished truth about Hollywood's golden years. Indeed, she became a film writer herself, contributing articles to *Sight and Sound* and *Film Culture*.

Top: Ford Sterling and Brooks in the now-lost feature, *The American Venus* (1926).

Bottom: Victor McLagen with Brooks in *A Girl in Every Port* (1928).

DOUGLAS FAIRBANKS (1883–1939)

Along with Mary Pickford, whom he married in 1920, and Charlie Chaplin, Douglas Fairbanks was a silent-era superstar. He was born in Denver, where his father, a former lawyer, abandoned the family when Fairbanks was only five. Before making his first film, *The Lamb*, in 1915, Fairbanks had a successful stage career.

He began by making comedies, in which he usually played a prosperous young man who overcomes all obstacles with good cheer and enthusiasm — he is reminiscent of Harold Lloyd. Among the best of his early films are *Wild and Woolly*, a Western spoof directed by John Emerson, and 1919's *His Majesty, the American* (directed by Joseph Henabery), an appropriate title for a member of America's new royalty. An oddity in this bunch is 1916's *The Mystery of the Leaping Fish*, directed by Emerson from a story by Tod Browning, in which Fairbanks plays detective Coke Ennyday, who shoots cocaine throughout the film.

After cofounding United Artists, Fairbanks made the eight dazzling silent swashbucklers for which he is best remembered today. We see him with hands on hips, head thrown back, flashing his million-dollar smile, laughing at the absurdity of . . . what — the plot obstacles, his outrageous good fortune, the universe? And we, irresistibly, laugh with him.

Fairbanks carefully oversaw the production of his silent adventure dramas — he even contributed to stories on a number of films under a pseudonym — which in the twenties slowed to one a year. They were extraordinarily entertaining, with great costumes, spectacular sets, and innovative special effects. He leaped and bounded effortlessly through *The Mark of Zorro* (1920), *Robin Hood* (1922), *The Thief of Bagdad* (1924), and *The Black Pirate* (1926). His acrobatic skill and ease were aptly summed up by Alistair Cooke, who extolled his "virtuoso use of the landscape as a natural gymnasium whose equipment is invisible to the ordinary man." The world was his playground. Orson Welles perhaps described the actor best when he said that he "had something that nobody ever equaled — a kind of charm, a kind of dash, a sort of innocent arrogance that has never been seen since on the screen."

It was difficult for his fans to separate the man from his screen persona, for he wrote eight inspirational tomes (we would call them self-help books today), with titles like *Laugh and Live* and *Initiative and Self-Reliance*. He made a few talkies, but they were unsuccessful — he was forty-seven when he made his first — and he retired in 1934, when his marriage to Pickford ended.

Top: Mary Pickford and Fairbanks pose in costume for a publicity photo between breaks from filming, circa 1920.

Bottom: Anna May Wong with Fairbanks in *The Thief of Bagdad* (1924).

MOTION.PICTVRE.

SEPTEMBER

Magazine

25 CTS

Douglas Fairbanks

GRETA GARBO

GRETA GARBO (1905–90)

Of all the screen goddesses, Greta Garbo was the most remote and enigmatic — like Artemis hunting in the moonlight — and the one cameras worshipped most ardently. And she *was* alone: she had an unhappy childhood, never married, left her native Sweden. But on-screen, her presence is so riveting, it's impossible to look away.

Born in Stockholm, Garbo left elementary school after only six years. She worked as a shopgirl in a department store and appeared in a short promotional film for it. After doing a few commercials, she got a scholarship to the Royal Dramatic Theater acting school. She was discovered by director Mauritz Stiller, who cast her as one of the leads in *The Story of Gösta Berling* (1924). It was a risk putting an unknown eighteen-year-old in Sweden's most expensive film to date, but Stiller saw something extraordinary in her (he also put her on a diet). The film was a hit in Europe, and Stiller, or "Moje" as Garbo called him, always claimed that he had made her a star.

After costarring with Asta Nielsen in G. W. Pabst's *The Joyless Street* (1925) in Germany, she moved to Hollywood with Stiller, who had signed a contract with MGM's Louis B. Mayer and insisted on bringing her with him. Garbo's star rose; Stiller's fell. When she arrived in the United States, she knew no English, but Stiller taught her to say, "I am a poor Swedish girl" and "God bless America."

Garbo with Conrad Nagel and Gustav von Seyffertitz in a scene from *The Mysterious Lady* (1928).

She made ten silent films at the studio — often mediocre, all successful — but she transcended her material by her mere presence. Her characters could be selfish and adulterous, but audiences didn't care — although she did. After making 1926's *The Temptress*, she complained, "I do not want to be a silly temptress. I cannot see any sense in getting dressed up and doing nothing but tempting men in pictures."

Clarence Brown, who directed Garbo seven times, twice in silents (*Flesh and the Devil*, 1926, which made her a superstar; and *A Woman of Affairs*, 1929), understood her appeal. "Garbo has something behind the eyes," he told Brownlow, "that you couldn't see until you photographed it in close-up. You could see thought. If she had to look at one person with jealousy, and another with love, she didn't have to change her expression. You could see it in her eyes as she looked from one to the other. And nobody else has been able to do that on screen."

Her relationship with John Gilbert began with *Flesh and the Devil* and their real-life affair added fuel to their many on-screen love scenes. They came within hours of marrying, but for some reason never fully explained, Garbo backed out. She starred in talkies throughout the thirties, and retired in 1942.

Top: Gaynor and Charles Farrell in *7th Heaven* (1927) and, bottom: in *Street Angel* (1928).

JANET GAYNOR (1906–84)

The diminutive, saucer-eyed Janet Gaynor, more wholesome than beautiful, sweet but not saccharine, was a late silent star whose career stretched well into the thirties. She moved to Hollywood after graduating from high school in San Francisco and worked as an extra and in bit parts in Hal Roach comedies and B Westerns before being cast in the 1926 hit feature *The Johnstown Flood*, which also starred George O'Brien.

At the end of the silent era, she scored a triple header — and the first-ever Best Actress Oscar — for her roles in Murnau's *Sunrise* and Frank Borzage's *7th Heaven* and *Street Angel*. In the last two, Borzage paired her with Charles Farrell, and like Garbo and Gilbert, they became famous screen lovers. In *7th Heaven*, for which Borzage also won Best Director, Farrell plays Chico, a Paris sewer worker who falls in love with Gaynor's Diane, a waif who is whipped and beaten by her cruel sister Nana. Chico takes her in and is promoted to street cleaner, but their tenuous happiness is shattered by the war, in which Chico is blinded in a bombing. The couple are reunited in the end, and the film remains a classic silent romance.

Gaynor easily made the transition to talkies; she was voted the top box-office female star in 1934. She starred in the first film version of *State Fair* (1933) and received an Oscar nomination for 1937's *A Star Is Born*.

JOHN GILBERT (1899–1936)

Along with Rudolph Valentino, John Gilbert was the silent screen's other "Great Lover," but unlike Valentino, Gilbert appealed to women without turning off men. He was a matinee idol before that became a pejorative term.

Gilbert began in films by playing bit parts for Thomas H. Ince in the mid teens, but within a few years he was getting more prominent roles, in films with Colleen Moore and Mary Pickford. It was when he signed with the brand-new MGM, in 1924, that his career blossomed. There he starred in Victor Seastrom's *He Who Gets Slapped*, a strange and wonderful film that also starred Lon Chaney and Norma Shearer; *The Merry Widow*, one of Erich von Stroheim's most successful features; and King Vidor's *The Big Parade*, one of the biggest box-office hits of the silent era (it made fifteen million dollars, a huge sum at the time). After *Parade*, MGM gave Gilbert a four-year, million-dollar contract.

The Big Parade combines love and war, but Gilbert's physical attractiveness, his ability to look good in a uniform or a tux, and his smoldering gaze drove him toward romantic roles. He was paired in a series of silent romances with Greta Garbo, with whom he had an offscreen love affair as well: *Flesh and the Devil* (1926), which made Garbo a star; *Love* (1927), an eviscerated version of Tolstoy's *Anna Karenina* that, in the American version, has a happy ending; and *A Woman of Affairs* (1929), by which time their offscreen affair had ended. The studio, of course, played up the on- and off-screen chemistry.

There are many explanations for why the fire of Gilbert's career, which burned so brightly for a few years in the mid to late twenties, turned to ash. An early and enduring version had it that talkies killed the silent star because he didn't have a good voice (still, he made eleven dialogue films, including one with Garbo, 1933's *Queen Christina*).

Bottom: Gilbert with frequent costar Renée Adorée in *The Cossacks* (1928).

Right: Gilbert and Greta Garbo in *Flesh and the Devil* (1926).

Another explanation is that he had alienated Louis B. Mayer, MGM's mogul. Certainly a factor in his fall was his worsening alcoholism. Vidor, who helped make Gilbert a star, offered as plausible an explanation as any for his demise: "The literal content of his scenes, which in silent films had been imagined, was too intense to be put into spoken words."

ROTOGRAVURE SECTION OF FAMOUS PLAYERS

PICTURE-PLAY

MAGAZINE

MARCH 1920 · 20 CENTS

LILLIAN GISH

PAINTED BY
HASKELL COFFIN

LILLIAN GISH

LILLIAN GISH (1893–1993)

John Barrymore considered Lillian Gish an actress on the level of Sarah Bernhardt, writer Edward Wagenknecht notes in an essay. Wagenknecht then goes on to refer to "the exaltation, the profound mysticism of Miss Gish's playing." Many critics and film writers have joined Wagenknecht in lauding her with exalted prose. Some, however, have argued that her persona, an ethereal beauty in late Victorian style, narrowed her range of roles. It's a purely subjective judgment call, but no one can deny her iconic status in silent-film history.

Abandoned by their father, Lillian and sister Dorothy both began acting on the stage by the age of five. In 1912, they visited the Biograph studio to see their friend Mary Pickford, and D. W. Griffith promptly cast them — and their mother — in a film, *An Unseen Enemy*. Gish played in twenty of Griffith's two-reelers over the next two years. She was the personification of Griffith's ideal heroine — a fragile beauty with an underlying strength of character — and she would star in many of his most successful films: as Elsie Stoneman in *The Birth of a Nation*, as The Woman Who Rocks the Cradle in *Intolerance*, as the battered waif in *Broken Blossoms*, and as the innocent driven out into the storm and onto the ice floes of the White River in *Way Down East*. She would costar with sister Dorothy in Griffith's epic *Orphans of the Storm*. Her fame made her too expensive for Griffith, although she always admired her mentor (and gave money to the Museum of Modern Art to preserve his films).

Donald Crisp and Gish in *Broken Blossoms* (1919).

She eventually signed with MGM, where she starred in several fine films, including King Vidor's *La Boheme*, with John Gilbert. Victor Seastrom directed her in *The Wind* with Lars Hanson. The story of a young woman transplanted to the desert, driven to the brink of madness by the constant wind and the emotional aridity of its denizens, is now considered one of the great classics of the late silent era. MGM, however, thought Gish out of date and did little to promote it. After making a couple of talkies, she found the stage more amenable. During World War II, she returned to film in character roles.

Gish's sister, Dorothy, was also an accomplished actress, although her career has been eclipsed by Lillian's notoriety. While Lillian's strong suit was drama and melodrama, Dorothy had a gift for comedy. Dorothy costarred with Lillian in *Romola* as well as *Orphans* and was directed by her sister in *Remodeling Her Husband*. She had a big box-office hit in the English film *Nell Gwynne* in 1926. As sound came in, Dorothy also returned to the theater. She died in 1968.

SESSUE HAYAKAWA (1889–1973)

Sessue Hayakawa was the son of a provincial governor in Japan and a graduate of the University of Chicago. He returned to Japan, where he performed with an acting troupe. While touring the American West in 1913, he was discovered by Thomas H. Ince and signed to a movie contract.

It was as the villain in Cecil B. DeMille's 1915 *The Cheat*, however, that he became Hollywood's first Asian star. His performance — as the Japanese art dealer who lusts after and brands Fannie Ward's Long Island society matron like a steer — is naturalistic and understated, given the sensationalistic material. (When the film was rereleased in 1918, protests by Japanese Americans forced the filmmakers to change Hayakawa's character to a Burmese ivory dealer.)

Hayakawa made dozens of films with considerable success, playing villains and romantic heroes. For a time, he had his own production company, Haworth Pictures. Although his Haworth films emphasized racial tolerance, he was often stereotyped, and his film romances with Caucasian women usually ended disastrously.

Typical is the Ince film *The Typhoon*, directed by Reginald Barker. Hayakawa plays Tokorama, a Japanese diplomat in Paris who is having an affair with a chorus girl, Helene (Gladys Brockwell). After an argument, Tokorama strangles Helene, and a young Japanese boy is forced to confess to the killing and is guillotined. Tokorama dies, and his papers are burned to protect Japan's interests. While films like this suggest the dangers of love between Caucasian women and Asian men, Hayakawa wrote that "public acceptance of me in romantic roles was a blow of sorts against racial intolerance."

In 1931, Hayakawa made his dialogue-film debut with Anna May Wong (the first Asian American film star) in *Daughter of the Dragon*, but it was poorly received. He moved to Europe, where he acted until after World War II, when he returned to Hollywood. He is perhaps best remembered today for his Academy Award–nominated performance as the Japanese prisoner-of-war camp commandant in *The Bridge on the River Kwai* (1957). He retired in the 1960s, becoming a Zen master.

Top: Hayakawa with his wife, Tsuru Aoki, in *Black Roses* (1921).

Bottom: Glass slide advertising *The City of Dim Faces* (1918).

EMIL JANNINGS (1884–1950)

Swiss-born Emil Jannings was, quite simply, one of the greatest actors of his generation, displaying a wide emotional range while only occasionally devolving into hamminess. He began in theater, acting for Max Reinhardt's prestigious theater company in Berlin. Stocky and bearlike in appearance, he often played royal or grandiose characters in films, from Louis XV in *Madame DuBarry* and Henry VIII in *Anna Boleyn*, both by Lubitsch, to Mephistopheles in F. W. Murnau's *Faust*.

Interestingly, however, he is best remembered for a series of films in which he plays a proud man who suffers humiliation: in E. A. Dupont's *Variety*, as a sideshow operator whose trapeze-artist wife cheats on him; in Murnau's *The Last Laugh*, as a puffed-up doorman at a posh hotel who is demoted to washroom attendant; in Josef von Sternberg's *The Last Command*, as a refugee czarist general reduced to working as a Hollywood extra; and in 1930's *The Blue Angel*, also by von Sternberg, as a pompous professor whose sexual obsession with a nightclub singer (Marlene Dietrich) leads him to perform as a clown.

Jannings's sojourn to Hollywood in the late twenties earned him the first-ever Best Actor Oscar, in 1929, for his work in Victor Fleming's *The Way of All Flesh* and *The Last Command* (the award was not given for a specific film). But his heavy accent forced his return to Germany with the advent of talkies. There, he became an enthusiastic supporter of the Nazis and appeared in many pro-German, anti-Semitic movies and was even named Artist of the State in 1941 by Joseph Goebbels. He became a pariah outside Germany after the war.

Bottom: Emil Jannings with Ruth Chatterton (making her screen debut) in the part-talking picture *Sins of the Fathers* (1928).

Left: Jannings and Ica von Lenkeffy in an advertisement for *Othello* (1922).

ΙΟΤΙΟΝ PICTURE

JANUARY — 25 CTS

Is It
Stardom
That
ills Them?
See Page 22

There's somethin
about an actress
that attracts
wealthy and title
men
See Page 19

MARLAND
STONE

COLLEEN MOORE

COLLEEN MOORE (1900–88)

"I was the spark that lit up flaming youth," wrote F. Scott Fitzgerald, that writer-naturalist who made a study of the 1920s species, the flapper, "and Colleen Moore was the torch." And in the film *Flaming Youth* (1923), Moore emblazoned the flapper in public consciousness.

The flapper was partly manufactured, partly a real reflection of the Jazz Age, but in the movies, it was a phenomenon to be carefully studied by women eager to learn how to look and (mis)behave. Moore quickly followed *Flaming Youth* with *The Perfect Flapper*, and with her boyish figure and Dutch boy bob, she embodied the look that made her career. At her peak, in 1927, she was earning $12,500 a week.

Flappers represented a liberation from Victorianism but rejected the male fantasy of vamps: they wanted to drive in fast cars, stay out all night, drink from flasks, listen to jazz, have madcap adventures and, perhaps, sex, but they weren't necessarily decadent — just fun loving. On the other hand, the movies demanded repentance. Of the fairly inconsequential story of *Flaming Youth*, the *New York Times* review declared, "The moral of this picture is to show the emptiness of the pace-killing life."

But before coming to symbolize this phenomenon — and cutting her hair — Moore played a fairly conventional ingenue, starring in oaters with Tom Mix and even in a couple of rural romances with country boy Charles Ray, looking innocent and demure. And in a late silent, the wartime picture *Lilac Time*, she abandoned her flappish ways for a sentimental drama with Gary Cooper.

After several talkies, she retired in the mid thirties. She shrewdly invested her earnings and wrote a book called *How Women Can Make Money in the Stock Market*. She also built an enormous dollhouse, which reportedly cost half a million dollars, complete with a library full of miniature literary classics. It is on display at Chicago's Museum of Science and Industry.

Top: Sam Hardy with Moore on a lobby card for *Orchids and Ermine* (1927).

Bottom: Glass slide advertising the romantic comedy *Irene* (1926).

IVAN MOSJOUKINE (1889–1939)

A sort of Russian Valentino, Ivan Mosjoukine — darkly handsome, slightly androgynous — was one of the most famous silent actors in France during the twenties. After studying law in Moscow for a couple of years, he quit to pursue a career in the theater. Mosjoukine turned to film in an unusual way. The Russians' love of tragedy made the happy endings of Western films unpalatable, so they were often reshot with sad endings using Russian actors. Mosjoukine broke into films playing the double of Western actors. He then went on to perform in films by the great pre-Soviet director Evgeni Bauer and by Yakov Protazanov. Mosjoukine's gaze — he often stared directly at the audience — became an artistic trademark.

In the wake of the civil war, much of the Russian film community moved first to the Crimea and then to France, where Mosjoukine arrived in 1919. He directed himself in a few films, including the surreal fantasy *The Burning Crucible*. He then starred in two remarkable films by fellow émigré Alexandre Volkoff — *Kean* (1924) and *Casanova* (1927). In *Kean*, a biopic about the eighteenth-century English actor Edmund Kean's wild life, the White Russian's amazingly rapid editing predated the Reds' staccato cutting. In *Casanova*, Mosjoukine plays the infamous womanizer with a light comic touch reminiscent of Douglas Fairbanks; the film's color sequences are captivating, with the characters given completely lifelike flesh tones.

Mosjoukine ventured to Hollywood at the end of the silent era but made only one film, Edward Sloman's *Surrender*, which was a flop. He returned to Europe, but because of his heavy Russian accent, he was unable to successfully make the transition to sound. He died of tuberculosis in a hospital for the poor.

POLA NEGRI (1894–1987)

The Polish actress Pola Negri is more famous for being famous than she is for her films. Negri was the first great European actress to come to Hollywood, and what made her attractive to American audiences — her dark beauty, her fierce sexuality and emotion, her grandiloquent acting style — now makes her seem dated. Still, she starred in several good films, most of them directed by Ernst Lubitsch, who toned down her histrionic tendencies.

Nee Barbara Appolonia Chalupiec, Negri trained at the Imperial Ballet School in St. Petersburg and the Philharmonia Drama School in Warsaw, then acted both on the stage and in films in Poland. In 1917, she moved to Berlin, where she starred in Lubitsch's *Carmen* (1918) and *Madame DuBarry* (1919).

When Americans got a look at this exotic creature in these films, retitled *Gypsy Blood* and *Passion*, respectively, a few years later, they were electrified. Of *Carmen/Gypsy Blood*, *Variety* simply declared: "This Negri is amazing." And she could act. When she portrayed the mistress of Louis XV (played by Emil Jannings) in *Madame DuBarry/Passion*, the *New York Times* praised her performance: "She makes DuBarry real. . . . She actually wins sympathy for a woman who cannot at any time be admired. This is an accomplishment." The film was a huge hit.

Adolph Zukor brought her over to Paramount in 1922, but her American films rarely reached the heights of her former glory. Her best performances were in another Lubitsch film, *Forbidden Paradise*, and in Stiller's *Hotel Imperial*, interestingly both directed by Europeans.

She lived the life of the silent-movie queen. Draped in furs and jewels, Negri drove around Hollywood, which she declared a backwater, in a white Rolls lined in white velvet, a Russian wolfhound ensconced on either side. (An animal lover, she could be seen promenading down Sunset Boulevard with her pet tiger on a leash.) She had affairs with Chaplin and Valentino, at whose funeral she made a spectacle of herself.

With the coming of talkies, her accent forced her return to Germany, where she continued to work through the thirties. She was offered the Norma Desmond role in *Sunset Boulevard*, but declined. Self-parody was not in her repertoire.

Bottom: Negri and Anders Randolf in *Three Sinners* (1928).

ASTA NIELSEN

ASTA NIELSEN (1881–1972)

Asta Nielsen was European cinema's first female movie star. Born in Copenhagen to working-class parents, she early on decided to become an actress and studied at the Royal Theater of Copenhagen. Beautiful, sensual, intelligent, she was also independent, and after completing her studies, she became pregnant and chose to be an unmarried mother.

Asta (her professional name was *Die Asta*, never Nielsen) had only modest success on the stage, but her film debut, 1910's *The Abyss*, was a huge hit, playing across Europe for months. Directed by Urban Gad, whom she later married, *The Abyss* is a melodrama about an unconventional music teacher who chooses a circus "cowboy" over a parson's son. The cowboy is a philanderer and wastrel, which leads her to kill him. But before she does, they engage in one of the most erotic scenes in silent cinema. In a stage act, she lassos him, ties him up, then brushes against him in her slinky black dress, rubbing her derriere against his pelvis.

Asta and Gad moved to Germany, where she made some seventy films, about half of them now lost. In addition to erotic melodramas, she played a variety of styles, including comedies and classics (she even crossed gender lines by playing Hamlet in 1920). Asta evoked ecstatic responses from her fans. "She is everything!" wrote the poet Guillaume Apollinaire. "She is the drunkard's vision and the lonely man's dream."

She is probably best known today for her role as a kept woman in Pabst's *The Joyless Street* (1925), in which she costars with Greta Garbo. Asta made only one sound movie, in 1932, and then withdrew from film.

MARY PICKFORD
"Little Lord
Fauntleroy"

Top: *Rags* (1915).

Bottom: A lobby card for *Little Lord Fauntleroy* (1921).

Right: *Little Annie Rooney* (1925).

MARY PICKFORD (1892–1979)

Growing up poor in Toronto, as plain Gladys Marie Smith, Mary Pickford first began performing on stage at the age of six. Beloved as "America's Sweetheart," Pickford was a force to be reckoned with. Not only was she America's first female film superstar (a star for twenty years, Pickford was named number one by *Photoplay* magazine for fifteen of them), but a shrewd businesswoman as well.

She talked herself into jobs with New York stage impresario David Belasco, who renamed her Mary Pickford, and later with D. W. Griffith at Biograph, where she appeared in dozens of one-reelers. When she was hired at Zukor's Famous Players, she started at five hundred dollars a week, and by 1916, she was making ten thousand dollars a week. Reportedly, she even told Zukor that she "couldn't afford to live on ten thousand dollars a week." In 1919, she cofounded United Artists with Fairbanks, Chaplin, and Griffith and was the business brains behind the enterprise. Her growing influence was not just about the money; she worked with the best in the industry — directors, writers, cameramen, and art directors.

Pickford has been stigmatized as a figure of sweetness and innocence, and like many stereotypes, it is only a half-truth. It is true that she played adolescents well into adulthood: in 1926's *Sparrows*, for instance, in which she plays a teen leading a troop of kids through a gator-infested swamp, she was already in her early thirties. But she played a large number of roles that transcended the formula of *Pollyanna*, in which her credo is "just be glad."

For Griffith, she played a prostitute and woman who asks to have her lover killed. In one of her best films, *Stella Maris*, directed by Marshall Neilan, she portrays two characters, Stella Maris, a sheltered rich invalid, and Unity Blake, a poor orphan girl. In Lubitsch's *Rosita*, she plays an adult, a Spanish street singer who becomes a countess. Molly Haskell argues in *From Reverence to Rape* that Pickford wasn't just a Cinderella or Snow White, "she was a rebel who, in the somewhat sentimental spirit of the prize pup as underdog, championed the poor against the rich, the scruffy orphans against the prissy rich kids. She was a little girl with gumption and self-reliance who could get herself out of trouble as easily as into it."

That's why the public loved her, and they did favor the adolescent roles. Pickford, too, recognized that she was the prisoner of her screen persona. "I left the screen because I didn't want what happened to Chaplin to happen to me. . . . The little girl made me. I wasn't waiting for the little girl to kill me."

Pickford was married three times: to Owen Moore (1911–20) and Douglas Fairbanks (1920–36), both of whom she divorced, and to Charles "Buddy" Rogers (from 1937 until her death, in 1979). Although she made a few talkies, she retired after 1933's *Secrets*.

MARY PICKFORD

Top: Ray and George Webb in *Alarm Clock Andy* (1920).

Bottom: Clara Horton with Ray in *Nineteen and Phyllis* (1920).

CHARLES RAY (1891–1943)

The son of a railroad worker, Charles Ray toured in plays as a teenager in the Southwest before landing a job as an extra for Thomas H. Ince in the early teens. After playing in dozens of films, he was cast as the lead in Ince's Civil War film *The Coward* (1915).

More typically, he played a charming hayseed in rural melodramas who gets out of town and makes good in the city. In *The Clodhopper* (1917), for example, he plays Everett, a small-town boy who is physically abused by his wealthy but miserly father. After running away to New York, he becomes a successful and rich cabaret dancer. When his father's bank is in trouble, he returns home to bail out his dad and marry his former sweetheart. Other films, with such titles as *Homer Comes Home*, follow a similar pattern. The formula was successful, and at the height of his fame in the late teens, he grew rich enough to establish his own studio.

But Ray grew restless and wanted to stretch a little after leaving Ince. He starred in *The Old Swimmin' Hole* (1921), a film entirely without intertitles (years before *The Last Laugh* used the same strategy). A pastoral idyll, in which his character, Ezra, spends his time fishing at the swimmin' hole or trying to stay awake in class, it is certainly transparent enough not to require titles, and it documents a simpler way of life that is gone forever. In a much bigger gamble, Ray put all of his money on an adaptation of Longfellow's *The Courtship of Miles Standish* (1923), a costume romance that tanked so badly that Ray lost his studio. His attempts at a comeback in the silent era were mostly unsuccessful, but he went on to play bit parts in talkies.

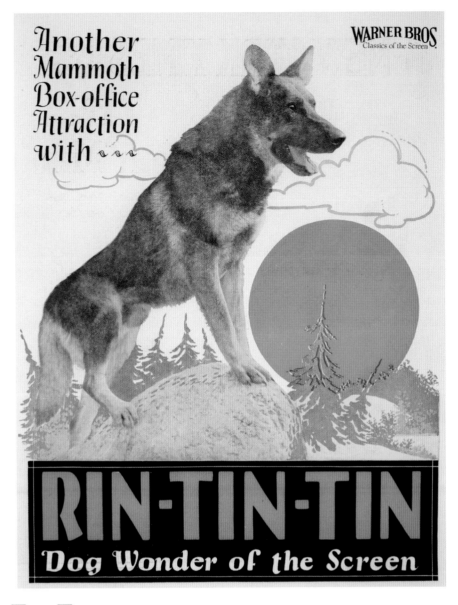

Another Mammoth Box-office Attraction with...

WARNER BROS
Classics of the Screen

RIN-TIN-TIN
Dog Wonder of the Screen

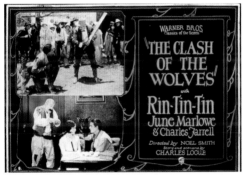

Glass slide for the Rin-Tin-Tin feature *The Clash of the Wolves* (1925).

RIN-TIN-TIN (1918–32)

The German shepherd Rin-Tin-Tin was not only cinema's greatest canine star but one of the biggest stars of the twenties, period. At the height of his fame, Rinty, as he was known to his fans, made six thousand dollars a month and received more than ten thousand fan letters a week. He helped to keep the fledgling, cash-strapped studio Warner Bros. afloat during the silent era, reportedly earning more than a million dollars at the box office.

Rin-Tin-Tin was rescued by a U.S. soldier, Corporal Lee Duncan, after he was abandoned by retreating Germans during World War I. Duncan, who named him after a good-luck doll that French peasants sold to American soldiers, trained him and took him to Hollywood. According to film legend, when Rinty collapsed in 1932, his neighbor, Jean Harlow, cradled him in her arms as he died.

His 1925 film *The Clash of the Wolves* was added to the National Film Registry in 2004. In that film, he is clearly the star, outshining the human cast. Rin-Tin-Tin plays Lobo, the leader of a wolf pack, although he is half-dog, half-wolf. He is tamed by a young prospector (played by Charles Farrell) and rescues him and his girlfriend (June Marlowe) from a villainous claim jumper. While the film is fairly routine, mixing melodrama and broad comedy, Rinty reliably does what he does best — saving the slow-witted good guys from the equally slow-witted bad guys with alacrity. It is hard not to anthropomorphize Rin-Tin-Tin, for he was a creature of intelligence, nobility, and grace.

GLORIA SWANSON (1897–1983)

It is hard to believe that the girl tied to the tracks and rescued from a speeding train by a dog (*Teddy at the Throttle*, 1917) became the glamorous clotheshorse of DeMille's postwar sex-and-fashion spectacles and much later the half-mad silent star Norma Desmond, preparing her comeback in *Sunset Boulevard* (1950). If Gloria Swanson didn't exist, a silent-film historian would have had to invent her.

She began her career as a teenager at Essanay in Chicago, then moved to Hollywood, where she made two-reelers for Mack Sennett. Swanson resented having to do slapstick, but she later

Above: *Manhandled* (1924).

Right: *Why Change Your Wife?* (1920).

acknowledged that comedy was a good school for drama. DeMille made her a new kind of star in a series of films (*Don't Change Your Husband*, 1919; *Why Change Your Wife?* 1920). She was neither virgin nor vamp but seemingly the quintessential modern woman questioning the age-old double standards. "Seemingly" is a necessary qualification, because her DeMille films aren't real — the Olympic-size bathrooms, the furs and the jewels, the orgiastic Babylonian sequences — and the denouements are familiar: the wandering wives and husbands come to their senses at the end. But Swanson was the perfect vehicle for sophisticated fantasy.

Swanson went on to make a number of romances before returning to comedy, under the deft direction of Allan Dwan, in such films as 1924's *Manhandled* and 1925's *Stage Struck*. The following year, she left her studio, Paramount, to produce her own movies. In one of her best films, *Sadie Thompson* (1928), directed by and costarring Raoul Walsh and set in the South Seas, Swanson plays a former prostitute running from her past, in love with a marine sergeant (Walsh) but in the thrall of a hypocritical preacher (Lionel Barrymore). The same year, she had to pull the plug on *Queen Kelly*, directed by Erich von Stroheim, who played his usual game of ignoring budgets and schedules. It was never released in the United States.

La Swanson lived life grandly. "We were making more money than we ever dreamed existed, and there was no reason to believe it would ever stop." It did stop, of course, but we still have the films.

GLORIA SWANSON

BLANCHE SWEET (1895–1986)

There are two kinds of stars: those who create a screen persona and stick with it and those who disappear into their characters. Blanche Sweet was of the chameleon variety. She was only fourteen when she joined Griffith at Biograph, acting in dozens of one- and two-reelers. Among her best-known performances was in 1911's *The Lonedale Operator*, one of Griffith's classic short films. She charms her engineer suitor, balancing on a railroad line while walking with him, then turns tough and resourceful when crooks try to steal the waiting payroll, holding them at bay with a wrench that they think is a gun. Griffith chose her from his bevy of adolescent actresses to star in his first feature, *Judith of Bethulia*, in which she beguiles and then beheads Holofernes, the leader of the Assyrians besieging her city.

After leaving Griffith, she continued her varied career, starring in DeMille's Civil War drama *The Warrens of Virginia*; *Tess of the D'Urbervilles*, directed by her then-husband Marshall Neilan; and the Ince production *Anna Christie* (1923), which playwright Eugene O'Neill preferred over the other screen adaptations of his play. In it, she shows off her protean talents — at times a whiskey-drinking, cigarette-smoking black hole of despair, then projecting a radiant innocence when she senses the possibility of love with the seafaring Mat Burke (William Russell). Sweet made a few unsuccessful talkies before turning to theater.

Eugénie Besserer (left) and Sweet in Thomas H. Ince's *Anna Christie* (1923).

NORMA TALMADGE (1897?–1957)

In the twenties, Norma Talmadge was one of the biggest stars in Hollywood. In 1924, she was making ten thousand dollars a week. She was married to movie mogul Joseph Schenck (1917–1930), whom she called Daddy and who produced her movies. When she retired, she had made more than 250 films. And yet, today she is virtually forgotten.

That is partly due to the unavailability of her films and partly due to the roles she played, which seem dated today. According to writer Jack Spears, Talmadge specialized in being, and indeed her fans demanded she be, "a brave, tragic, and sacrificing heroine, [amid] lavish settings and beautiful clothes, and [shedding] buckets of tears before the eventual redemption at the fadeout."

Talmadge and her sisters, Constance and Natalie, were raised by their formidable stage mother, Margaret, whose husband deserted her. Talmadge began acting at Vitagraph when she was just fourteen. She went on to form her own production company in 1917 with Schenck and director Allan Dwan. She usually played traditional, contemporary women's roles in weepies, although she made the occasional comedy. In *Panthea*, for instance, directed by Dwan and produced by Schenck, Talmadge plays a brilliant Russian pianist married to a composer going mad because he can't get his opera produced. She sacrifices herself to a rich, elderly baron to get the opera on the boards. The work is a success, but she is unjustly arrested for being part of a nihilist plot and sent to Siberia. The couple eventually travels to England to begin a new life.

Talmadge's sister Constance was also an actress, best known for her outstanding performance as the Mountain Girl in Griffith's *Intolerance*. Natalie had less success as an actress; she married Buster Keaton in 1921 and starred opposite him in *Our Hospitality* (1923).

Norma Talmadge's career crashed with the advent of sound. She made two dialogue films, which did poorly, and then retired.

Top: Actor George Nichols scolds his daughter, played by Norma Talmadge, in this scene from *Secrets* (1924).

Center: Talmadge and Eugene O'Brien in *The Only Woman* (1924).

Bottom: Glass slide for *Kiki* (1926), one of Talmadge's rare comedy features.

MOTION PICTURE

SEPTEMBER — 25 CTS

A BREWSTER PUBLICATION

CRAZY QUILT

A Big Human Story

Have You an Idea For A Movie?

See Page 28

FLOHRI
HOLLYWOOD

They Are Not What They Seem

RUDOLPH VALENTINO

RUDOLPH VALENTINO (1895–1926)

Rudolph Valentino, born Rodolpho Guglielmi di Valentina d'Antonguolla, is in the peculiar position of being the first major star to die young. And he was *very* famous during his brief career on-screen. Although he made only a few memorable films, which are rarely revived today, he is more well known than many other actors of the silent era. A sign of his notoriety is that in histories of the twenties, in which stars such as Mary Pickford and Richard Barthelmess might get a passing nod, Valentino's funeral — along with the trial and execution of Sacco and Vanzetti, gangland violence in Chicago, and Charles Lindbergh's transatlantic flight — is invariably described. When he died suddenly, in 1926, at the age of thirty-one of peritonitis, some thirty thousand mourners turned out. They were "in large part women and girls," according to the *New York Times*, "rioting . . . without precedent in New York."

After arriving in America from Italy, in 1913, Valentino was employed as a gardener, petty thief, gigolo, and professional dancer before breaking into movies as an extra and in several small roles. His first big hit, and it was huge, was Rex Ingram's World War I film *The Four Horsemen of the Apocalypse* (1921). It was an incredibly lucky break for Valentino, who particularly shone in a scene in which the Latin Lover dances — what else? — the tango.

Later the same year, the film that would fix him permanently in the firmament and history books, George Melford's *The Sheik*, was released. The film is a farrago of nonsense. Valentino plays Sheik Ahmed Ben Hassan, who kidnaps an Englishwoman, Lady Diana Mayo (Agnes Ayres). Several plot twists save Lady Diana's virtue — it's a rape fantasy without the rape — and the sheik turns out to be a well-bred European, not an Arab at all. It was an enormous hit, one of the most successful movies of all time.

Top: Valentino and Vilma Bánky in *The Eagle* (1925).

Bottom: Valentino as the brooding Sheik in his final film, *The Son of the Sheik* (1926).

On the other hand, the sequel — George Fitzmaurice's *The Son of the Sheik* (1926) — is a genuinely entertaining film, perhaps Valentino's best. It has more action and swashbuckling adventure, as well as romance, which takes some of the strain off Valentino to play the Latin Lover, and some wit and self-mockery make it more palatable. It was released posthumously, like James Dean's *Giant*, a publicity hack's dream.

Valentino was considered a "woman's actor," appealing especially to older women. For many of them he represented, as Adela Rogers St. Johns put it aptly, "the lure of the flesh." Many men at the time, however, detested (or felt threatened by) his ambiguous sexuality. An article in the *Chicago Tribune* sneered at the pernicious influence of the "pink powder puff." The mostly male reviewers didn't get it, but it didn't matter anyway.

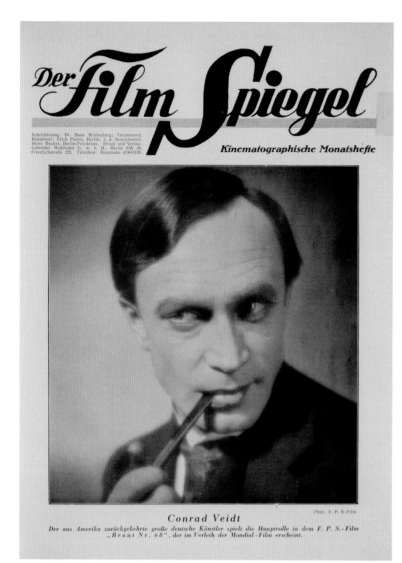

Conrad Veidt

Der aus Amerika zurückgekehrte große deutsche Künstler spielt die Hauptrolle in dem F. P. S.-Film „Braut Nr. 68", der im Verleih der Mondial-Film erscheint.

CONRAD VEIDT (1893–1943)

In many of his Expressionist silent-film roles, the German actor Conrad Veidt seems like a character straight out of Edgar Allan Poe — tall and gaunt and in the grip of powers, imagined or real, out of his control. If he had played only one role, the somnambulist Cesare in Wiene's *The Cabinet of Dr. Caligari,* he would be forever remembered in film history. "No matter what roles I play," he said, "I can't get *Caligari* out of my system." That's probably an exaggeration, for over Veidt's career he showed a versatility that allowed him to transcend the Expressionist acting style he helped invent. Indeed, before such Expressionist films as *Caligari, Orlac's Hands,* and *Waxworks,* he worked with the director Richard Oswald, who produced so-called enlightenment films, which dealt with the dangers of sex but were often simply soft-core pornography. But with Oswald, Veidt produced another cinematic milestone in *Different from the Others* (1919), in which he played what may be film's first explicitly homosexual character.

In 1927, he went to Hollywood, where he starred in *The Man Who Laughs,* directed by his friend Paul Leni and costarring Mary Philbin. In the film, set in seventeenth-century England, Veidt's character is horribly disfigured in childhood by gypsy surgeons and given a grotesque permanent smile so that he could work in freak shows. He gives an extraordinary performance, able to evoke a range of emotions with his eyes and body language (Batman's creator, Bob Kane, used Veidt's appearance as the inspiration for the character of the Joker).

After returning to Germany, the staunchly anti-Nazi Veidt left with his wife for England, in 1933. He later returned to Hollywood, where he was, ironically, often cast as a Nazi, most famously as Major Strasser in *Casablanca.*

Bottom: Veidt with Olga Baclanova in *The Man Who Laughs* (1928).

CONRAD VEIDT

PROMOTION and THE PRESS

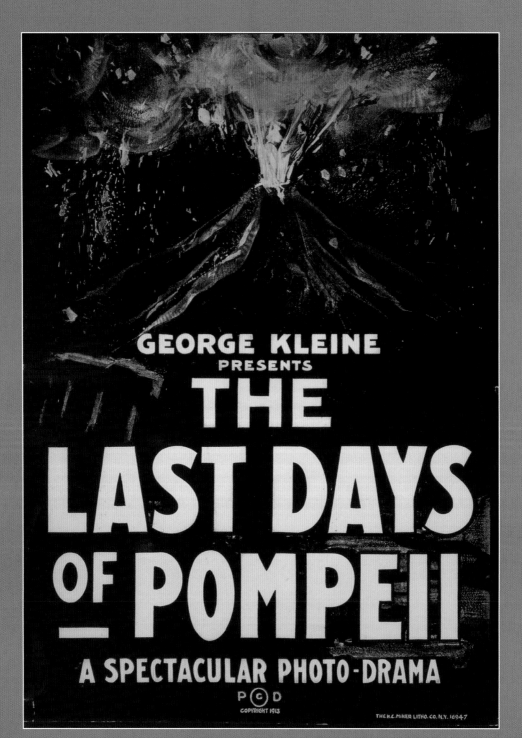

GEORGE KLEINE
PRESENTS
THE
LAST DAYS
OF POMPEII
A SPECTACULAR PHOTO-DRAMA
P C D
COPYRIGHT 1913

PRINT PROMOTION

THE ART OF THE SPIN BEGAN EARLY IN HOLLYWOOD HISTORY. IT STARTED AS BUSINESS-TO-BUSINESS MARKETING, AS IT IS CALLED TODAY, CONSISTING MAINLY OF FILM-COMPANY CATALOGS SUCH AS *EDISON FILM* AND *BIOGRAPH BULLETIN*. THEY CONTAINED PLOT SUMMARIES AND OCCASIONALLY PICTURE STILLS. SUGGESTIONS FOR THE ORDER OF THE FILMS OR INFORMATION FOR LECTURES TO ACCOMPANY THEM MIGHT BE INCLUDED. SMALL ADS WERE PLACED IN TRADE JOURNALS.

Above: The screen's first star with a fabricated background, the Vamp Theda Bara (circa 1916), who, according to the studio was the daughter of an Arabian princess, was actually born Theodosia Goodman in Cincinnati, Ohio.

Left: American poster for the Italian epic *Gli Ultimi giorni di Pompeii* (1913).

Initially, films were marketed to audiences by studio brand. During Griffith's tenure at Biograph, its brand carried considerable cachet. But as the cameras moved closer, individual actors became more recognizable, and their fans wanted to get closer still. Production companies were reluctant to identify actors in their films because they knew higher salary demands would soon follow; they relented because stars were valuable commodities. They began to promote them in the press, and spin became an art form.

Carl Laemmle and Robert Cochrane of the IMP Company famously promoted Florence Lawrence, one of their new actresses and one of the first genuine movie stars, in an ad in the March 12, 1910, edition of *Moving Picture World.* In "We Nail a Lie," they wrote a response to fake death notices that the studio itself had almost certainly planted: "The blackest and at the same time the silliest lie yet circulated by enemies of the 'Imp' was the story foisted on the public of St. Louis last week to the effect that Miss Lawrence (the 'Imp' girl, formerly known as the 'Biograph' girl) had been killed by a street car. . . ."

Irving Asher, the first press agent for Warner Bros., told Kevin Brownlow: "I don't know of any publicity that was truthful in those days. . . . Anything I wrote and sent to the papers, they'd print. They'd print anything to do with movie stars. Ninety percent of it was manufactured. . . . Everyone made a million dollars a minute and had six Rolls-Royces and every picture cost a million dollars. Few pictures in those days cost a million. A picture cost a hundred, two hundred thousand dollars, and that was a big super production."

Perhaps one of the most egregious examples of studio inventiveness is that of Theda Bara. Born Theodosia Goodman, from Cincinnati, Ohio, she was the daughter of a Jewish tailor who had emigrated from Poland. After a lackluster theater career, she made her film debut as a seductress and destroyer of men in 1915's *A Fool There Was*, directed for Fox by Frank Powell. The film was derived from a stage play, which in turn was inspired by Burne-Jones's famous painting *The Vampire* and Rudyard Kipling's poem of the same name, which is quoted extensively in the film's intertitles. Theda Bara was not the first screen vamp (Alice Hollister in Kalem's 1913 *The Vampire* may have that honor), but she was the most famous.

Top: Exterior of the Théâtre Français in Bordeaux, France, with a promotional display for Clara Bow's feature *It* (1927).

Bottom: Exterior of a theater showing Harold Lloyd's *Speedy* (1928).

Right: Promotional contest for Douglas Fairbanks's *The Black Pirate* (1926).

Fox hired press agents Johnny Goldfrap and Al Selig to give the unknown actress a new name (supposedly an anagram for "Arab death") and a new biography, as a French-Arab exotic who was born under the Sphinx. Film historian Terry Ramsaye, writing from the perspective of a few years later in *A Million and One Nights*, cynically described the press agents' creation: "This deadly Arab girl was a crystal gazing seeress of profoundly occult powers, wicked as fresh red paint and poisonous as dried spiders." The word *vamp* came into common parlance, and Ramsaye opined, "This verb may prove to be the only permanent contribution of the Fox-Theda barrage to the world."

The film will strike most modern viewers as fairly ridiculous; Theda Bara overacts terribly, but to be fair it was her first film. Many liked it because of or despite the hype, for it was a big hit for Fox. The reviewer for the *New York Dramatic Mirror* was, to put it politely, enchanted by her performance: "To come in contact with her is like touching the third rail. . . . She has enough sex attraction to supply a town full of normally pleasing women."

When studio publicity departments weren't busy inventing fictions as interesting as their directors' work, they used stunts to promote films. Press agent Harry Reichenbach was famed for the outrageousness of his stunts: for example, to promote 1920's *The Return of Tarzan*, he succeeded in letting a lion loose in New York City's Belleclaire Hotel. During the summer of 1921, when Erich von Stroheim was hemorrhaging money filming *Foolish Wives*, much to Universal's dismay the studio put up a three-story electric sign at Broadway and Forty-fifth Street in New York reading, "The cost of *Foolish Wives* up to this week," with the figure updated weekly.

But the work of promotion was often more mundane and the stunts more homespun. The Hollywood publicity machinery routinely produced exhibitor campaign books for upcoming films, which included an array of marketing materials, including plot summaries, ads, advance features, reviews and snappy shorts suitable for placement in local papers, and a panoply of posters.

Promotional stunts were also proposed for theater management. For Goldwyn's *Made in Heaven*, directed by Victor Schertzinger and starring Tom Moore, about an Irish immigrant who becomes a New York fireman and marries into society's inner circle, the press book suggests theater owners get local fire department glee clubs to sing at evening showings, in uniform, of course. The press book for the Marguerite Clark–starrer *Three Men and a Girl* had sample advance-mail advertising, one piece of which starts with the come-on, "Dear Madam: Aren't men peculiar? With some girls they're daring Romeos. With others, they are grouches. You can make them daring Romeos if you know Sylvia's secret."

Similar booklets, directed at the audience as souvenirs, were often quite sophisticated and well executed. The souvenir booklet for *The Phantom of the Opera*, for instance, is twenty-four pages

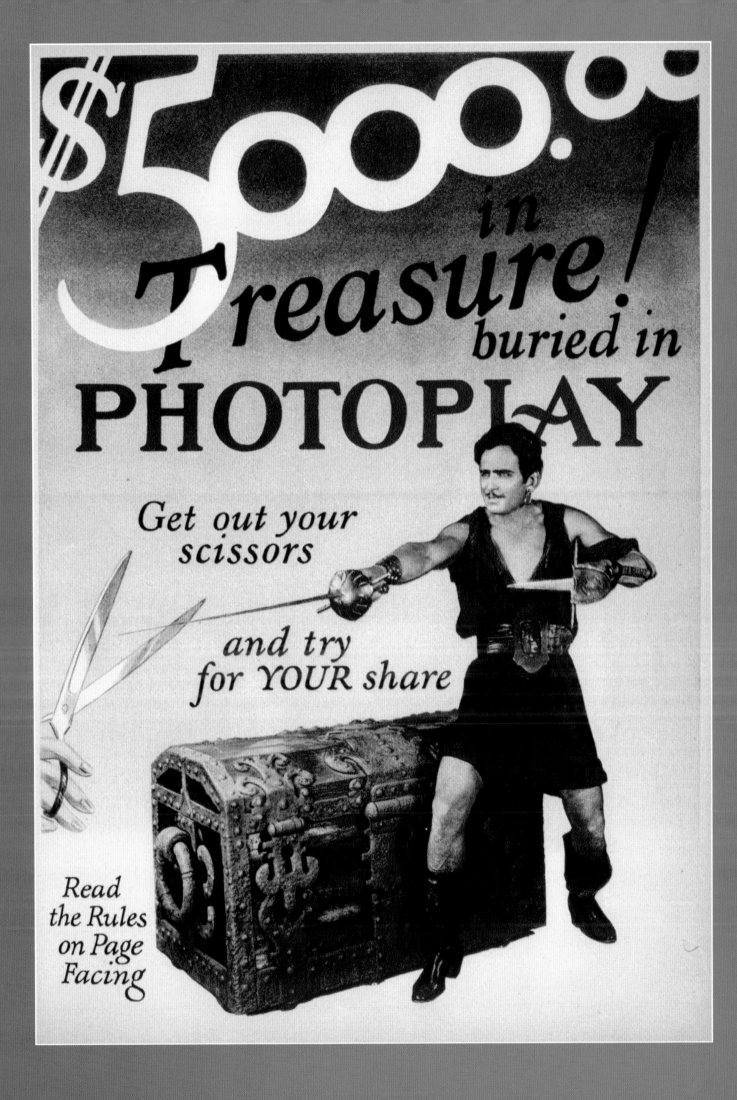

"THE PHANTOM OF THE OPERA"

Grand Staircase of the Paris Opera House,
the Largest Setting Ever Built
for a Motion Picture

PRICE 25 cents

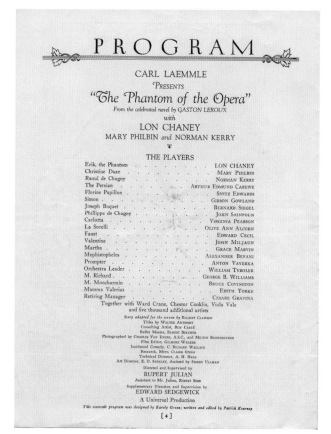

PROGRAM

CARL LAEMMLE
Presents

"The Phantom of the Opera"
From the celebrated novel by GASTON LEROUX
with

LON CHANEY

MARY PHILBIN and NORMAN KERRY

THE PLAYERS

Erik, the Phantom	LON CHANEY
Christine Daae	MARY PHILBIN
Raoul de Chagny	NORMAN KERRY
The Persian	ARTHUR EDMUND CAREWE
Florine Papillon	SNITZ EDWARDS
Simon	GIBSON GOWLAND
Joseph Buquet	BERNARD SIEGEL
Phillippe de Chagny	JOHN SAINPOLIS
Carlotta	VIRGINIA PEARSON
La Sorelli	OLIVE ANN ALCORN
Faust	EDWARD CECIL
Valentine	JOHN MILJAUN
Martha	GRACE MARVIN
Mephistopheles	ALEXANDER BEVANI
Prompter	ANTON VAVERKA
Orchestra Leader	WILLIAM TYROLER
M. Richard	GEORGE B. WILLIAMS
M. Moncharmin	BRUCE COVINGTON
Mamma Valerius	EDITH YORKE
Retiring Manager	CESARE GRAVINA

Together with Ward Crane, Chester Conklin, Viola Vale
and five thousand additional artists

Story adapted for the screen by ELLIOTT CLAWSON
Titles by WALTER ANTHONY
Consulting Artist, BEN CARRÉ
Ballet Master, ERNEST BELCHER
Photographed by CHARLES VAN ENGER, A.S.C. and MILTON BRIDENBECKER
Film Editor, GILMORE WALKER
Incidental Comedy, C. RICHARD WALLACE
Research, META CLAISE STERN
Technical Director, A. H. HALL
Art Director, E. D. SHELLEY, Assisted by SIDNEY ULLMAN
Directed and Supervised by
RUPERT JULIAN
Assistant to Mr. Julian, ROBERT ROSS
Supplementary Direction and Supervision by
EDWARD SEDGEWICK
A Universal Production
This souvenir program was designed by Karoly Grosz; written and edited by Patrick Kearney

[4]

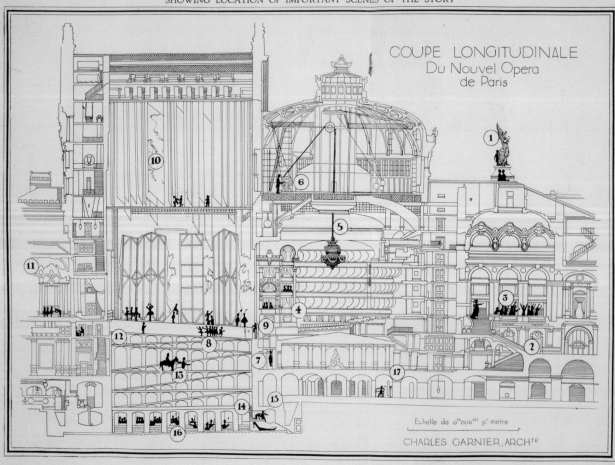

CROSS SECTION OF THE PARIS OPERA HOUSE

Reproduced from the original drawing by the architect, CHARLES GARNIER
SHOWING LOCATION OF IMPORTANT SCENES OF THE STORY

COUPE LONGITUDINALE
Du Nouvel Opera
de Paris

Echelle de 0^m006^ml p^r metre

CHARLES GARNIER, ARCH^TE

1. Statue of Apollo on top of the Opera House. Here the Phantom hears Christine and Raoul planning to elope.

2. The entrance and grand foyer—the portals to the world's centre of beauty and splendor.

3. The grand staircase, the richest setting in the world. It is here that the Phantom terrifies the thousands of maskers.

4. Box Five—the Haunted Box, which no one dares to enter because of the Phantom's threats.

5. The great 16,000 pound crystal chandelier, which the Phantom's malevolence causes to fall during a performance of "Faust."

6. The secret room from which the Phantom manipulates the fall of the chandelier.

7. The property room where Joseph Buquet is found dead—because he knew too much of the Phantom's secrets.

8. Another property room, where the ballet girls are terrified by seeing the weird shadowy figure.

9. Prompter's Box, from which the Phantom kidnaps Christine during a performance.

10. Lofts, where Christine and Raoul flee from the Phantom.

11. Foyer de la Danse, where the ballet girls receive admirers.

12. The Phantom's secret passage from the cellars to Christine's dressing room from which, unseen, he sings and speaks to her.

13. The five labyrinthine cellars below the Opera, through which the inflamed mob pursued the Phantom.

14. Trap in fifth cellar through which Raoul and Persian fall into the torture chamber.

15. The Phantom's torture chamber, in which Raoul and the Persian are held captive.

16. The lowest cellar, containing the underground lake which floods the cellars at the Phantom's command.

17. The Phantom's palatial apartments below the Opera, from which, by superhuman powers, he makes or mars human lives.

Theater program for *The Phantom of the Opera* (1925).

and is laid out like a big feature in *Premiere* or *Entertainment Weekly*. It features a "main bar" story on the making of the film, an article by the book author Gaston Leroux, scenes from the picture, a schematic drawing of the Paris Opera showing where key scenes take place, a profile of Lon Chaney, and fun facts about the movie ("seven blocks of Paris streets were built in complete detail"). Modern-day entertainment journalists can feel either humbled by the lack of innovation and distinction in their craft or part of a grand tradition.

POSTERS AND VISUAL DISPLAYS

Film was an art as well as a business, but from the earliest days of cinema another art enhanced commerce: the poster. Originally posters advertised the company providing the films — Lumière, Edison — rather than the films themselves (which was convenient because the film bill changed frequently, and the posters could be recycled). The art also was intended to convey that the performance was a film, not a play, so posters often featured a beam of light streaming from the projector to the screen.

One of the first posters to show an actual moving picture was for the Lumières' comedy *The Sprinkler Sprinkled*. More frequently, stock posters were used with a woman holding a card listing the film program. The card could be replaced as the program changed.

After the Trust was formed, in 1909, its distribution arm, the General Film Company, signed a contract with the A. B. See Lithograph Company in Cleveland to produce one-sheet posters for each film. Each company branded its posters with stock borders, and in the center of the sheet, ABC, as it was known, printed the film's title, plot, studio logo, and a still from the movie. Independent printers produced generic, often lurid posters that could be used by theater managers over and over, even if they had little to do with the film then showing.

As the films got bigger, so did the posters. In 1911, the American Printers' Congress adopted formats for posters that would become standard: the one-sheet (27" x 41") was the most common, but three-sheets (41" x 81") and six-sheets (82" x 81") were used in special displays. There was even a twenty-four-sheet format used on billboards. Also printed were lobby cards (11" x 14") and window cards (14" x 22"), to be displayed in shop windows.

After 1915, big studios kept a staff of artists for designing posters and cards, and they were often quite good even if they toiled in relative obscurity. Poster art became a more important part of the marketing mix. The wordy plot summaries and generic art were discarded for glamorous star

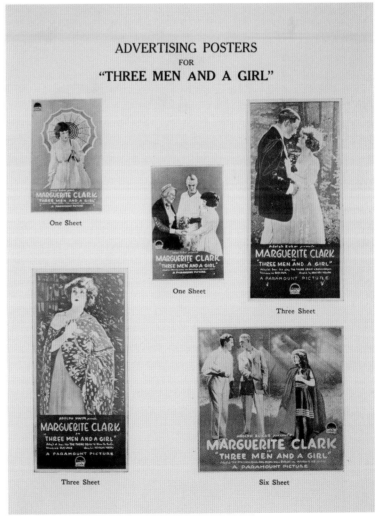

Various-sized movie posters for exhibition in movie theaters.

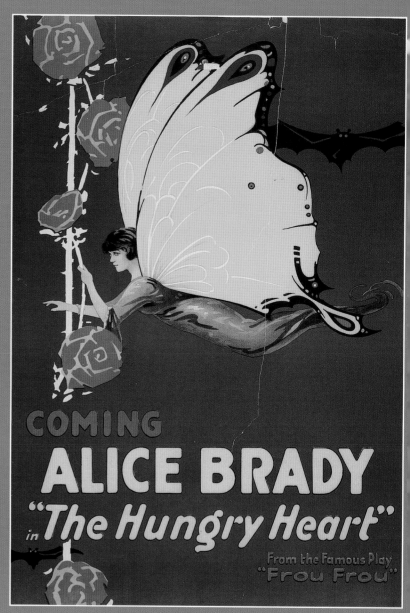

Top left: Rex Ingram wrote, produced, and directed this 1917 dramatic feature.

Top right: Actress Alice Brady, best known today as the scatterbrained mother in *My Man Godfrey* (1936), began her career in dramatic films like *The Hungry Heart* (1917), produced by her father, William A. Brady, one of the cofounders of the World Film Corporation.

Bottom: An early advertisement for Pathé productions, promoting cinema as family entertainment.

Poster for the English-language release of the French film *La Passion de Jeanne d'Arc* (1928).

Poster for a lost 1912 short starring Mabel Normand and Mack Sennett.

images with their names prominently displayed. Paramount chief Adolph Zukor set great store by posters. "Paramount has found that best results are usually achieved by large dramatic figures, brilliant coloring and a small amount of letters," he told *Poster* magazine in 1928.

In the twenties, the studios distributed their own posters and cards. A theater owner would pick up not only a movie at the exchange but a plethora of lobby cards and posters in several sizes. A popular film might have several different versions of posters: *The Phantom of the Opera* had eight different one-sheets, six three-sheets, and four different billboard-size posters.

The poster work of such serious artists as Henry Clive, C. V. Millard, and Louis Fancher remained mostly anonymous (an exception is Clive's signed poster for *The Sheik*, which evokes the film's exotic romance with a lovely portrait of Valentino's costar Agnes Ayres writing in the sand). American poster art emphasized stars. In a poster for Chaplin's *The Kid Auto Race*, the Tramp is painted standing against a white background with the film title crossing the center of the poster and his name beneath. There is no hint of the movie's plot, but in another poster, for *The Vagabond*, Chaplin plays the violin for Edna Purviance near a gypsy wagon, which suggests major elements of the story.

But a poster could convey a story more subtly, without the star's compelling presence. In a dramatic and sinister art nouveau poster for Maurice Tourneur's *A Girl's Folly*, about a country girl lured to the city by a jaded actor, a woman appears about to be devoured in the maw of a malevolent demon.

Posters for European and Russian films were less star driven and were often more boldly artistic. In two posters for Dziga Vertov's *The Man with a Movie Camera*, both use a montage style: a German version has a cameraman riding a speeding motorcycle with his camera mounted on the handlebars, while a Russian version, by the Russian brothers Georgii and Vladimir Sternberg, features a woman's legs with her torso cut off, a camera lens filled with an eye, and men aiming cameras that look more like guns.

A poster for *The Cabinet of Dr. Caligari* depicts the doctor and his somnambulist, Cesare, at a country fair, emphasizing the film's skewed angles. A poster for Fritz Lang's *Metropolis*, perhaps one of the most famous films of the silent era, shows only the feminine head of a robot. Because the image is so iconic, one version doesn't even bother to include the film's title or any print whatsoever.

These film artifacts offer a colorful window on the world of the silents. The quality of poster art has waxed and waned over the decades, but its importance as a marketing tool and as an art form

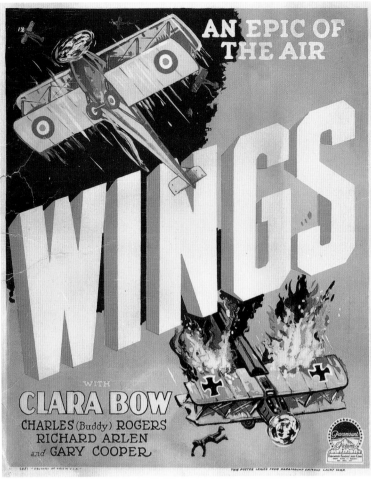

Poster for William Wellman's *Wings* (1927), starring Clara Bow and Charles "Buddy" Rogers.

The now iconic image of the robot Maria in Fritz Lang's *Metropolis* (1927).

Russian movie posters designed by artists Vladimir and Georgii Sternberg in the late 1920s for Mary Pickford's *Little Lord Fauntleroy* (1921) and Douglas Fairbanks's *Don Q, Son of Zorro* (1925).

DeMille's *Saturday Night* (1922), starring Leatrice Joy and Conrad Nagel.

A poster for *Salome* (1923), starring Alla Nazimova.

has diminished because so many other outlets exist for movie promotion: the plethora of stars promoting their latest vehicles on television chat shows and the easy availability of movie trailers on the Internet have speeded the decline of the poster.

Of course, movie trailers themselves are hardly new. They are called trailers because when they were first introduced — the earliest surviving one is from 1914 — they followed the feature. Initially, they weren't particularly creative, merely offering snippets from a couple of scenes. But in the twenties, they became more compelling, looking forward to the minimovies of today.

Trailers for coming attractions were a valuable promotional tool, but, sadly, they are sometimes merely the visual remnants of films that are now considered lost. One example is the trailer for 1926's *The American Venus*. It doesn't tell the viewer all that much about the missing film, but it features the first credited screen appearance by Louise Brooks, then nineteen, as a beauty contestant whose kimono is ripped off by a lusty businessman who then kicks her behind a door to hide her from his wife.

A Paramount Picture

VIVIAN MARTIN
IN
"The Fair Barbarian"

ROSES

Paramount Pictures

The Fair Barbarian (1917) starring Vivian Martin.

GLORIA SWANSON IN AN ALLAN DWAN PRODUCTION WAGES OF VIRTUE

A Paramount Picture

The Wages of Virtue (1924) directed by Allan Dwan.

Nell Shipman's Production
THE GRUB-STAKE
Distributed by
American Releasing Corp.

Actress Nell Shipman wrote and produced *The Grub-Stake* (1923).

LOBBY CARDS
In 1908, movie houses began promoting screenings with advertising placards, called lobby cards, displayed on easels in the lobby or near the box office. The first cards were simply poor reproductions of 8" x 10" movie stills printed in sepia or tinted by hand on heavy paper stock. As the style and techniques used to make movies evolved, so did the promotion of films. Lobby cards were now used to highlight key sequences or promote favorite stars. The size of the cards increased to 11" x 14" (there was also a jumbo 14" x 17"), and they were packaged for display in sets of eight to sixteen. High-quality images were made colorful (though films were largely shot in black and white), and even the borders were stylishly decorated with advertising art. Lobby cards remained an important part of movie promotion through the 1980s.

Everett Butterfield and Herbert Prior in *The Magic Skin* (1915).

Reginald Denny stars in "Widower's Mite," an episode from the Universal series *The Leather Pushers* (1922).

A 1926 feature with Laura La Plante and Norman Kerry.

Alice Joyce joins W. C. Fields in this 1926 comedy feature.

Corinne Griffith was both producer and star of *Mademoiselle Modiste* (1926).

Ronald Colman and Vilma Bánky, a popular romantic screen couple, in *Two Lovers* (1928), their last film together.

Getting Gertie's Garter (1927) with Marie Prevost and Charles Ray was remade in 1945 by director Allan Dwan.

Dorothy Gish in the comedy *I'll Get Him Yet* (1919).

GLASS SLIDES Glass advertising slides were used in theaters to provide information to the patron or to promote upcoming programs. The slides (a standard 3" x 4" or smaller) were made from two panes of glass, one with a hand-painted image and one clear to protect the first. They were projected via a magic lantern between film reels in the early years and later, when feature-length films became the norm, before the programs began. Glass slides remained a popular form of theater advertising through the 1950s.

Matinee idol Thomas Meighan in the romance *The Man Who Saw Tomorrow* (1922).

Realart Pictures capitalized on the ten-day jail sentence of actress Bebe Daniels for numerous speeding violations in the 1921 feature *The Speed Girl*.

Norma Shearer, the queen of the MGM studios lot in the 1930s, appeared in an estimated forty silent features, including *The Demi-Bride* (1927).

Betty Compson on the cover of *Exhibitors Trade Review*, January 1922.

TRADE MAGAZINES

Between the reviews and reporting of mainstream newspapers and magazines and the promotional vehicles of the film producers were the trade magazines. Magazines that covered general entertainment — *Variety*, the *New York Clipper*, the *New York Dramatic Mirror* — began covering moving pictures early on.

Later, several trade publications were devoted solely to film. The first, *Views and Film Index*, debuted in 1906. Others included the *Moving Picture World*, *Moving Picture News*, *Exhibitor's Trade Review*, and *Exhibitor's Herald*. They offered news, plot summaries, reviews, and box-office returns.

Because the films came and went so quickly, writers offered general essays as well as synopses and reviews. Some of the articles, many of which were anonymous, were remarkably insightful. Frank Woods, an ad salesman for the *Mirror*, convinced the theater journal to start reviewing films, then wrote a column of film commentary under the pseudonym "The Spectator" from 1909 to 1912. Woods also sold scenarios to Biograph and later moved to California with Griffith. M. O. Lounsbury says in *The Origins of American Film Criticism, 1909–1939* that Woods's work for the *Mirror* "started as an apology for the film manufacturers [and] became the earliest exploration into a number of important esthetic and social issues concerning the motion picture." Indeed, the trade magazines helped to shape the evolution of film in many significant, often positive, ways.

FAN MAGAZINES

Fan magazines appealed to the audiences that the industry was trying to entice. *Motion Picture Story Magazine* and *Photoplay*, two of the earliest fan magazines, were launched in 1911. They were full of plot synopses, portraits of stars, and popularity contests.

Although the generic description "fan magazines" has a pejorative sound, leading one to expect fluffy features and tame reviews, that was not always the case. James R. Quirk, who became vice president of *Photoplay* in 1915 and then editor in 1920, brought a journalistic sensibility to the magazine (he had previously edited *Popular Mechanics*). *Photoplay* began publishing real film reviews and serious features and interviews. Scenarist and writer Adela Rogers St. Johns penned articles, as did Terry Ramsaye, author of the early, epic history of silent film, *A Million and One Nights*. Quirk

MOTION PICTURE

JUNE — 25 CTS

A BREWSTER PUBLICATION

From
Stardom
to
Extra
Roles

Ramon Novarro on the cover of a 1926 fan magazine.

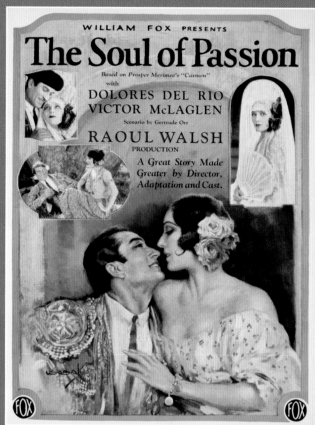

Ads for two 1927 Fox features, the comedy *Pajamas* (1927) and the romantic drama *Loves of Carmen* (1927).

Director Rex Ingram's seafaring war drama *Mare Nostrum* (1926).

She (1925), starring Betty Blythe, was one of three silent screen adaptations of the H. Rider Haggard novel *She: A History of Adventure*.

MAGAZINE ADS In the early twentieth century, before the birth of commercial radio and long before the invention of television, magazines and newspapers were the largest disseminators of popular culture. The translation of movie culture from the big screen to the small page was an important factor in the success of the movie industry. Movie magazines such as *Photoplay*, *Motion Picture Magazine*, and *Motion Picture News* were some of the most popular publications of their era, and their circulations ranged from a few hundred thousand to more than two million. Full-page advertisements in these magazines were major promotional tools for production companies, as evidenced by this collection of elaborate movie ads from the silent era.

Marion Davies, one of silent cinema's great comediennes, stars here in the melodrama *Buried Treasure* (1921).

Constance Talmadge produced and starred in the sophisticated comedy *Breakfast at Sunrise* (1927).

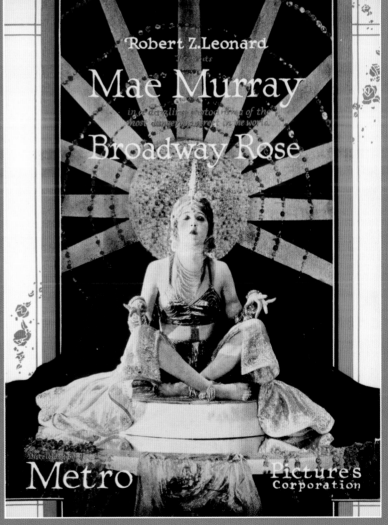

Broadway Rose (1922) features Mae Murray, who was known as the girl with the bee-stung lips.

PHOTOPLAY

The World's Leading Moving Picture Magazine

Magazine

March

20 Cents

If Christ
Went to the
Movies

Alice Joyce

Actress and renowned beauty Alice Joyce in 1920.

himself held strong opinions, as in his diatribe against Stroheim's *Foolish Wives*, which he deemed "an insult to every American."

Motion Picture Story, later simply called *Motion Picture*, also sometimes offered high-class journalism, as when writer Katherine Anne Porter interviewed Charles Ray, the popular star of rural dramas.

NEWSPAPER AND MAGAZINE FILM JOURNALISM

Coverage of film showings during their novelty phase was more about the event than the films themselves. Reporters described the audience's reaction and the theater as well as what occurred on-screen. An anonymous review in the *New York Times*, dated April 24, 1896, is typical:

The new thing at Koster and Bial's last night was Edison's vitascope, exhibited for the first time. The ingenious inventor's latest toy is a projection of his kinetoscope figures, in stereopticon fashion, upon a white screen in a darkened hall. In the center of the balcony is a curious object, which looks from below like the double turret of a big monitor. In the front of each half of it are two oblong holes. The turret is nearly covered with the blue velvet brocade which is the favorite decorative material in this house. The white screen used on the stage is framed like a picture. The moving figures are about half life-size.

After giving a brief description of the films themselves, the writer notes: "So enthusiastic was the appreciation of the crowd long before this extraordinary exhibition was finished that vociferous cheering was heard. There were loud calls for Mr. Edison, but he made no response." The writer then describes the rest of the vaudeville bill.

As they focused more on the films themselves, newspapers offered brief, unsigned reviews. The most carefully preserved, those of the *New York Times*, are often pedestrian. By the twenties, more newspaper reviews carried bylines. Today, the most famous newspaper film critic of the silent era is Carl Sandburg, who wrote reviews and features from 1920 to 1927 for the *Chicago Daily News*. He is renowned for his poetry, not his criticism, but he was curious and enthusiastic about the medium, which comes across in his writing.

Established magazines such as the *New Republic* and the *Nation* offered serious film criticism of high caliber. But certainly one of the best contemporary critics was Robert E. Sherwood, who wrote film reviews for *Life* magazine from 1920 to 1928. He was honest, wise, and witty — strong assets for any film writer. In his rave review of 1921's *The Four Horsemen of the Apocalypse*,

Actress Betty Bronson on the cover of industry magazine *The Hollywood Vagabond*, 1927.

A press book with marketing suggestions for *Hotel Imperial* (1927).

he writes: "Praise is difficult to compose, for it is always easier to be harsh than it is to be ecstatic. The reviewer's task would be much simpler if every movie was of the caliber of [the now-forgotten] *Man-Woman-Marriage*, for instance. . . . *The Four Horsemen of the Apocalypse* is a living, breathing answer to those who still refuse to take motion pictures seriously."

And Sherwood reveals a lighter side in his review of *The Three Musketeers*, released the same year. "When Alexandre Dumas sat down at his desk, smoothed his hair back, chewed the end of his quill pen, and said to himself, 'Well, I guess I might as well write a book called *The Three Musketeers*,' he doubtless had but one object in view: to provide a suitable story for Douglas Fairbanks to act in the movies." Sherwood goes on to call Fairbanks's performance "marvelous."

As the movies matured, so did film criticism. In film's early years, writers played a significant role in prodding filmmakers to aspire to greater things.

PHOTO[I]

The Shadow Stage

(Continued from page 72)

Stanley Olmstead wrote the scenario, telling his story consistently.

DR. JEKYLL AND MR. HYDE—
Pioneer

THE version of "Dr. Jekyll and Mr. Hyde" with Sheldon Lewis playing the harassed soul who gave himself up to the devil, hurriedly screened to take advantage of the interest aroused by Jack Barrymore's appearance in the same role, does not reflect great credit upon its producers. It is typical movie stuff, with little artistry and less imagination to commend it. In this version the good Dr. Jekyll dreams a dream. In the dream he sees himself testing his theory that it is possible for a man to be controlled by his baser self. He swallows the concoction compounded in his laboratory, suffers a growth of hair and a mouth full of buck teeth, and achieves a passion for frightening defenseless females and setting fire to buildings. He is a less sensual and less ferocious Mr. Hyde than the Barrymore exhibit. Neither does his particular compound equal in strength that discovered by the other Mr. Hyde, who was immediately transformed into a repulsive degenerate with an elongated cranium, knotted knuckles and protruding finger-nai's. The picture is cheaply set. Mr. Lewis' performance is that of a competent but uninspired actor, and there is little attempt at cleverness in tricking the change from one character to the other. The ending, too, by the employment of the dream idea, is conventionally happy.

THE ROUND UP—
Paramount-Artcraft

I SHOULD say that Roscoe Arbuckle's plunge into the five reelers has been successfully negotiated in "The Round-up." As "Slim" Hoover, the sheriff, the genial comic waddles in and out of the story, plays straight when he has to, falls off a horse when he can do so safely, without fracturing either his histrionic ambitions or the plot, and emerges finally the pathetically humorous philosopher who allowed that nobody ever loves a fat man. I don't suppose anyone could possibly take "Fatty" seriously as a sheriff with notches on his gun, but it is something of a triumph for him that he keeps the faces of his audience straight while he is suggesting the possibility. George Melford has extracted a reasonably interesting Western romance from the old melodrama in which Maclyn Arbuckle starred. In it Irving Cummings is permitted to escape temporarily from his curly-headed deviltries with women and become more or less a normal he-man.

The story is one of alternate fights with Apaches, bank robbers and such, mingled with the romance of two pals who loved the same square little heroine. She married one, thinking the other dead, and, finding he wasn't, sent her husband to find him and explain. This involves another big fight with the Indians and their renegade chief, and results in the elimination of the extra lover. If the fighting were on the level the cast would have been wiped out in the first reel. Which would be sad, for it is a good cast.

Tom Forman plays the sub-hero (and he also wrote the scenario, which provides a second feather for his Scotch bonnet); Mabel Julienne Scott is the heroine. Wallace Beery is again the fighting renegade, and the others are all capable. The scenic shots are excellent and the fighting excessive but lively.

Above: Press book cover for *The Big Parade* (1925).

Left: Reviews found in the fan magazine *Photoplay*.

A small Quaker community learns the perils of the sea firsthand, confronting sharks, murder, kidnapping, and mutiny in *Down to the Sea in Ships* (1922), directed by Elmer Clifton.

Agnes Ayres and Antonio Moreno lead the cast of *The Story without a Name* (1924), directed by Irvin Willat, but it seems a trick title produces an even trickier plot.

Wallace Beery (right) and Raymond Hatton as Powderhorn Pete and Deadeye Dan, snake-oil salesmen who run afoul of feuding Ozark clans in *The Big Killing* (1928), directed by F. Richard Jones.

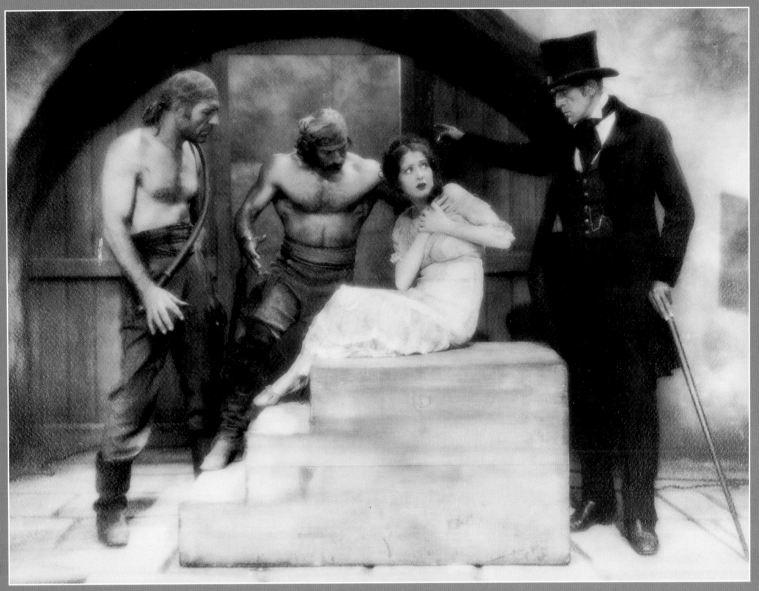

Billie Dove recoils from Boris Karloff and his two bare-chested henchmen in *The Love Mart* (1927), directed by George Fitzmaurice.

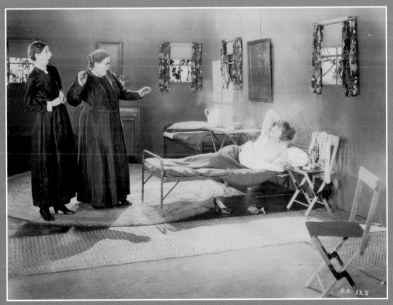

Pauline Starke causes consternation to her appalled company in *The Streets of Shanghai* (1927), directed by Louis J. Gasnier.

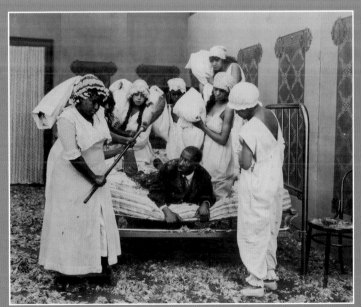

Unidentified Ebony Film Company comedy, circa 1917.

PROMOTIONAL STILLS play the same role today as they did in the silent era. During shooting, the actors would stop and pose for the photographer before resuming the action. The resulting stills were used purely for publicity — in lobbies, magazines, trade journals, and newspapers — to sell the film to an audience.

Madame X (1920), directed by Frank Lloyd. Pauline Frederick stars as a woman thrown out of her house by her jealous husband. She is charged with killing a man who wants to harm her son. Her son unknowingly defends her in court.

The Passionate Pilgrim (1921), directed by Robert G. Vignola, is a complicated story of a hidden family history of murder, starring Matt Moore, Julia Swayne (center), and Mary Newcomb (right).

A famous opera star, played by Louise Dresser, loses her voice when she has a child in *The Goose Woman* (1925), directed by Clarence Brown. When a murder occurs near her house, she seeks to regain the spotlight, inventing a story that implicates and imprisons her son.

Archdukes abound, as does murder, in *Yellow Lily* (1928), directed by Alexander Korda, with Clive Brook and Marc McDermott.

In *Rose-Marie* (1928), a Canadian tale directed by Lucien Hubbard, James Murray and Joan Crawford become involved in a murder and a love rectangle.

THE
DIRECTORS

I N THE EARLY TEENS, THE CULTURAL LANDSCAPE WAS CHANGING SIGNIFICANTLY, ESPECIALLY IN EUROPE, WHERE THE ARTISTIC AVANT-GARDE WAS ON THE MOVE ON SEVERAL FRONTS. IN 1911, GERMAN THEATER DIRECTOR MAX REINHARDT PREMIERED KARL GUSTAV VOLLMÖLLER'S PLAY *THE MIRACLE* IN LONDON'S MAMMOTH OLYMPIA EXHIBITION HALL WITH SOME TWO THOUSAND MUSICIANS, ACTORS, AND DANCERS IN A SPECTACLE OF MYTH AND RITUAL. IN THE YEARS LEADING UP TO THE WAR, PICASSO AND BRAQUE DEVELOPED CUBISM, ONE OF THE TWENTIETH CENTURY'S MOST IMPORTANT ART MOVEMENTS, WHICH FRAGMENTED OBJECTS INTO GEOMETRIC FORMS. IN PARIS, IN 1913, THE DEBUT OF IGOR STRAVINSKY'S BALLET *THE RITE OF SPRING* PROVOKED A NEAR RIOT.

But if the cinema was still offering slapstick one- and two-reelers and melodramas, it was also revealing more clearly than ever its own artistic potential. The new feature-length films gave directors the opportunity to develop characters, weave more complex plots, and offer the nuance and depth of literature and theater (indeed, many of the films were based on stage dramas, and moviemakers liked to call their productions photoplays because the term lent moving pictures the legitimacy of theater). Film was evolving quickly — technically and creatively — and it would soon offer explicitly artistic efforts as well as mass entertainment (*The Cabinet of Dr. Caligari* would be released in 1920, and avant-garde artists adopted film as a medium in the twenties).

By 1915, all but the most patronizing of cultural elitists had begun to accept cinema as an art form. Indeed, one of the first books of serious film aesthetics, published that year by poet Vachel Lindsay, says it all in its title: *The Art of the Moving Picture*. Lindsay saw the transforming power of this new art: "Edison is the new Gutenberg," he wrote. "He has invented the new printing."

However, the cataclysm of World War I, which began in the summer of 1914, was an enormous setback for the European film industry. (The United States wouldn't enter the war until 1917.) When the Treaty of Versailles was signed in 1919, 90 percent of all films screened in Europe (with the exception of Germany, which had been cut off from American film producers throughout the war) were American.

Above: Glass slide for D. W. Griffith's 1921 feature *Orphans of the Storm*.

Left: Billy Bitzer cranks the camera while D. W. Griffith directs Henry B. Walthall in a scene from *The Avenging Conscience: Thou Shalt Not Kill* (1914).

Wanting to make feature-length films, D. W. GRIFFITH left Biograph in 1914 to head the feature production company Reliance-Majestic. His first film there, begun in late 1914, was *The Birth of a Nation*, an epic about the Civil War and Reconstruction, which was released early the following year. Its impact was so extraordinary that the silent-film era can be divided into two parts — pre- and post-*Birth*.

At twelve reels, clocking in at three hours, it was at least twice as long as the average feature. It was hugely successful: the top-grossing film of the silent era, it ran for an unprecedented forty-

Heroines Elise Stoneman (Lillian Gish) and Margaret Cameron (Miriam Cooper) ride through town with the Ku Klux Klan in *The Birth of a Nation* (1915).

eight weeks at the Liberty theater in New York City, where it was eventually seen by 825,000 people in the metropolitan area alone. (It is impossible to say exactly how many people saw it worldwide or how much money it made during its first run. Richard Schickel, in *D. W. Griffith: An American Life*, estimates that it made some sixty million dollars. Not bad for a film whose negative cost was about one hundred thousand dollars.) It was the first film to be screened at the White House. *The Birth of a Nation* was more than a film; it was a milestone event in the history of cinema.

More than a hugely successful spectacle, it was a masterpiece — using Griffith's trademark cinematic techniques and combining emotional intimacy with epic sweep — but it was a deeply tainted one. Its racism — consciously intended by the filmmaker or not — makes parts of *Birth* extremely difficult to watch today.

Drawing on the works of Southern clergyman Thomas Dixon Jr. — the novels *The Leopard's Spots* and *The Clansman* and the latter's subsequent stage adaptation — *The Birth of a Nation* follows the intertwined fates of two families, the Southern slaveholding Camerons and the Northern Stonemans, led by Austin Stoneman (Ralph Lewis), a character based on Thaddeus Stevens, a Republican congressman and famous abolitionist who was an advocate for radical Reconstruction. Part One of the film depicts the events leading up to the Civil War, the war itself, with stirring battle scenes, the South's surrender, and Lincoln's assassination. Griffith made a case for the film's historical fidelity; the director studied Mathew Brady's photographs and mixed real-life figures such as President Lincoln and his assassin, John Wilkes Booth, and generals Lee and Grant with fictional characters.

But after offering a reasonably balanced portrait of the war as an enormous human tragedy, Part Two, focusing on Reconstruction, takes a more ideological turn. As one intertitle puts it, quoting then-president Woodrow Wilson, the vengeful movement attempts "to crush the White South under the heel of the Black South."

After the war, unruly blacks take control of the state legislature — drinking and putting their feet up on their desks in the august legislative building — and pass a law permitting the intermarriage of blacks and whites. Colonel Cameron, dismayed by such "outrages," forms the Ku Klux Klan to defend Southern white womanhood.

A lobby card for *The Birth of a Nation*.

Jesus carrying the cross in Griffith's *Intolerance* (1916).

Gus, a renegade black soldier played by Walter Long, finds Flora Cameron (Mae Marsh) alone in the woods and asks her to marry him. Whether he is sincere or merely wants to rape her is unclear, but from the film's point of view both are equally horrific, and Flora leaps off a cliff to her death rather than face either fate. Silas Lynch, Stoneman's mulatto protégé, traps Elsie Stoneman (Lillian Gish) in a room and proposes that she rule his black empire with him. She denies him but is rescued at the last minute by Colonel Cameron and the Klan, dressed in white-sheet regalia and racing on horseback to Wagner's "Ride of the Valkyries."

Actually, the racism of Dixon's novel *The Clansman* is toned down in the film. In the book, Flora Cameron and her mother are gang-raped by blacks, and both commit suicide for "the shame that neither they nor the world can forget."

The civil rights organization the National Association for the Advancement of Colored People (NAACP) mounted protests, fighting the film in courtrooms and before the National Board of Censorship. In a succession of local legal battles, the NAACP succeeded in getting only a few cuts. Still, the NAACP's organized protests gained the group stature and spurred its growth. Unfortunately, the Klan, which was basically moribund at the time of *Birth*'s release, grew substantially in numbers and influence in the wake of the film. (Both Dixon and Griffith disdained the contemporary Klan, saying that it had been necessary only during Reconstruction.)

At some point in 1915, Griffith decided that the small film he had begun before *Birth*, called *The Mother and the Law*, would become one part of another epic, called *Intolerance* (1916). Perhaps he felt that expectations were so high that he couldn't follow *Birth* with a small film. Karl Brown, the assistant cameraman on *Birth* and *Intolerance*, has said that Griffith rushed off to watch the Italian epic *Cabiria* and, after seeing it, began *Intolerance*.

In ambition and scope, *Intolerance* dwarfs even *Birth*. Intercutting among four separate stories — a contemporary story of social injustice *(The Mother and the Law)*, the St. Bartholomew's Massacre of the Huguenots in sixteenth-century France, the Crucifixion of Christ, and the fall of Babylon to the Persian forces of Cyrus the Great in 539 B.C. — it remains astonishing even today. But perhaps even more astonishing is that Griffith shot and edited *Intolerance* without a script — the film's concept evolved organically. The film ends on a utopian note: an epilogue depicts airships bombing New York City and soldiers fighting before scores of angels appear to stop the carnage with an end title reading "And Perfect Love shall bring peace forever more." As a connecting motif, Lillian Gish appears in transitions between story lines, rocking a cradle, although that connective tissue is dropped as the tempo of the editing speeds up for the climactic scenes of all four stories.

Initially *Intolerance* did well, but the box office fell off after a few months, and Griffith withdrew it from release. Contemporary critics perceptively laid out the film's many merits and shortcomings. Frederick James Smith, writing for the *New York Dramatic Mirror*, called it "stu-

The filming of *Orphans of the Storm* (1921).

Lillian Gish in the famous ice floe sequence from *Way Down East* (1920).

pendous," asserting that *Intolerance* "stands at the outpost of the cinema's advance. It has an idea. It has a purpose. From a structural standpoint, the handling and weaving of four plots are revolutionary."

But Alexander Woolcott of the *New York Times*, while granting the film's spectacle, found its "idea" unsubstantiated. "Unprecedented and indescribable splendor of pageantry is combined with grotesque incoherence of design and utter fatuity of thought to make the long-awaited new Griffith picture at the Liberty an extraordinary mixture of good and bad — of wonderful and bad."

Griffith went on to direct twenty-six features after *Intolerance*. The poetic *Broken Blossoms* (1919), set in London's Limehouse district, is small and intimate in scale compared to Griffith's epics, and it offers several memorable, moving performances. Lillian Gish plays Lucy, the fifteen-year-old daughter of an abusive, drunken prizefighter, Battling Burrows (Donald Crisp). Richard Barthelmess is "the Yellow Man," a gentle Asian who takes care of her after she is savagely beaten by her father. But when Burrows learns where she is, he drags her back home and prepares to beat her again. She hides in a closet, and in one of the most disturbing scenes in silent cinema, she runs around like a terrified trapped animal, as Burrows smashes his way in and then beats her to death. The Yellow Man, betraying his pacifist philosophy, kills Burrows and then commits suicide.

Griffith then turned an old stage play into the hugely popular melodrama *Way Down East* (1920), which again starred Gish and Barthelmess. Gish, as the impoverished Anna Moore, is tricked into a fake marriage and abandoned with child by a playboy (Lowell Sherman). Just when she seems to have found happiness as a servant in the house of Squire Bartlett, her "dark" past is exposed, and she is turned out in a blinding snowstorm and stumbles onto a frozen river, which is just breaking up.

Her rescue on the ice floes by the squire's son David (Barthelmess), who has fallen in love with her, is yet another iconic scene from the silent era. The realism of the filming certainly helped, as Griffith shot during a real blizzard and blew up a frozen river (he was injured by the blast, and Elmer Clifton filmed the rest of the ice floe sequence).

The box-office success of *Way Down East* afforded Griffith the opportunity to build his own studio in Mamaroneck, New York, where he produced two more historical epics, *Orphans of the Storm* (1921) and *America* (1924), set during the French and American revolutions, respectively. Both films sketch personal dramas against the backdrops of larger panoramas of historical events, mixing fictional and real-life characters. *Orphans*, which starred the Gish sisters, was an artistic and critical success, but that did not translate to a box-office hit; *America* was dramatically less compelling and again was not the success Griffith needed. The director could no longer afford to keep his own studio, and he became a contract studio director. Griffith made a few talkies, 1930's *Abraham Lincoln* and 1931's *The Struggle*, but the latter was a financial flop and his final film.

Although he stopped directing in the early 1930s, Griffith continued to live in Hollywood, the town without pity, until his death, in 1948. French writer Paul Valéry once famously penned that "a poem is never finished, only abandoned," and Griffith apparently felt the same way about his films — he refused to leave them alone. At revivals of his works, he could often be found reediting them in the projectionist's booth, and after donating his films to the Museum of Modern Art, he returned repeatedly to reedit them, until he was finally barred from doing so. Griffith was an artist steeped in the values of the Victorian era, and his works began to lose appeal in the go-go twenties, but his legacy remains huge and undeniable.

OSCAR MICHEAUX was an African American writer, producer, and distributor who directed an estimated forty independent feature films between 1919 and 1948. His production company, Oscar Micheaux Book and Film Company, which later became the Micheaux Pictures Corporation, made *The Homesteader* (1919). Adapted from Micheaux's 1917 novel of the same name, *The Homesteader* was the first feature-length race picture (a film made for black audiences). His films promoted the educational and economic uplifting of black Americans and addressed such controversial subjects as lynching, passing, and interracial romance. Micheaux's company produced more race movies than any other film corporation and was the only one to make the transition from silent to talking pictures.

Oscar Micheaux (circa 1913).

Only three of Oscar Micheaux's silent films are known to exist today. *Within Our Gates* (1920) and *Symbol of the Unconquered* (1920) were found in Europe, where his work had minor distribution. *Body and Soul* (1925), which boasts the screen-acting debut of Paul Robeson, was found in the United States and is the only surviving material with Micheaux's original intertitles. Due to their taboo subject matter, the films were ripe for attack by state censor boards and also were criticized by both the black and white communities.

Left: Poster of the black rodeo cowboy Bill Pickett in the 1922 Norman Film Company feature production *The Bull-Dogger*.

Top right: African American actor Noble Johnson, pictured here with actor Albert MacQuarrie in the Universal short *Mr. Dolan* (1917), founded the Lincoln Motion Picture Company. The Lincoln Company was the first to produce and distribute race movies to a national audience.

Center: Lobby card for a 1921 feature film by Reol Productions, a white-owned race movie company that employed a celebrated group of black actors from Harlem's Lafayette Theater, starring actress Edna Morton.

Bottom: The cast (African American) and crew (white) of the Ebony Film Company, circa 1917.

RACE FILMS

African Americans had few opportunities to see people of their own race in films. It was not unusual to have white actors in blackface cast in black roles, and when African American actors were hired, it was typically to play bit parts as servants, porters, chauffeurs, boxers, or criminals. Black- and white-owned independent film companies, including Lincoln Motion Picture Company, Colored Players Film Corporation, and Reol Productions, filled the void and began to make what became known as race films, featuring black casts in comedies, Westerns, and melodramas, and in stories relevant to African American audiences.

The race film studios, based mostly in the Northeast, Midwest, and even in the South, provided work for not only black actors but also black directors, producers, and writers, including Noble M. Johnson, Oscar Micheaux, and Spencer Williams. Between 1910 and 1950, race films were shown throughout the country in black movie houses and sometimes in white theaters that had segregated seating.

Just as black actors were stereotyped by Hollywood, so too were Asian actors. Although Hollywood's fascination with the Far East produced such film stars as Sessue Hayakawa and Anna May Wong, Asians were frequently stereotyped as villains, dragon ladies, opium dealers, and addicts. One Asian American production company, the Wah Ming Motion Picture Company, produced *Lotus Blossom* (1921), in part to counter negative images. *Lotus Blossom* producer James B. Leong, like race filmmaker Oscar Micheaux, was interested in film as a tool for education. Leong expected to reach the mainstream American movie audience and also voiced the desire to reach the "Chinese in China" with his message.

Black race film producers had a sizable African American audience to draw upon and were able to establish an industry "separate from Hollywood." The small size of the various Asian American communities did not offer such a base and, without mainstream distribution or overseas sales, were unable to continue production.

Top left: Japanese actress Tsuru Aoki on the cover of *Reel Life*, an industry trade magazine, promoting the Majestic Company two-reeler *The Oath of Tsuru San* (1913).

Top right: A production still from a recently rediscovered Chinese American feature, *The Curse of Quon Gwon* (1917), written and directed by Marion Wong.

Center: Vaudeville entertainer Lady Tsen Mei in the Asian American production *Lotus Blossom* (1921).

Bottom: Popular Chinese American actress Anna May Wong was featured in numerous silent films and made the transition to sound films.

Top: A frame enlargement from *Within Our Gates* (1920) of the attempted rape of the African American Sylvia Landry by a white man. The scene is Oscar Micheaux's response to the racist imagery used by D. W. Griffith in the attempted rape scene of the white Flora Cameron by a black man in *The Birth of a Nation* (1915).

Bottom: Newspaper advertisement for the Chicago run of what is arguably Micheaux's most controversial film.

OSCAR MICHEAUX'S
SCREEN MASTERPIECE

"WITHIN OUR GATES"

A STORY OF THE RACE WITH AN
ALL-STAR COLORED CAST!
—FEATURING—

EVELYN PREER

AND OTHER CAPABLE ARTISTS
The Greatest Preachment Against Race Prejudice and the Glaring
Injustices Practiced Upon Our People

IT WILL HOLD YOU SPELLBOUND!
FULL OF DETAILS THAT WILL MAKE YOU

GRIT YOUR TEETH IN SILENT INDIGNATION

On Account of Enormous Rental of This Picture Prices Will Be
ADULTS 30c, CHILDREN 15c, INCLUDING WAR TAX

THURS., FRI. AND SAT., JAN. 29, 30 AND 31

HAMMOND'S
PICKFORD THEATER
35th St. at Michigan Ave.

In the last reel of *Within Our Gates* Micheaux provides a back story for his lead character, Sylvia Landry, that is an obvious challenge to the racist narrative and imagery of D. W. Griffith's *The Birth of a Nation*. Scenes about the lynching of an innocent black couple take direct aim at the glorification of the Klan's vigilantism; the attempted rape of a young African American woman by a white man (who realizes from a scar on her breast that he is her father) audaciously counters Griffith's depiction of a black man attempting to rape a white girl. Micheaux's scenes were approved by censors in Chicago, where *Within Our Gates* premiered in January 1920. But racial tensions, already exacerbated by the previous summer's violent race riots, made all of the citizens of Chicago uneasy with the film's controversial content.

There were also other complaints. Both *Body and Soul* and *Within Our Gates* offended blacks with their depiction of African American ministers. In the latter film, Micheaux takes a swipe at his own community for allowing the hope of a better afterlife prevent them from demanding a good life on earth. Some African American audiences also felt that Micheaux favored light-skinned over dark-skinned blacks (a criticism of his work even today) and that many of his characters depicted racial stereotypes. Whites were obviously uncomfortable with films that addressed issues of sex and violence between the races from an African American perspective. Still, his portrayal of whites was not all critical (in fact, he desired a white audience for his movies). The goal of his work was not to condemn the white community, but to provide a realistic and rich representation of black life and character.

Like Griffith, THOMAS H. INCE was another film pioneer who began his career as a small-time stage actor. He appeared in one Biograph film before moving to the IMP Company, where he directed Mary Pickford in several shorts in 1911. That same year, Ince was hired by the New York Motion Picture Corporation to run its California studio. Over the next few years, he used the state's scenic diversity to lend authenticity to and reinvigorate Civil War and Western films when audiences had grown tired of "Eastern" Westerns shot in New Jersey. As his studios expanded, Ince increasingly assigned writing and directorial duties of the films to others, while closely overseeing them as a production supervisor. Today, he is probably best known for his genre films, for establishing a prototype of the studio production system, and for the "mystery" surrounding his early death, in 1924.

In 1915, the year *The Birth of a Nation* was released, Ince wrote and produced a Civil War feature, *The Coward*, which was directed by Reginald Barker. While Ince eschewed the epic scale of *Birth*, this intimate drama used many of the techniques for which Griffith was noted. Charles Ray plays a young Virginian who is afraid to join the Confederate Army until his father (Frank Keenan), a colonel and Mexican War veteran, forces him to fight. Ray deserts his post and returns home, and Keenan, fearing disgrace to his family, takes his place as a private. In following father and son, the film tells their stories through parallel editing to build narrative momentum and uses close-ups to

Top: Micheaux's film about the murder of Mary Phagen and the mob lynching of Jewish suspect Leo Frank.

Bottom: An advertisement from the black newspaper the *Chicago Defender* for the Micheaux-directed melodrama *The Dungeon* (1922).

Magazine advertisement for producer Thomas H. Ince's feature *The Hottentot* (1922).

evoke emotion and psychological insight. The following year, Ince released *Hell's Hinges*, starring William S. Hart and codirected by Hart and Charles Swickard.

But Ince's films ranged widely in subject. In early 1916, the year of *Intolerance*, he released his own epic, *Civilization*, an antiwar screed set in a mythical country, which he produced and co-directed. It was a hit, and *Intolerance* was a miss, and some historians attribute this to the trick of timing: Ince's film came out when antiwar sentiment was still strong in the United States, while the pacifist *Intolerance* came out later in the year, as public opinion was moving closer to joining the war in Europe. In 1923, a year before he died, Ince released the first film version of Eugene O'Neill's play *Anna Christie*. Blanche Sweet offers a powerful performance as the title character.

Ince productions were popular in the United States (*Photoplay* magazine once called him the "Rodin of shadows"), and he was even more highly regarded in Europe. He died prematurely, at the age of forty-two. The circumstances of his death have been the subject of conjecture for decades, inspiring a play, *The Cat's Meow*, filmed by Peter Bogdanovich. In November 1924, Ince joined William Randolph Hearst on his yacht, the *Oneida*. Other guests included Hearst's mistress, Marion Davies, Charlie Chaplin, Elinor Glyn, and Louella Parsons. Stricken ill, Ince was dropped off in San Diego, where he died two days later.

The cause of death was declared heart failure, although there was no autopsy. Rumors spread that either Chaplin or Ince had made a pass at Davies and that shots had been fired. But Brian Taves, a Library of Congress film scholar who is writing a book on Ince, calls him a poster boy for

Enid Markey in Ince's epic drama *Civilization* (1916).

Top left: Star and producer Mary Pickford gets the final word with her director Maurice Tourneur in this advertisement promoting *The Pride of the Clan* (1917).

Top right: Shirley Mason as Jim Hawkins and Charles Ogle as the pirate Long John Silver in Maurice Tourneur's *Treasure Island* (1920).

Bottom: Clara Kimball Young and Chester Barnett in a scene from Tourneur's 1915 feature *Trilby*.

cardiac arrest, noting that it was not unusual for hospitals at the time to skip autopsies when the cause of death was obvious. Although this makes a nice piece of Hollywood legend, there may not be any mystery at all.

Among the most lyrical, and least well known, of early silent-feature directors was MAURICE TOURNEUR, who made several outstanding films in the teens. Tourneur began his career as an artist and stage actor in France before moving to the United States, in 1914. Late that year, he released the charming *The Wishing Ring*, subtitled *An Idyll of Old England*. Shot in New Jersey, it nevertheless convincingly evokes nineteenth-century England. The story is whimsical, involving a ne'er-do-well son of an earl who is banished until he can redeem himself. While working as a gardener at a neighboring estate, he falls in love with a parson's beautiful daughter. Their wishes come true through the influence of a magic ring gotten from a gypsy. The film is framed theatrically, even opening and closing with a curtain, but there is nothing theatrical about the acting, which is quite natural.

A proscenium arch, either literally with a curtain or, more naturalistically, with a cave's mouth, was a signature technique derived from Tourneur's theater background (in 1918's *The Blue Bird*, based on the Maeterlinck story, he even used painted backdrops). He was also a master of the use of deep focus and natural lighting.

Perhaps Tourneur's best-known extant film is 1920's *The Last of the Mohicans*, a splendid screen adaptation of the James Fenimore Cooper novel (Tourneur was injured during filming, and Clarence Brown completed the movie, but the film's style is clearly Tourneur's). Tourneur also directed two Mary Pickford films, *The Pride of the Clan* and *The Poor Little Rich Girl*, both 1917.

Tourneur directed as an independent, and his individualism made it difficult for him to work within the constraints of the studio system. He quit in the middle of filming *The Mysterious Island* (1927), when MGM required that he have a producer. He returned to France, where he continued to make films until the 1940s. Tourneur's son Jacques became famous as a director of such artful horror movies as *Cat People* and *I Walked with a Zombie*.

Two Maurice Tourneur features, top: *Lorna Doone* (1922) with John Bawers and Nadge Bellamy, and bottom: *The Closed Road* (1916) with House Peters (second from right).

Leatrice Joy stars in DeMille's dramatic spectacle *Manslaughter* (1922).

Another director who rose to fame in the twentieth century's second decade was CECIL B. DeMILLE, a flamboyant filmmaker who created his own larger-than-life persona. In near self-parody, he sported breeches and high boots and not infrequently had a gun strapped to his hip on the set. Early in his career, he produced some enduring, artful works, but his later pandering to the audience's lowest common denominator brought him the opprobrium of many peers and film critics. The P. T. Barnum of film at least had a sense of humor about it: "Every time I make a picture, the critics' estimate of American public taste goes down ten percent." But a number of filmmakers detested his work. As director King Vidor put it, "When I saw one of his pictures, I wanted to quit the business."

But in the beginning, DeMille could be very, very good. His 1915 feature *The Cheat* tells the story of a frivolous society woman (Fannie Ward), who, after borrowing Red Cross funds, is forced in turn to borrow from an Asian businessman (Sessue Hayakawa). When she tries to pay him back in cash, he expects sexual favors. In a scene that is still shocking today, he then brands her like one of his possessions. Her husband shoots Hayakawa, and to save him Ward reveals her brand in court. With its chiaroscuro lighting, its Oriental production design, and the sensationalistic branding of its heroine, the film introduced the audience to a different world.

After the war, DeMille made a series of lavish sex comedies, *Old Wives for New* (1918), *Don't Change Your Husband* (1919), and *Why Change Your Wife?* (1920), which treated sexual affairs and divorce with flippant amusement. During this time, DeMille made an enchanting comedy, *Male and Female,* adapted from the play *The Admirable Crichton*, by J. M. Barrie, of *Peter Pan* fame. When a British aristocratic family is shipwrecked on a cruise, the rigid class system is turned topsy-turvy, and they find themselves ruled by their butler (Thomas Meighan) because they are clueless at surviving on their own. Spoiled rich girl Gloria Swanson falls for him — until they are rescued and the old order is restored. It features two iconic scenes with Swanson, one in which she steps down into her pool-like bath and one, during a Babylonian fantasia, in which Swanson is thrown to the lions.

After the Hays Office was established, DeMille cleverly used religious spectacles, the first of which was 1923's *The Ten Commandments*, as cover for sex and violence. DeMille's brother William viewed the cinematic conversion with some amusement: "Having attended to the underclothes, bathroom and matrimonial irregularities of his fellow citizens, he now began to consider their salvation."

Where DeMille's melodramas donned a morality that many considered suspect, no one could

Why Change Your Wife? (1920), with Thomas Meighan and Bebe Daniels, and *Don't Change Your Husband* (1919) with Gloria Swanson, are just two of a series of sex comedies Cecil B. DeMille made during the teens and twenties.

Top: Wallace Reid, Geraldine Farrar, and William Elmer in DeMille's *Carmen* (1915).

Bottom: A magazine ad for DeMille's 1917 World War I drama *The Little American* starring Mary Pickford.

Far right: Mildred Harris dances in DeMille's *Fool's Paradise* (1922).

384-294

Top: Claire Winsor stars as a society lady who falls for a rough-mannered oilman, played by Louis Calhern, in Lois Weber's feature *What's Worth While?* (1921).

Bottom: Claire Winsor stars as the daughter of a struggling professor who finds herself pursued by three men in *The Blot* (1921).

doubt the moral earnestness of LOIS WEBER, one of the most successful American directors during the war years. Weber worked for a while as a street evangelist in Pittsburgh, and she brought her missionary zeal to films of social comment.

She began her show-business career on the stage, and it was while working in the theater that she met and married her husband, Phillips Smalley. In 1908, Weber began working at the Gaumont studio in New York, where she wrote, directed, and acted in one-reelers. Collaborating with her husband, they began making films together (originally they took joint credit, although gradually Weber took on more and more responsibility). She had found her calling in film: "Now," she said, "I can preach to my heart's content."

In 1915, they released their first big hit, *The Hypocrites*, a four-reel allegory that exposes many of society's moral shortcomings. It stirred considerable controversy at the time because Weber used a nude actress (Margaret Edwards) to portray Truth.

Weber's films continued to deal with social issues, such as birth control and abortion (*Where Are My Children?* 1916), child labor (*Shoes*, 1916), and capital punishment (*The People vs. John Doe*, 1916). By 1916, she was one of the most successful directors in the United States. Universal was paying her five thousand dollars a week, and *Where Are My Children?* made three million dollars at the box office. Her best-known film today is 1921's *The Blot*, which depicts the struggles of a poor professor's family.

Weber's popularity waned swiftly in the early 1920s, however, as Jazz Age audiences sought entertainment rather than moral messages. The years following World War I brought a new sensibility, and the great filmmakers of the teens, Griffith and Ince, began to seem old-fashioned, although DeMille managed to ride the postwar zeitgeist with his Swanson sex comedies.

The times were changing. The stock market began its long bull run, and the United States was undergoing a cultural renaissance. Ernest Hemingway, F. Scott Fitzgerald, and John Dos Passos were coming of age and offering an entirely new kind of writing (whether at home or as expats in Europe). The Harlem Renaissance produced such African American literary luminaries as Langston Hughes and Zora Neale Hurston, while Harlem jazz clubs were packed with blacks and whites.

With the passage of the Nineteenth Amendment in 1920, women at last got the right to vote. With help from the crusader Margaret Sanger, contraception was more widely practiced. There

Top: Lois Weber directed a number of social-problem films, including *Where Are My Children?* (1916), which addresses the controversial subjects of birth control and abortion.

Bottom: Lois Weber with Anna Pavlova on the set of *The Dumb Girl of Portici* (1916). This was the Russian ballet star's only film.

Top: Considered one of the industry's most successful female directors, Dorothy Arzner worked in both silent and sound films.

Bottom: Universal Film Company employed a number of female directors during the silent era, including Cleo Madison, who made both short and feature-length films.

was much talk of the "new woman," whose sexual and cultural mores reflected a new independence. Still, such independence was usually afforded to the economically more fortunate. Some ten million women joined the workforce in the 1920s, but relatively few were professionals, and many of the jobs, low-level positions in stores or offices, paid poorly.

Fitzgerald describes the twenties in an essay, "Echoes of the Jazz Age," from the not very great distance of November 1931. His observations of the culture of the times are cynical but insightful: "It was an age of miracles, it was an age of art, it was an age of excess, it was an age of satire," he writes, describing "a whole race going hedonistic, deciding on pleasure." He continues:

Contrary to popular opinion, the movies of the Jazz Age had no effect upon its morals. The social attitude of the producers was timid, behind the times and banal — for example, no picture mirrored even faintly the younger generation until 1923, when magazines had already started to celebrate it and it had long ceased to be news. There were a few feeble splutters and then Clara Bow [sic] in Flaming Youth; *promptly the Hollywood hacks ran the theme into its cinematographic grave. Throughout the Jazz Age the movies got no farther than Mrs. Jiggs, keeping up with its most blatant superficialities.*

A decade after *Flaming Youth*, Fitzgerald had forgotten that it starred Colleen Moore, not Clara Bow. Nevertheless, he was certainly correct in noting that films have rarely started social trends — they merely follow them, however belatedly. But it is also true that after World War I, new directors and new stars emerged with the rapidly changing culture and at least reflected the new cultural climate.

One of the strangest figures working in Hollywood during the silent era, and certainly one who could never have made his films in the more innocent prewar era, was ERICH VON STROHEIM. He directed a series of films — *Blind Husbands* (1918); *The Devil's Passkey* (1919); and *Foolish Wives* (1922) — that covered the same artistic territory as Hemingway and Fitzgerald — Americans in Europe — but they obsessively, compulsively run through the maze of adulterous sexual triangles. The films deal explicitly with sexual and moral corruption.

Stroheim, the Viennese son of a Jewish merchant, reinvented himself as an aristocrat and military officer. He began his career as an actor who found a niche during World War I playing Prussian villains. He was so good at these roles that he was promoted as "the man you love to hate." In Universal's *The Heart of Humanity*, for example, he portrays a Hun of such savagery that, while trying to rape a Red Cross nurse, he throws her crying baby out the window.

As a director, Stroheim acquired a reputation for running over budget and behind schedule in an almost autistic pursuit of perfect detail. In *Foolish Wives*, he built two huge sets re-creating the Mediterranean resort of Monte Carlo, one on the lot at Universal and another on the Monterey Peninsula, showing the sea side of the buildings.

In addition to directing *Foolish Wives*, Stroheim played the part of a mundane sexual villain,

Poster for Erich von Stroheim's *The Wedding March* (1928).

Von Stroheim had lavish sets built to re-create the glamorous gambling resort of Monte Carlo for his 1922 feature *Foolish Wives*.

though he was dissatisfied with the role. Playing a fake Russian count while trying to seduce the wife of an American diplomat, he is obviously having sex with his two "cousins" and with his maid, from whom he's borrowed money with a promise to marry her. When he tries to rape the retarded daughter of an old counterfeiter, her father kills him and throws him into a sewer. The script's punishment seems extreme, but Stroheim, perhaps ingenuously, argued that it was necessary to punish his character to get the film past the censors.

While *Foolish Wives* did well at the box office, Stroheim's profligate spending caused him to clash with his producers at Universal. (He did, for a while, have a talent for getting defenestrated at a studio, then, like a cat, landing on his feet at another — unfortunately, he eventually ran out of studios. His nemesis, Irving Thalberg, who kicked him off several films, dogged him.)

Stroheim went on to Goldwyn, later MGM, to adapt American naturalist writer Frank Norris's novel *McTeague* as *Greed* (1924), regarded by many critics as one of the best films ever made. Stroheim's rough cut was about forty-five reels, which he succeeded in reducing to twenty-two. When he found he couldn't cut it anymore, he asked his friend, the director Rex Ingram, to trim it further. Ingram and his editor, Grant Whytock, whittled it down to fifteen reels. When the studio still found this version too long, it was slashed to ten reels. This is the version we know today, a skeleton of its original, with many subplots completely eliminated, but it is still a milestone of cinema.

Stroheim sought to capture Norris's stark, often grim realism and filmed *Greed* entirely on location, in San Francisco, at the Big Dipper Mine in northern California, and in Death Valley in midsummer, with temperatures reaching 142 degrees Fahrenheit. A San Francisco dentist, McTeague (Gibson Gowland), marries Trina (Zasu Pitts), who obsessively hoards five thousand dollars she won in a lottery. Her jealous former beau, Marcus Schouler (Jean Hersholt), reveals that McTeague is practicing without a license, and he loses his job. Faced with a life of squalor because Trina refuses to part with her money, McTeague kills and robs her, fleeing to Death Valley with her gold. Marcus follows him, and in a struggle, McTeague kills Marcus. Only then does he realize they are handcuffed and that he, too, is doomed.

It is a bleak picture, and critical reaction was almost entirely negative. *Life*'s Robert E. Sherwood blamed Stroheim for making such a long film in the first place, famously calling the director "a genius . . . badly in need of a stop watch." The film lost money at the domestic box office and did poorly overseas — surprisingly, because Europeans were supposedly more open-minded about artistic films.

Stroheim regained credibility at MGM with the box-office success of *The Merry Widow*, but

Top: Von Stroheim and his crew working on location in the desert while making *Greed* (1924).

Bottom: Zasu Pitts plays the frugal lottery winner Trina in *Greed* (1925).

Top: Betty Compson and George Bancroft in von Sternberg's *The Docks of New York* (1928).

Bottom: Magazine advertisement for von Sternberg's *The Salvation Hunters* (1925), starring Georgia Hale and George K. Arthur.

cost overruns, busted production schedules, and/or thematic sexual audacity led to his being removed from *The Wedding March*, *Queen Kelly*, and *Walking Down Broadway*. Thereafter he worked as a writer and actor in the United States and France, where he lived out his last days. He is well remembered today for his strong performances as the prison commandant in Jean Renoir's *The Grand Illusion* and as ex-director, ex-husband, and butler to faded silent star Norma Desmond (Gloria Swanson) in Billy Wilder's *Sunset Boulevard*.

When Griffith died, the BBC asked Stroheim for a eulogy. In part, he could have been talking about himself as much as Griffith when he said: "In Hollywood, you're as good as your last picture. If you didn't have one in production within the last three months, you're forgotten, no matter what you have achieved. If you live in France, and you have written one good book, or painted one good picture, or directed one outstanding film, fifty years ago, and nothing ever since, you are still recognized as an artist and honored accordingly. They do not forget."

Like Tourneur, JOSEF VON STERNBERG was one of silent cinema's great visual stylists, although he was often the kind of poet who sees the moon reflected in a wet gutter. Like Stroheim, von Sternberg turned himself into another "man you love to hate," but in his case, not as a character but as a person. Both of them, however, used it as a self-marketing ploy. "The only way to succeed," he was often quoted as saying, "is to make people hate you. That way they remember you."

George Bancroft in a scene from *Underworld* (1927), Josef von Sternberg's classic gangster film.

His directorial debut, *The Salvation Hunters* (1925), is a grim picture about a boy, a girl, and a child who live on a steam dredge. They escape from the bleak landscape and brutal dredgeman to the city, only to be accosted by a pimp who tries to make the girl a prostitute. They flee from him, hoping to find a better life. The film was made on a shoestring budget of five thousand dollars, but it got von Sternberg noticed.

He made four silents for Paramount in the late twenties; the first was *Underworld* (1927), a gangster film that not only established what would become that genre's clichés (including a gangsters' ball) but inspired a cycle of crime films that would reach its apotheosis in the thirties. Von Sternberg's film romanticizes crime and criminals, for which he was criticized at the time.

Von Sternberg's *The Docks of New York* (1928) is one of the great silents, coming just at the end of

From one in a crowd of baby bassinets (above) to one in a crowd of pencil pushers (right), King Vidor's *The Crowd* (1928) highlights the struggle for upward mobility and human connection within the landscape of a densely populated industrial city.

the era. Bill (George Bancroft), a stoker on a steamer, comes ashore on eight hours' leave. He saves the life of a woman, Sadie (Betty Compson), who has thrown herself into the water in despair over her sordid life in sailors' bars. They spend a wild night together, which climaxes in a barroom wedding. After abandoning her, he realizes he loves her and jumps ship. He ends up going to jail for two months for stealing clothes for her and asks if she'll wait for him. "I guess I'd wait forever, Bill," she says.

The Docks of New York has vivid characters and clever lines, but what makes it unforgettable is its dark, gritty look and spartan lighting, offering the rare, stray ray by which to glimpse the occasional flash of goodness. Von Sternberg went on to direct five films with Marlene Dietrich, including *The Blue Angel* (1930) and *The Scarlet Empress* (1935), for which he is better remembered. But *The Docks of New York* may be his masterpiece.

KING VIDOR was another director who really came into his own in the mid to late twenties, although his career continued to flourish well into the forties. He produced several outstanding films in the late silent era, including the war film *The Big Parade* (1925), the urban drama *The Crowd* (1928), and a Hollywood satire *Show People* (1928).

A third-generation Texan, born in Galveston in 1895, he started making films there in the early days before regional filmmakers were virtually erased by Hollywood's hegemony. In 1915, he headed for

Hollywood in a Model T with his wife, Florence Vidor, who would become a very successful actress.

Vidor was a lifelong Christian Scientist, and he set out to make positive films. He took out an ad in *Variety* titled "A Creed and a Pledge" after building his own independent studio, Vidor Village, on Santa Monica Boulevard. "I believe in the motion picture that carries a message to humanity," he wrote. While most of his early melodramas are lost or forgotten, Vidor evolved beyond simplistic dogmatism. Although he couldn't afford to keep his studio going and signed with MGM, he had an extraordinary gift for preserving his personal vision while working within the studio system.

The Big Parade, the story of ordinary doughboys encountering the horrors of World War I, was a huge success for Vidor — and MGM. John Gilbert plays Jim Apperson, a rich idler who enlists amid the heedless patriotism of his fiancée and buddies. Shipped to France, he falls in love with a village girl, Melisande (Renée Adorée), before being sent to the front. Apperson, wide-eyed, and his working-class army comrades, Bull and Slim, march through the sun-dappled Belleau Wood, utterly exposed to sniper fire. After savagely bayoneting a German soldier, Apperson finds that he can't kill him, instead offering him a cigarette before he dies.

Although *The Big Parade* powerfully depicts a war fought not by heroes but by ordinary men, it is not pacifist. "In the Great War many were wondering why in an enlightened age we should have

to battle," Vidor told the *New York Times* at the time. "I do not wish to appear to be taking any stand about war. I certainly do not favor it, but I would not set up a preachment against it."

The Crowd was critically acclaimed but did less well at the box office (although it made a modest profit). About an urban everyman coping with work and marriage in New York City, it has aged well and is now seen as one of the classics of the late twenties. The aptly named John (minor actor James Murray) and Mary (Vidor's then-wife, Eleanor Boardman) struggle to get by on John's salary as a clerk in a large company. In an early scene, the camera sweeps up a skyscraper, then swoops in a window and across a sea of identical desks to reinforce the anonymity of the film's hero; in homage to Vidor, Billy Wilder used a similar shot at the beginning of *The Apartment*.

When John and Mary's daughter is run over by a car and dies, John has trouble concentrating at work and impulsively quits. In despair and disgust, he takes jobs and quits them and is eventually reduced to wearing a clown suit and sandwich board. Mary, fed up, decides to leave him, but on her way out the door, John implores her to go with him and their son to a vaudeville show. The film ends with them in the midst of a laughing audience. The apparently happy ending is ambiguous. Questions linger provocatively: Will the couple stay together? Will John get a decent job? MGM and Vidor were apprehensive about the equivocal ending, however, and released a second version as well. Both were offered to exhibitors. The other ending is explicitly happy: John becomes a successful adman. Only one exhibitor chose the alternative ending.

Vidor also had a gift for comedy, and in a few films starring Marion Davies, the mistress of media mogul William Randolph Hearst, he drew on her talents as a comedienne. Davies will probably forever be stigmatized by Orson Welles's *Citizen Kane*, which had Charles Foster Kane, a stand-in for Hearst, foisting his talentless mistress, Susan Alexander (Davies), on the public as an opera singer. While Hearst did maneuver Davies into serious costume dramas, for which she was ill suited, she positively shined in silent comedies, including Vidor's *Show People* and *The Patsy*.

In *Show People*, Davies plays a Georgia girl, Peggy Pepper, who seeks her fortune in Hollywood. After the usual struggling actress travails, she breaks into slapstick comedies, but she wants to act in "serious" dramas. When she does get a chance at "High Class Pictures," she changes her name to Patricia Pepoire, and fame and money do their dirty work. In the end, of course, she comes to her senses. The film is amusingly self-reflexive, and many real celebrities appear as themselves, including Charlie Chaplin and Elinor Glyn, as well as Vidor and Davies playing themselves — Patricia Pepoire doesn't think that much of Davies either. *Show People* satirizes Hollywood as a small pond with a lot of big frogs who quickly come to admire their own amphibian splendor. Things have not changed that much over the decades.

The epic battle scene from Vidor's *The Big Parade* (1925).

INTERNATIONAL CINEMA

THE GREAT WAR CHANGED CULTURAL AS WELL AS POLITICAL LANDSCAPES. THE DEVASTATED ECONOMIES OF EUROPE GAVE HOLLYWOOD AN OPPORTUNITY FOR GLOBAL HEGEMONY IN CINEMAS. ENGLAND AND ITALY, WHICH HAD THRIVING FILM INDUSTRIES BEFORE THE WAR, FADED IN IMPORTANCE.

Kevin Brownlow has especially harsh words for English filmmaking of the postwar silent era: "English films, with few exceptions, were crudely photographed; the direction and acting were on the level of cheap revue, they exploited so-called stars, who generally had little more than a glimmer of talent, and they were exceedingly boring. The silent-film industry in Britain never advanced beyond the atmosphere of the barns and glass houses in which it began."

As Brownlow notes, however, there were exceptions: Alfred Hitchcock, who was just beginning his long, illustrious career (*The Lodger*, 1926); and Anthony Asquith, who produced some fine films at the end of the silent era (*Underground*, 1928; *A Cottage on Dartmoor*, 1929).

Filmmaking spread around the world, to India and Japan, to Brazil and Australia, but because films from these countries were not widely distributed, they had little influence on the world scene. Their contributions are beyond the scope of this survey. But several nations entered a golden age of cinema, producing masterpieces that we can only marvel at today. Directors in Denmark, Sweden, Germany, France, and the Soviet Union brought filmmaking to the level of fine art.

SCANDINAVIA

Above: *The Lodger* (Great Britain, 1925), directed by Alfred Hitchcock.

Left: Bartolomeo Pagano in *Maciste all' inferno* (Italy, 1925).

Two relatively small countries, Denmark and Sweden, loom large in silent-cinema history. Before World War I, Denmark's Nordisk company was, after France's Pathé, the world's second largest film producer. Danish films were distributed widely — in Europe, in the United States, and in Russia. Among the more noted directors were August Blom, whose 1913 feature *Atlantis* concerned the sinking of an ocean liner; and Urban Gad, whose sexually frank *The Abyss* made Asta Nielsen Europe's first film star. Denmark also produced two directors who would gain worldwide recognition in the twenties: Benjamin Christensen and Carl Theodor Dreyer.

Sweden's film scene came to prominence between 1917 and 1923, at least partly because of its neutrality in the war. The two most important Swedish directors were Victor Sjöström and Mauritz Stiller, both of whom worked for the film studio Svenska Biografteatern, which became Svenska Filmindustri, one of the biggest studios in Europe.

Originally a stage actor, Sjöström turned to directing in 1912, becoming, according to Dreyer, "the father of the Swedish art film." His 1913 realist social drama *Ingeborg Holm* was based on a true story. After her husband dies suddenly, Ingeborg is placed in a poorhouse, and her children are taken away from her. Years later, her grown son visits her, finding her mad from grief and cradling a board like a baby. He shows her an old photograph of herself, and it slowly dawns on her who he is. The film is

Gerda Lundequist and Greta Garbo in Mauritz Stiller's *The
Legend of Gösta Berling* (Sweden, 1924).

still powerful today, and it had such tremendous impact that it caused Sweden to reform its poor laws, a rare and striking instance of the power of film.

Sjöström often played out human dramas of emotion against the larger landscape of nature, as in 1918's *The Outlaw and His Wife*, in which an escaped convict and his spouse flee to the freedom of remote mountains. Fearing capture by the authorities, the woman kills their child, then in despair collapses in the snow, to be joined by her husband in icy death.

In the intense, supernatural *The Phantom Carriage* (1921), a wastrel who dies at midnight on New Year's Eve is given a second chance by Death's messenger to reform. After seeing a vision of his wife about to poison their children and then commit suicide, he vows to change and returns just in time to stop her. The film is made spooky by spectral multiple exposures. "I was deeply shaken by the film," said Ingmar Bergman in an interview in the 1970s, "not because I understood it or for any other reason. But I think I was quite simply affected by its tremendous cinematographic force. It was a totally emotional experience."

Mauritz Stiller's war drama *Hotel Imperial* (Sweden, 1927), about an Austrian officer trapped behind Russian lines.

Stiller, a Finnish-Russian Jew, at first preferred social comedies, such as the film-industry satire *Thomas Graal's Best Film* (1917) and the cynical 1920 comedy of manners *Erotikon*, about the love affairs of a woman married to an entomologist too devoted to bugs. But some of his best films would be dramas based on the novels of Selma Lagerlöf, the first woman to win the Nobel Prize for Literature. In *Sir Arne's Treasure* (1919), set in the sixteenth century, three Scottish thieves plunder a castle, slaughtering everyone but a young woman who later unknowingly falls in love with one of them. *The Legend of Gösta Berling* (1924), the most expensive Swedish film made to that date, tells the story of a dissolute defrocked priest, Gösta Berling, redeemed by the love of an Italian countess, played by the luminous Greta Garbo.

The Nordic love of nature is revealed in the work of both directors, which contains unforgettable scenes filmed on location, with the elements like characters in the dramas: the couple in *The Outlaw and His Wife* slowly buried by the gently falling snow, Garbo in a sleigh being chased by wolves at night in *Gösta Berling*, a funeral cortége snaking across a frozen bay at the end of *Sir Arne's Treasure*.

Svenska Filmindustri recruited the Danes Christensen and Dreyer. Christensen began his career as an opera singer and stage actor before joining Denmark's booming film industry,

Sir Arne's Treasure (*Herr Arnes pengar*, Sweden, 1919), directed by Mauritz Stiller.

becoming one of film's first actor-directors. In 1913's *The Mysterious X*, he plays a naval officer falsely accused of espionage, and 1915's *The Night of Revenge* has him playing a circus performer, who after a long sentence in prison returns to find his daughter. Both films reveal his obsession with chiaroscuro effects and a strong sense of narrative. After moving to Sweden, he directed the bizarre pseudodocumentary *Häxan: Witchcraft Through the Ages* in 1922, which has become a cult classic.

Journalist, film critic, and filmmaker, Dreyer was a bit of a maverick. He was also an admirer of Sjöström's, noting that "through Sjöström's work film was let into art's promised land." If Sjöström was film art's Moses, Dreyer was silent film's Old Testament visionary prophet. He directed two films in Denmark, including *Leaves from Satan's Book* (1921), in which Satan tempts mortals into betrayal in four different epochs — the time of Christ, the Spanish Inquisition, the French Revolution, and contemporary Finland during the struggle between the Red and White armies.

But Dreyer made his first great film, *The Parson's Widow* (1920), for Svenska Filmindustri. When a young minister takes a new position, tradition demands that he marry the former clergyman's ancient widow. He and his girlfriend, whom he calls his sister, plot to kill her. But it turns out that the old woman is warm and understanding, and when she dies, the couple has a fuller understanding of love. The vagabond Dreyer worked all over Europe, but he made his masterpiece, *The Passion of Joan of Arc* (1928), in France. It is, quite simply, one of the most beautiful films ever made, and its cumulative emotional power is overwhelming (Jean-Luc Godard in *Vivre Sa Vie* has Anna Karina weep in a theater while watching Maria Falconetti as Joan of Arc).

The Passion of Joan of Arc was released in the same year as another French film, *The Marvelous Life of Joan of Arc*. While *Life*, a traditional epic, was a huge hit in France, *Passion* was not. Nevertheless, it is Dreyer's *Joan* that remains one of the best films of the twenties, and one of its most radical. Based on the actual records of the girl-warrior's trial, *Passion* is an anti-epic, a psychological study told through a series of remarkable close-ups. The iconography of the faces of Joan's accusers and torturers and indeed of Joan herself presents both a vision of fifteenth-century realpolitik, where religion and politics collide, as well as psychological portraits of almost unbearable intensity. The cinematography of both *The Parson's Wife* and *The Passion of Joan of Arc* is so finely detailed it's almost like daguerreotypy.

Top: Maria Falconetti gives one of the silent cinema's greatest performances in Carl Theodore Dreyer's *The Passion of Joan of Arc* (*La Passion de Jeanne d'Arc*, France, 1928).

Bottom: Helge Nissen and Johannes Meyer in *Leaves from Satan's Book* (*Blade af Satans bog*, Denmark, 1921). As in *Intolerance*, four stories from Christ to modern times are woven together.

GERMANY

German film production was negligible before World War I; most theaters showed foreign films. After the war, Germany's economy was in a shambles, but its film industry grew rapidly and enjoyed a renaissance, in part because of an embargo on U.S. films until 1921.

It also helped that, during the war, the German state created a huge film-production conglomerate, the Universum-Film Akteingesellschaft (UFA), for commercial and propaganda purposes. UFA was privatized when the hostilities ended and made several films that are now part of the silent-film canon, including *The Last Laugh* and *Metropolis*. Still, having been on the losing side in the war, German films initially had to overcome considerable prejudice to get exported. One strategy was to produce lavish costume dramas set in other countries.

Ernst Lubitsch directed a number of these spectacles (*Madame DuBarry*, 1919; and *Anna Boleyn*, 1920), which helped to put the Germans back on the cinematic world stage. Lubitsch, a native Berliner, started out as a member of Max Reinhardt's acting company, and in 1913, he made his film acting debut. In his historical epics, he had a talent for mixing huge crowd scenes with intimate settings with his stars. In *Madame DuBarry*, released as *Passion* in the United States, Pola Negri plays the titular French courtesan who sleeps her way to the top — here, King Louis XV, played by Emil Jannings. In one scene, the king is so in her thrall that he kisses her calves and feet, even licks her toe and clips her toenails. When the Revolution comes, however, the people want to cut off her head, not her nails. *Madame DuBarry* is what all great epics aspire to — grand moments that show the sweep of history mixed with touches of intimacy to humanize the drama.

Robert Wiene's Expressionist masterpiece *The Cabinet of Dr. Caligari* (1920) also helped to take German film beyond its borders, especially in Europe. It tells the story of Cesare, a somnambulist serial murderer controlled by an evil mountebank, Dr. Caligari. The original scenario, written by Carl Mayer and Hans Janowitz, was subsequently given a framing tale — to which the writers strenuously objected — that reveals that the story is told by a madman and that Dr. Caligari is actually the reasonable director of a mental institution. The film's bizarre, stylized sets reflect his deluded patient's fevered imagination.

Expressionism, which tried to convey psychological states through décor, shaped other films,

Top: Ernst Lubitsch's delightful fairy tale *The Doll* (*Die Puppe*, Germany, 1919).

Bottom: Werner Krauss and Conrad Veidt in the German Expressionist masterpiece *The Cabinet of Dr. Caligari* (*Das Cabinet des Dr. Caligari*, Germany, 1920).

Pola Negri as the title character in Lubitsch's *Madame DuBarry* (Germany, 1919).

*Der Regisseur Fritz Lang spielt Heinrich George vor, wie er Brigitte Helm packen soll.
(Aus dem Film „Metropolis")*

Heinrich George spielt die Szene

Top left: Brigitte Helm as False Maria, with her creator, Rotwang (Rudolf Klein-Rogge, right) in one of the silent cinema's greatest achievements, Fritz Lang's *Metropolis* (Germany, 1927).

Top right: A 1927 magazine advertisement for *Metropolis*.

Bottom: At left, Fritz Lang directs Henrich Georg and Brigitte Helm, and at right, the two actors incorporate Lang's instruction into their performances.

including Wiene's *Raskolnikov* (1923), inspired by Dostoevsky's *Crime and Punishment*, and Paul Leni's *Waxworks* (1924). In *Waxworks*, a poet is hired to write stories about the figures in a fairground wax museum. The writer (William Dieterle) imagines scenarios involving the hedonistic caliph of Baghdad, Haroun al-Rashid (Emil Jannings), Ivan the Terrible (Conrad Veidt), and a spectral Jack the Ripper. With its all-star cast, stylized sets, strange tales, and plot twists, *Waxworks* is immensely entertaining.

The other three great filmmakers of the Weimar era were Fritz Lang, F. W. Murnau, and G. W. Pabst. (Lang and Murnau later worked successfully in Hollywood, while Pabst made only one film there — 1934's *A Modern Hero*, with Richard Barthelmess — but it flopped, and he returned to Germany.)

Top: The counterfeiters' workshop in Fritz Lang's
Dr. Mabuse (1922).

Bottom: Fritz Lang's *Woman in the Moon* (*Frau
im Mond*, Germany, 1929).

Lang, born in Austria, was an artist before becoming a filmmaker. He was wounded in the war and, while recovering, began writing scenarios. The versatile director made genre pictures — the serial *The Spiders*; science fiction like *Metropolis*; crime dramas, from *Dr. Mabuse, the Gambler* (1922) to the American film noir classic *The Big Heat* (1953); and even Westerns in Hollywood — but he also explored allegory and myth in striking productions. In *Destiny* (1921), for instance, Death appears in a village "lost in time" to take the fiancé of a young woman. He then offers her three opportunities to regain her lover if she can save the life of one of three men about to die. In all three stories (one set in a Muslim country, one in Renaissance Italy, and the third in ancient China), the man is her lover, but she fails each time to overcome fate. Death reunites them, then disappears. The ending is ambiguous: are they joined together in death or in life?

The film made Lang's reputation and proved influential both commercially and aesthetically. Douglas Fairbanks bought the U.S. rights to the film to delay its American release so that he could re-create some of its effects for *The Thief of Bagdad*. The picture inspired other directors as well. In his autobiography, *My Last Breath*, Luis Buñuel writes, "When I saw *Destiny*, I suddenly knew that I wanted to make movies. It wasn't the three stories themselves that moved me so much, but the main episode — the arrival of the man in the black hat (whom I instantly recognized as Death) in the Flemish village — and the scene in the cemetery. Something about this film spoke to something deep in me; it clarified my life and my vision of the world." The world-weary Death figure, played

Bernhard Goetzke as Death in Fritz Lang's *Destiny* (*Der Müde Tod*, Germany, 1921).

by Bernhard Goetzke, prefigures Death in Bergman's *The Seventh Seal*, played by Bengt Ekerot.

Lang returned to crime drama with the two-part *Dr. Mabuse, the Gambler*. Set in a city that appears to be decadent postwar Berlin, it pits Mabuse, a sinister crime lord, against state prosecutor von Wenk. The actor who played the diabolical criminal, Rudolf Klein-Rogge, described his character as "a symptom of a Europe that was falling apart . . . a guiding force, a creator, if only in destruction."

Lang's next production, *Die Nibelungen* (1924), also released in two parts (*Siegfried* and *Kriemhild's Revenge*), mined Teutonic legend, drawing on the medieval epic poem *Das Nibelungenlied*, Wagner's opera cycle, and other sources. In the first part, the heroic Siegfried (played by Paul Richter) travels through the mist-shrouded Woden Wood, slays a fire-breathing dragon and a dwarf-king, and takes the king's treasure. At the court of the Burgundians, he must help King Gunther win the warrior-queen of Iceland, Brunhild, in order to marry Gunther's beautiful sister, Kriemhild. Siegfried is killed by the treacherous Lord Hagen, which sets off a cycle of tragic violence in Part Two.

In *Kriemhild's Revenge*, Siegfried's widow is driven to fury in seeking vengeance. She marries Attila, lord of the Huns, then invites the Burgundians to visit when she bears a child. In a finale of chaos and carnage, the Burgundians barricade themselves in Attila's court. The fortress is set aflame, and nearly everyone is slaughtered.

The epic grandeur of *Siegfried* is utterly remarkable. While the film moves at a languorous pace, scene after scene takes one's breath away. The monumental buildings, the geometrical designs of the costumes, the ride through the spooky Woden Wood, the dwarves being turned to stone — all create a universe of mystery, myth, and wonder against which the tragic passions of the actors play out. As Thea von Harbou, Lang's wife and coscreenwriter, said, the film reveals "the inexorability with which the first guilt entails the last atonement."

Lang said in interviews that he wanted the heroic diptych to give a psychological boost to the Germans, who were struggling under a war-battered economy (he dedicated the film to "the German people"). At the same time, its grandiosity prefigured Nazi propaganda films (it was one of Hitler's favorites).

Lang then topped himself with his sci-fi epic *Metropolis*, which was a worldwide hit, but so costly that it lost money. From pulp to allegory, film critic Andrew Sarris aptly summed up Lang's oeuvre by saying, "His cinema is that of the nightmare, the fable and the philosophical dissertation."

La Vengeance de **KRIEMHILD** par Fr. LANG
LES NIBELUNGEN (II)   Superproduction **U. F. A.**

Margarete Schön as Kriemhild in Lang's *Die Nibelungen* (Germany, 1924).

Lil Dagover, Werner Krauss, and Emil Jannings in F. W. Murnau's *Tartuffe* (*Herr Tartüff*, Germany, 1926).

Murnau studied art history, philosophy, and literature at the universities of Heidelberg and Berlin. He joined the theater director Max Reinhardt's company as an actor and assistant before serving as a combat pilot in the war and later making propaganda films. Making his feature film debut in 1919, Murnau's early works were influenced by Expressionism. He directed a version of the Jekyll and Hyde story, 1920's *Janus-Faced*, which starred Bela Lugosi and Conrad Veidt.

But while Murnau's *Nosferatu: A Symphony of Horror* (1922), the first film adaptation of Bram Stoker's *Dracula* and perhaps his most famous work, has a few Expressionist elements, it is more remarkable for its realistic approach to the supernatural. Much of it was filmed on location, and its depictions of landscapes and daily life make the collision of the real and fantastic just that much more frightening. Murnau was a restless experimenter, and *Nosferatu* has some startling visual effects: negative images of white trees against a black sky and deliberately speeded-up movements.

The visual style of Murnau's *The Last Laugh* (1924), not its simplistic story, made it one of the masterpieces of the Weimar era. Emil Jannings plays the doorman of a posh hotel who is demoted to washroom attendant because of his age. The loss of his position and his fancy, quasi-military uniform is emotionally shattering for him. "This is pre-eminently a German tragedy," writes Lotte Eisner in *The Haunted Screen*, "and can only be understood in a country where uniform is King, not to say God. A non-German mind will have difficulty in comprehending all its tragic implications."

Emil Jannings in Murnau's *The Last Laugh* (*Der Letzte Mann*, Germany, 1924).

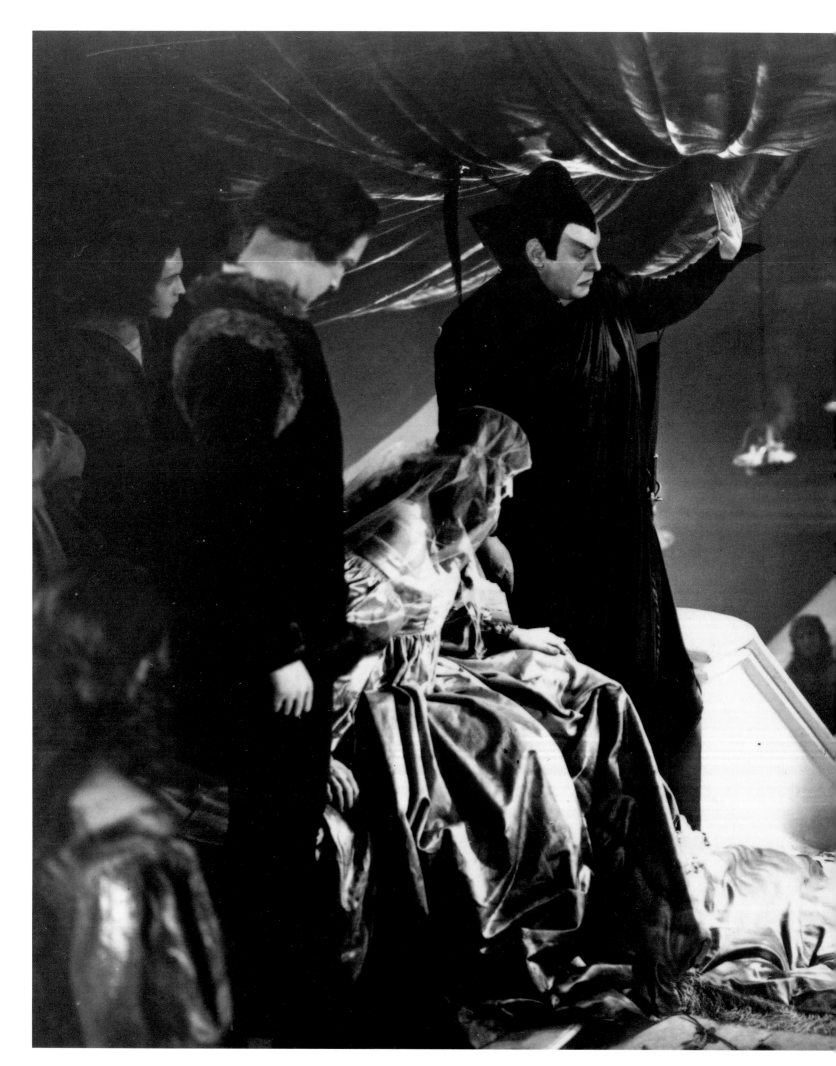

A scene from Murnau's *Faust* (Germany, 1926).

French miners desperate to be rescued in *Kameradschaft* (Germany, 1931), directed by G. W. Pabst.

The film was an international hit, so obviously foreign audiences could empathize with his humiliation. But *The Last Laugh*'s striking freedom of camera movement, what scenarist Carl Mayer memorably called the "unchained camera," aided in its phenomenal success and influence. The extraordinary cinematographer Karl Freund moved his camera through the hotel lobby and corridors, down city streets, and into tenements by using a variety of innovative techniques to convey the main character's point of view — putting the camera on a bicycle, tying it to overhead wires, and even, in one scene, strapping it to his ample belly and stumbling across the set to convey the doorman's drunken stagger.

Another point suggests the story's universality. The entire film has just one intertitle, which comes at the end to introduce a tongue-in-cheek happy ending, in which the protagonist, through the most implausible means, becomes fabulously rich, and all of the people who had scorned him become sycophants. The mobile, subjective camera tells the story so well that words are almost unnecessary. As Murnau remarked, "The camera is the director's pencil." Freund would show similar flair in filming E. A. Dupont's 1925 *Variety*, about a love triangle of trapeze artists, depicting the soaring acrobats from every angle.

Murnau's last two German films, *Tartuffe* (1926) and *Faust* (1926), both starring Jannings, were lush and atmospheric. *Faust* once again evokes the supernatural, in a masterful play of light and shadow. The story, about a scholar (Gösta Ekman) who sells his soul to the devil (Jannings), is loosely based on Goethe. Art director Robert Herlth and cameraman Carl Hoffmann brilliantly create the magisterial realms of heaven and hell and the woods and villages of the puny humans caught in between.

G. W. Pabst represented a distinctly different style, the so-called new objectivity. Through location shooting, he brought a sense of realism to his psychological melodramas, using his camera as a sort of X-ray. Iris Barry, the former curator of the Film Department at the Museum of Modern Art, describes Pabst's *The Love of Jeanne Ney* (1927) as "in no sense picturesque, it is photographic. His setting and his individual scenes are quite as carefully composed as those of the more obviously artistic German films, but the craftsmanship is less apparent, the spectator is led to feel 'how true' rather than 'how beautiful.' "

Lulu (Louise Brooks, right) dances with Daisy d'Ora as her paramour, Dr. Schon (Fritz Kortner), watches in the Jazz Age cautionary tale *Pandora's Box* (*Die Büchse der Pandora*, Germany, 1929), directed by G. W. Pabst.

A relative latecomer to German silent film, Pabst studied in Vienna before becoming a stage actor, performing in Germany, Austria, and America. His first film, *The Treasure*, was released in 1923. His first success as a director was *The Joyless Street* (1925), which depicts postwar, inflation-ridden Vienna with uncompromising realism, contrasting the luxury and decadence of the rich with the despair of the impoverished middle class.

The film stars Asta Nielsen as a kept woman and Greta Garbo as a bourgeoise whose family's desperate financial situation drives her to become a nightclub dancer and to flirt with the possibility of prostitution. Interestingly, D. W. Griffith had just the year before released *Isn't Life Wonderful*, much of it shot on location in postwar Germany and showing the grimness of life there.

Two of Pabst's finest films were made with American actress Louise Brooks, who clearly was the director's muse: *Pandora's Box* (1929) and *Diary of a Lost Girl* (1929). Critics who don't hold Pabst in great esteem credit Brooks with the films' success. Eisner, who rapturously eulogizes Brooks, writes that "she succeeded in stimulating an otherwise unequal director's talent to the extreme." Nevertheless, it was in Pabst's films that Brooks became immortal.

In *Pandora's Box*, Brooks is mesmerizing as Lulu, an innocently erotic creature who succeeds in destroying the lives of those around her as well as her own. A masterpiece of silent cinema that flung a gauntlet at the censors, the film has it all: murder, prostitution, gambling, blackmail, and lesbianism (Lulu, at her wedding, dances with Countess Geschwitz — played by Alice Roberts — who is one of the screen's first lesbians).

The implausible plot mirrors Lulu's whimsical nature. When Lulu is told by her lover, a rich newspaper magnate, that he is going to marry someone else, she takes up with his son, whom she weds. In an argument, she kills the father, and the couple flees on a cruise ship. At the end, turning to prostitution in London, Lulu has the bad luck to pick up Jack the Ripper, who murders her. It's not a moral ending in which she must die for her sins; like her entire life, it just happens.

Toward the end of the German silent era, mountain movies became the rage. Filmed on location on snowy summits, motion pictures such as *The White Hell of Pitz Palu* (1929), codirected by Pabst and Arnold Fanck, and *The Holy Mountain* (1926), directed by Fanck — both starring the young, beautiful Leni Riefenstahl — entailed a sort of mystical communion with nature, in the form of mountains, sky, and sex.

Werner Krauss in *Napoleon auf St. Helena* (Germany, 1929), directed by Lupu Pick.

The plot of *Holy Mountain* is elemental. Two best friends love the same girl, a dancer (Riefenstahl), but discover the fact only as they are climbing the brutal north face of the region's highest mountain during a snowstorm. When they are trapped — one of them suspended by a rope over a cliff — Riefenstahl braves the night storm to reach a cabin to alert other skiers of their plight. Pabst insisted on realism, and Riefenstahl recalled that he demanded that she endure a planned avalanche scene two or three times to get the right shot. While the simple story moves at a glacial pace, the imagery of rock and ice, snow and cloud is awesome.

FRANCE

While France's film industry was shattered by the Great War, it had started to decline even before. Restrictions created by the American Trust, a conglomerate of motion picture companies that had a virtual monopoly on the industry, had cut Pathé's percentage of film footage released in the United States to 10 percent by 1911. Two years later, the Americans were making substantial inroads in French cinemas. By the end of the war, American films were in French theaters everywhere, leading the publisher of the weekly trade journal *Le Film*, Henri Diamant-Berger, to wonder if France wasn't becoming a "cinematographic colony" of the United States. After the war, the old guard, such as Pathé and Gaumont, gave way to smaller companies, which merged to form a new order in France. Many Franco-German productions were produced to pool capital and to compete in the world market.

In the early twenties, the Société des Films Historiques was formed to lavishly evoke France's glorious history. Its first production was Raymond Bernard's 1924 epic *The Miracle of the Wolves*, the most expensive French film made up to that date. Set during the fifteenth century, it centered on the struggle between Louis XI and Charles the Bold. While it was an enormous hit in France, it was a box-office dud. Many other French films focused on European history, among them Henry Roussel's *Imperial Violets* (1924), set during the splendor of the Second Empire; and Marco de Gastyne's epic *The Marvelous Life of Joan of Arc* (1928). Gastyne painted his child-warrior in the midst of a huge canvas of battles and sweeping landscapes.

In contrast to these epics were a number of realistic films that set human dramas against either the cityscape of Paris or rural settings. A series of films dealt with barge life, such as Jean Epstein's *The Beautiful Nivernaise* (1924), which was shot on the Seine and inspired Jean Vigo's *L'Atalante* (1934). Pastoral films include André Antoine's *La Terre* (1920) and Jacques Feyder's *Visages d'enfants* (1925).

La Terre, based on an Emile Zola novel, captures the novelist's naturalistic style, revealing the characters' viciousness and greed. Shot on location with documentary realism in rural France, it tells the *Lear*-like story of patriarch Père Fouan, who divides his land between his worthless sons, who in turn vie with each other in ingratitude and treachery. The beautiful landscape is in stark

A magazine advertisement for Pierre Marodon's *Salammbô* (France, 1923).

The World War I epic *J' Accuse!* (France, 1919), directed by Abel Gance.

contrast to the brutality of the characters, and the land and farm life are not romanticized. The tragic ending is a foregone conclusion but remains wrenching nonetheless.

Originally an actor, Feyder worked for Feuillade. Feyder's *Visages d'enfants*, beautifully filmed in the Swiss Alps, uses the mountain peaks, icy glaciers, and swift rivers as a backdrop to an intense tale of childhood loss and redemption. Jean, played by Jean Forest in a striking performance that rivals Jean-Pierre Léaud's in *The 400 Blows*, is grief stricken by his mother's death. When his father remarries, he steadfastly rejects his stepmother and her daughter, and in a fit of anger, he drops the girl's favorite doll in the snow. When she goes out one winter night to look for it, she becomes lost and nearly freezes to death. Racked with guilt, Jean throws himself into an icy river but is rescued by his stepmother. Inner passions are reflected in the turbulence of nature — an avalanche that nearly kills the girl and the swirling waters Jean tries to kill himself in.

Some of the most interesting films in France in the twenties were produced by Russian exiles who had fled Russia for Paris during the civil war. They included directors Viktor Tourjansky and Alexandre Volkoff and actor Ivan Mosjoukine. Volkoff directed the 1927 *Casanova*, in which Mosjoukine plays the seducer-adventurer with a light comic touch. The film opens in Venice, where Casanova is busy fending off creditors in between liaisons. He escapes to Russia, where he romances Catherine the Great. The film is beautifully shot, evoking eighteenth-century Venice in all its magnificence, and the hand-colored Carnival fireworks are captivating.

Abel Gance is the giant of French silent cinema — some may dispute his genius, but his importance has to be acknowledged. Gance worked, unhappily, as a law clerk, slipping away to the library whenever he could to read Rimbaud, Poe, and Nietzsche. Eventually he made his break, first in theater, then in film, writing scenarios and directing his first movie in 1911. He continued making

Magazine advertisement for the U.S. release of *J' Accuse!*
(France, 1919).

Abel Gance's epic tragedy *The Wheel* (*La Roue*, France, 1921) had an original running time of eight and a half hours.

films, such as *The Torture of Silence* (1917) and *The Tenth Symphony* (1918), garnering a growing recognition, throughout the war (he had been before seven recruiting boards and was rejected each time on medical grounds).

Gance was eventually mobilized in the Cinematographic Section, and that would lead to the antiwar drama *J'accuse!* (1919). Gance filmed American and French troops fighting at the front, and later, for a sequence called "Return of the Dead," he filmed French soldiers on leave who had just returned from Verdun. In a disturbing allegorical scene, the soldiers, who appear to be dead, rise up to ask if the war has been of any use. Chillingly, the real-life soldiers were soon to return to the front and almost certain death. *J'accuse!* — a hit on both sides of the Atlantic — made Gance's international reputation.

Gance spent years filming *La Roue* (1923), which centers on a strange love triangle: Sisif (Séverin-Mars), a railroad engineer, and his son, Elie (Gabriel de Gravone), a sensitive violin maker, are both in love with the beautiful Norma (Ivy Close). Sisif found her as a baby after a rail crash and has raised her as his daughter, so Elie believes that she really is his sister.

Against the background of the grimy railway yards at Nice (a cottage was built on the site), the story plays out with tragic consequences. After Elie learns that Norma is not his sister, he is killed in a fall over a cliff. Sisif, partially blinded in an accident, attempts suicide by wrecking his train, but survives; he is demoted to driving a funicular train in the mountains. There he gradually goes completely blind and is occasionally visited by Norma. He is last seen staring blindly, cradling a model train.

While the story is melodramatic and sometimes sentimental, *La Roue* is historically important as it continues the fast cutting that Gance used in *J'accuse!* Flashing images of train wheels spinning, pistons pounding, smoke, tracks diverging and converging, and power gauges intercut with close-ups of the characters create an extraordinary rhythmic and emotional intensity. Gance discovered the power of fast cutting before Sergei Mikhailovich Eisenstein, one of the greatest Soviet directors of the century.

But Gance was to take his innovations to the limit with his magnum opus, *Napoléon* (1927); if he had made nothing but this monumental historical epic, he would be indelibly inscribed in film history. It follows Napoléon's life from a snowball battle at school, won by the savvy strategy of the budding military genius, to the film's climax, in which he rallies the French troops to advance into Italy. From battle scenes to balls, from a storm at sea to the storm of the French Revolution, the

Albert Dieudonné as Napoléon.

film moves like a boat swept up in the torrent of history. Even when viewed on video, one feels like cheering at the end, if not singing the "Marseillaise." After watching the film, it is hard not to recall actor Albert Dieudonné as Napoléon rather than paintings of the real-life historical figure.

Napoléon is a virtual encyclopedia of film technique. The rapid editing, the innovative mobile camera movements (Gance strapped a camera on a horse, tied it to a pendulum, hung it from wires) and the triptych ending — which used three screens, sometimes showing a panorama, sometimes separate but thematically linked images, tinted with the red, white, and blue of the French flag — leave one amazed.

Unfortunately, because of its length and the technical difficulty of using three screens, *Napoléon* appeared as it was intended in only eight cities in Europe. MGM bought it but never used the three-screen format, which Gance called Polyvision, in the United States. Instead the film was drastically cut and was poorly received in America by audiences and critics alike. Gance made several sound films but never again had the opportunity to reveal his audacity and brilliance as he did with *Napoléon*.

RUSSIA AND THE SOVIET UNION

Even many aficionados of silent film think of Russian movies as the fruit of the Russian Revolution, emerging in the twenties. But in recent years, film scholars have revisited pre-Soviet cinema: Yakov Protazanov, who directed Mosjoukine in several films (such as *The Queen of Spades* and *Satan Triumphant*), and Evgeni Bauer, whose brief, four-year career ended when he died of pneumonia, in 1917, are two examples of pre-Soviet directors. Bauer's films, with their themes of doomed love and death, evoke Edgar Allan Poe, while evincing a technical mastery — impressive sets, fluid camera movements, and innovative lighting — as advanced as that of any contemporary director in the West.

Bauer made more than eighty films, and at least twenty-six are extant. In 1915's *After Death*, adapted from a Turgenev story, a young photographer, Andrei, leads a hermetic life, living with an old aunt and memories of his dead mother. Dragged to a soiree, he meets an actress, Zoia,

The slaughter of helpless citizens by the Cossacks in one of the most famous scenes from Sergei Eisenstein's masterpiece *The Battleship Potemkin* (*Bronenosets Potyomkin*, Soviet Union, 1925).

Lev Kuleshov's *By the Law* (*Po zakonu*, Soviet Union, 1926).

who is deeply and immediately attracted to him. He rejects her advances, and after she poisons herself, he finds himself haunted by visions of her and wastes hopelessly away into death. In a striking example of Bauer's art, the camera follows Andrei at the party in a three-minute, uninterrupted tracking shot.

Most of the prerevolutionary filmmakers dispersed to Europe in the wake of the Russian civil war. (The Bolsheviks, led by Vladimir Lenin, seized power in October 1917, a long civil war ensued, and it was not until 1922 that Communist power was consolidated in the Union of Soviet Socialist Republics.) Lenin and other Bolsheviks recognized film as a unifying propaganda medium. Lenin asserted that "the cinema is for us the most important of the arts," and the Soviet film industry was nationalized in 1919.

The All-Union State Institute of Cinematography was founded to train filmmakers to replace the old guard that had fled. Students learned to edit existing newsreels for the purpose of agitation and propaganda (agitprop), and so-called agit-trains carried propaganda materials, including films, to remote parts of Russia; at the same time, rural life was documented and the film edited when it came back. But the film school was short on even the most basic resources, like film stock and cam-

Eisenstein's first attempts at montage occurred in *Strike* (*Stachka*, Soviet Union, 1925).

eras, so students often produced "films" without cameras by writing, directing, and acting out films as if they were performing before cameras.

Among the film school's most important teachers was agit-filmmaker Lev Kuleshov, who, along with Vsevolod Pudovkin, produced an experiment known as the Kuleshov effect: using close-up shots of an expressionless actor (Mosjoukine in an old film), Kuleshov juxtaposed them with three different shots — a plate of soup, a dead woman in a coffin, and a child playing. Invariably audiences thought the actor's expression had changed in reaction to the juxtaposed shots, expressing hunger, sadness, or affection, respectively. The experiment affirmed the importance of editing and of montage — which combines or juxtaposes different shots to create an impression or an association not conveyed by individual shots alone. The Soviets learned valuable lessons from Griffith, studying his epic *Intolerance* endlessly. In fact, Eisenstein, one of Kuleshov's students, wrote remarkably insightful film criticism on Griffith.

Eisenstein studied engineering before the revolution. Later he would become a painter and designer for agit-train theatrical productions. He made four important silent films, which cumulatively cover a broad sweep of revolutionary history: *Strike* (1925) and *Battleship Potemkin*

(1925) recount prerevolutionary uprisings, *October* (1928) concerns the Bolshevik revolution, and *Old and New* (1929) is set during the period of farm collectivization.

His first directorial effort, *Strike* (1925), was filmed by the cinematographer Eduard Tisse, which began a relationship not unlike that of Griffith and Bitzers, and it uses a large catalog of cinematic techniques — wipes, dissolves, superimpositions, irises, montage, and briefly, even reverse motion. For an artist like Griffith, montage was used to indicate parallel action or to create natural associations. For Eisenstein, who was also a prolific writer and film theorist, montage frequently involved violent juxtapositions. In *Strike*, Eisenstein shockingly intercuts the police massacre of strikers with the slaughter of cattle (in an homage in *Apocalypse Now*, Francis Ford Coppola intercuts between the ritual sacrifice of a water buffalo and Colonel Kurtz's killing).

In *Strike*, which follows a simple arc — strike, struggle, final massacre — the masses of workers are the central character. Proletarians and the fat-cat capitalists who exploit them are not developed as personalities. Its sweep of movement remains stirring, even without the melodrama of individual characters.

Battleship Potemkin (1925), however, is more intimate. One of the world's most famous films, it centers on the 1905 mutiny on the ship *Potemkin* and the killing of the mutineers' supporters in Odessa. In *Potemkin*, Eisenstein uses more close-ups of individuals to create an emotional, as well as an intellectual, connection: soldiers forced to eat mag-

The End of St. Petersburg (Konets Sankt-Peterburga, Soviet Union, 1927), directed by Vsevolod Pudovkin.

goty meat, a terrified mother with her baby carriage as the Cossacks attack the protestors on the Odessa steps. This sequence, in which citizens are decimated by czarist troops as they move in grim, stately formation down the steps — the baby carriage bouncing down precipitously before them — is one of the most imitated and parodied scenes in cinema (for example, in Brian De Palma's *The Untouchables*). As Roger Ebert has pointed out, it's more likely that a filmgoer will have seen one of these "homages" than the original film that inspired them.

Stalin, who famously described the role of the artist as an "engineer of human souls," repudiated Eisenstein's later silents, *October* (1927) and *Old and New* (1929). Eisenstein left for Hollywood in 1930, although he produced no films there, and his efforts to produce an epic in Mexico, subsidized by American writer Sinclair Lewis, were cut short (a version, not edited by Eisenstein, was subsequently released as *Que Viva Mexico*). He returned to the Soviet Union and made the spectacle *Alexander Nevsky* (1938), codirected with Dmitri Vasiliev, and the first two parts of the proposed baroque trilogy *Ivan the Terrible* (1945, 1958).

Pudovkin's *Mother* (*Mat*, Soviet Union, 1926), based on a novel by Maxim Gorky, concerns a strike during the revolution of 1905 and features a stirring performance by Vera Baranovskaya in the title role.

Left: The mother waters the head of her drunken husband.

Bottom: The mother mourns the death of her son.

Pudovkin was a more personal director than Eisenstein and, like Griffith, mixed his stories of epic events with human dramas. A student of chemistry and physics at Moscow University, Pudovkin was wounded in World War I and spent three years as a German POW. Inspired by a screening of *Intolerance*, he studied film at the state institute under Kuleshov, and, combining art and science, made *The Mechanics of the Brain* (1925), a documentary about Pavlov. Around the same time, he codirected a short comedy — a genre rare among Soviet films, although the Russians adored Chaplin — called *Chess Fever*, in which a woman comes to grips with her lover's chess obsession . . . by becoming a chess addict herself.

Pudovkin's silent features are among the most celebrated of the Soviet era. *Mother* (1926), based on a novel by Maxim Gorky, is the story of a woman who unknowingly leads the authorities to her son, a trade-union activist. In *The End of St. Petersburg* (1927), a family of peasants moves to the city, where they are caught up in the tidal events of World War I and the assault on the Winter Palace, in 1917. Pudovkin's use of montage can be extraordinarily apt — as in *Mother*, when a revolutionary march is crosscut with scenes of a frozen river breaking up — or overly obvious, as in *St. Petersburg*, when Russians being killed at the front are juxtaposed with frenzied war profiteers at the stock exchange.

Earth (*Zemlya*, Soviet Union, 1930), a poetic film about the trials of Ukrainian farming life, directed by Alexander Dovzhenko.

Perhaps Pudovkin's greatest work is the stunningly photographed *Storm Over Asia* (1928), filmed on location in Mongolia. It is set during the Russian civil war, when the British had occupied Soviet territory in the east. A naive young Mongol, shot for being a partisan and left for dead, is revived after the British come to believe that he is a descendant of Genghis Khan's — they want to make him a puppet ruler. He sees through their hypocrisy and eventually leads the Mongols in an uprising.

One of the film's most extraordinary scenes documents a real Buddhist ritual celebrating a new lama (it was not in the original scenario), giving an ethnographic record of the indigenous culture. In a cleverly incorporated montage, a British delegation solemnly shows its respect for the ceremony while their troops are stealing Mongol cattle.

Born of illiterate peasants in northeastern Ukraine, Alexander Dovzhenko joined the Red Army during the civil war. He entered the diplomatic service and was sent to Berlin in the early twenties, where he studied art. When he returned to Ukraine, he worked as a graphic artist

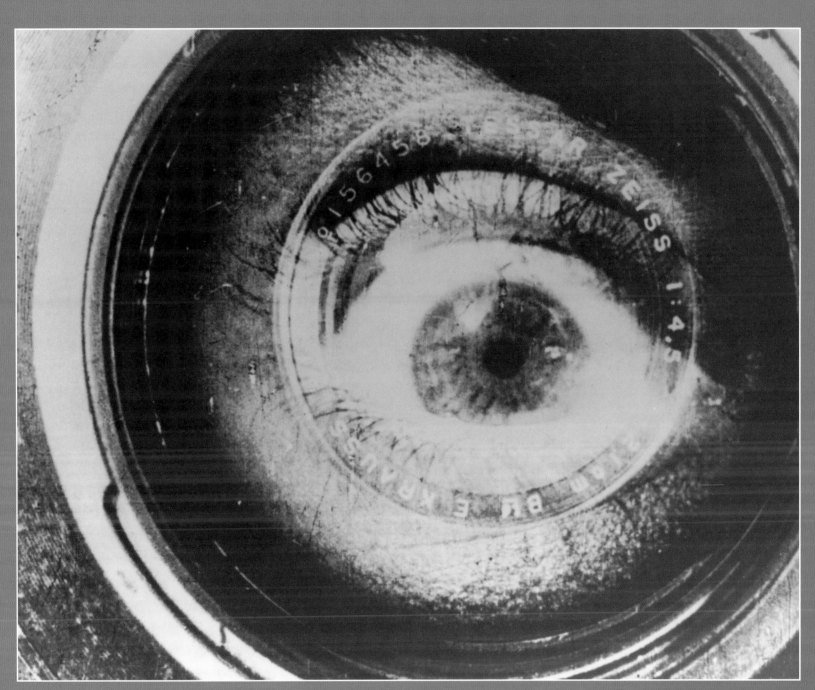

Kino-Eye (*Kinoglaz*, Soviet Union, 1924), a documentary depicting the merits of Soviet life, directed by Dziga Vertov.

A scene from Eisenstein's *October* (*Oktyabr,* Soviet Union, 1928).

and painter before becoming a filmmaker.

Dovzhenko's international reputation rests on his silent "Ukrainian trilogy" (*Zvenigora*, 1928; *Arsenal*, 1929; and *Earth*, 1930), although he continued making films into the forties. In his elliptical montage style, *Zvenigora* — the name of a mountain in Ukraine, so the film has always gone by its original title — mixes Ukrainian legends and contemporary revolutionary history. *Arsenal* uses odd camera angles, cartoon images, and parallel action to vividly depict the revolution in Ukraine.

The extraordinarily beautiful *Earth* is his masterpiece. Ostensibly a story about rural collectivization, its plot is so slight it barely exists: an old peasant dies, the farmers delight in a new communal tractor, the film's hero is shot and killed by a kulak (a wealthy landowner). Dovzhenko's lyrical film, more pantheistic than socialist, portrays fields of ripe grain, billowing cumulus clouds, trees weighed down by fruit glistening from a shower, a peasant dancing alone in the moonlight. It is a hymn to the earth and the peasants who live in mystical closeness to it.

A soldier in Eisenstein's *October* (1928), which depicted the events of the 1917 Russian revolution.

Earth was also controversial. Soviet critics charged that its beauty and philosophy did not sufficiently advance the collectivization cause. But the film was acclaimed in premieres in Berlin, Paris, and New York, and it remains an important part of the Soviet silent canon.

Dziga Vertov, born in Poland to a book dealer, played piano and violin and wrote poetry as a child and later studied neurology and human perception. In 1918, he began editing documentary footage, soon becoming editor of *Kinonedelya*, the first Bolshevik newsreel. All of his films were documentaries, but he brought a poetic sensibility to his film editing. Vertov despised fiction filmmaking: "The film drama is the Opium of the people . . . down with Bourgeois fairy-tale scenarios . . . long live life as it is!" he wrote. (He was much taken with producing manifestos.)

His experiments with frenetic montage, unusual camera angles, split screens, and superimpositions did not endear him, however, to party hacks. But his work, such as the feature *Kino-Eye: Life Caught Unawares* (1924), was lionized by European avant-gardists. Yet, when he was ready to begin his best-known film, the marvelous *The Man with a Movie Camera* (1929), Moscow film apparatchiks refused to back him. He got funding from a Ukrainian film studio.

While Vertov was never really persecuted by the doctrinaire authorities, in later years he was limited to producing innocuous industrial documentaries. His vision survived, however, as he influenced later directors as various as Jean-Luc Godard and Lars von Trier.

Soviet silent film was critically well received in the United States and influential. Its passion and craft made it possible to overlook its blatant propaganda. Gilbert Seldes, writing in the *New Republic* in 1929 about several Soviet films, explained:

> *The first point is that all of them are possessed of moral fervor far more intense than we are accustomed to, not only in our films (which almost entirely lack any element of morality), but in all of our arts. . . . Obviously the films are propaganda. I dislike propaganda in works of art. . . . The reason the Russian propaganda is acceptable is that you never feel the picture is being twisted to give a communist happy ending. While the pictures unroll, you feel intellectually what the directors obviously feel spiritually: that the triumph of Soviet Russia is the single desirable thing in the world, making all things right. . . . If you do not share their theories of economics, you may find that passion misdirected; but you will not find it feeble.*

From our vantage point in history — knowing about the horrors during farm collectivization, the Gulags — one can't help but bring an even greater measure of skepticism than Seldes had at the time. But the best of Soviet cinema holds up remarkably well artistically. And its influence is immeasurable. Want an example of metaphorical montage? Watch the ending of *The Godfather*, which cuts between the baptism of a child and the slaughter of the heads of the mafia families.

EUROPEANS IN HOLLYWOOD

When Lubitsch's *Madame DuBarry* was first shown in the United States, at New York's big Capitol Theatre in 1920, it was a roll of the dice. It was renamed *Passion* and originally promoted as an Italian film, then as "European," to try to deflect the anticipated anti-German sentiments lingering from the war. Associated First National Pictures purchased the rights for a paltry forty thousand dollars. But it was, despite the distributor's qualms, a sensation. Pola Negri, who played the title character, became a star in America almost overnight.

The review in the *New York Times* noted that Negri was a strange, new kind of cinematic creature. "It is not physical beauty that wins for her. She is lovely in many scenes, it is true, but some of her features are not beautiful, and she makes no apparent effort to pose becomingly without regard to the meaning of her performance. She is expressive. That is her charm. . . . She actually wins sympathy for a woman who cannot at any time be admired. This is an accomplishment."

ANNOUNCEMENT EXTRAORDINARY

Ernst Lubitsch

DISTINGUISHED SHOWMAN PRODUCER OF MANY FAMOUS HITS!

Coming:

Two Ernst Lubitsch Special Productions

PRODUCED by this de luxe wizard of the box office in the characteristic masterly Lubitsch manner. With all-star Paramount casts and backed by the limitless resources of this organization. A new epoch in Mr. Lubitsch's great career.

Paramount Pictures

Signs with Paramount

In 1927, movie magazines announced Ernst Lubitsch's signing with Paramount in Hollywood.

Mary Pickford stars in Ernst Lubitsch's first American production, *Rosita* (1923).

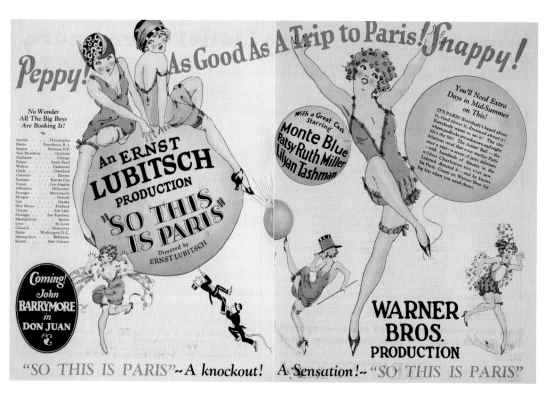

Lubitsch comedy *So This Is Paris* (1926) for Warner Bros.

Other Lubitsch films — *Anna Boleyn*, renamed *Deception*; and *Carmen*, which also starred Negri, retitled *Gypsy Blood* — were shown in the United States in 1921, and Hollywood began to get jittery about the quality and distinctiveness of Lubitsch's work. "This 'German Invasion' fright is the oldest and silliest of alarms," Adolph Zukor told *Photoplay*. "One would think that the Germans had some magical recipe for making great pictures." But as Paramount's honcho was pooh-poohing the Germans, he was on his way to Europe to sign Negri to a contract. And Mary Pickford brought Lubitsch to Hollywood to direct her in the grand costume drama *Rosita* (1923), a box-office and critical hit, that Pickford notoriously disliked. ("It's the worst picture I ever did," she declared.)

In America, Lubitsch went on to make a cycle of comedies of manners. The urbane sophistication of *The Marriage Circle* (1924), with its lighthearted treatment of divorce and love affairs, affirmed that silent comedy didn't have to be based on slapstick and sight gags — indeed, it could be quite subtle.

Reportedly Lubitsch's favorite film, *The Marriage Circle* draws a love pentangle: Parisian doctor Franz Braun (Monte Blue) and his wife, Charlotte (Florence Vidor), are deeply in love. Another married couple, however, Dr. Stock (Adolphe Menjou) and his wife, Mizzi (Marie Prevost), are deeply unhappy. Mizzi, Charlotte's best friend, begins flirting with Braun, while Stock, desperate for a divorce, hires a detective who seems to suspect everyone of infidelity. In the end, Stock gets his divorce, and Mizzi gets her man, although not the one she had hoped for.

The film was a success at the box office and with critics. Iris Barry's enthusiastic review of the film in the London *Spectator* at the time (May 17, 1924) is worth quoting at length:

A really efficient comedy — in which there is perception behind the wit and a perfect rounding of the action so that nothing irrelevant or forced mars the bright sparkle — is a rare thing. The very word recalls so pat our appreciation of writers like Sheridan, Molière or Congreve that it comes as a surprise to find in The Marriage Circle *... something on the screen in their tradition; a surprise even though one had held that the cinema was capable of delineating pictorially comedies as witty as anything in the theatre's repertory. Hitherto the cinema has shown us, in Harold Lloyd, Larry Semon and the late John Bunny, for example, only the succulent fun of* the music-hall and the circus, not the dry wit of true comedy; it has provoked laughter by physical peculiarities, acrobacy, clowning. Even Chaplin as an actor is hardly an exception: his mixture of farce and pathos has always been conceived too emotionally, too little cerebrally, to be right comedy. It was however, Chaplin, producer of A Woman of Paris, who opened the way for what has now been done.

As the reviewer in Motion Picture Classic summed up the film: "It is as light as moondust — and it sheds a radiance of capricious moods and shadings. It is gay, sparkling and smart." This could describe the director's other comedies and his style, which came to be known as the Lubitsch touch. Lubitsch followed with such films as Forbidden Paradise (1924), So This Is Paris (1926), and an adaptation by another master of the comedy of manners, Oscar Wilde's Lady Windermere's Fan (1925).

Emil Jannings, shown here in Josef von Sternberg's The Last Command (1928).

Lubitsch went on to have a successful career in talking pictures in Hollywood, making Ninotchka with Garbo (1939) and The Shop Around the Corner (1940), among many others.

"Why compete when you can hire the competition?" is an old business axiom, and Hollywood was an industry town. In 1927, Murnau left for Fox in California, where he made the masterwork Sunrise (1927). Fox didn't give Murnau a budget and told him to take his time. While the film was a box-office disappointment, it was an extraordinary artistic success, which was recognized at the first Academy Awards ceremony, where it shared top honors with Wings (two Best Picture awards were given that year: Wings won for best production and Sunrise for best artistic quality of production). Sunrise also helped Janet Gaynor get her Best Actress Oscar and garnered Best Cinematography awards for cameramen Charles Rosher and Karl Struss. There was an unusual synergy between the German and American filmmakers in Sunrise, marrying fatalism and optimism, but the extraordinary fluidity of the camera work certainly came from the German side of the film's family.

The story of Sunrise has the simplicity of a fable: the Man (George O'Brien) is a farmer who is lured away from his wife, the Woman (Gaynor), by the Woman from the City (Margaret Livingston), a vamp who beguiles him with tales of the bright lights in the big city. She convinces him to murder his wife and return to the city with her. He nearly kills his wife in a boat but can't go through with it, leaving her terrified of him. They travel to the city, where he gradually regains

A movie magazine advertisement for *He Who Gets Slapped* (1924), a film directed by Victor Seastrom, starring Lon Chaney and Norma Shearer.

her trust. They have a lovely day together, but on the trip back across the lake, a storm comes up and capsizes their boat. The Man believes his wife drowned, but she has survived, and the Woman from the City is banished. The couple watch the sunrise together.

Murnau made one more great work, *Tabu* (1931), before he died tragically in a car accident a few weeks before the movie's general release. Its stunningly lyrical photography — it was filmed entirely on location in Tahiti with nonactors — won a Best Cinematography Oscar for cameraman Floyd Crosby. *Tabu* was originally a collaboration between Murnau and documentary-filmmaker Flaherty. They cowrote the original script, but once filming started, they decided their styles were too different, and Flaherty bowed out.

Another German emigrant whose career was cut short by an early death was Paul Leni, who had directed the Expressionist film *Waxworks* (1924). For Universal, he made the classic haunted-house comedy *The Cat and the Canary* (1927), praised by the *New York Times* "as one of the finest examples of motion picture art," and the disturbing *The Man Who Laughs* (1928), with Conrad Veidt and Mary Philbin.

Lang didn't emigrate to Hollywood until after making two talkies, *M* (1931), with Peter Lorre as a child murderer, and *The Last Will of Dr. Mabuse* (1932), which has the mad Dr. Mabuse ranting Nazi philosophy. The latter forced Lang to move to France and then to the United States, where he had a long career. (Lang and his wife, Thea von Harbou, split up, and she worked as a filmmaker under the Nazis.)

The Man Who Laughs (1928), directed by Paul Leni.

The Devil's Circus (1926), directed by Benjamin Christensen for MGM.

Many Scandinavian filmmakers and actors also heeded the siren call of Hollywood, and because of the defections, the Swedish film industry was eviscerated.

Sjöström left for Hollywood in 1923. Among his several successes was *He Who Gets Slapped* (1924), the very first release of the newly formed MGM. Lon Chaney, Norma Shearer, and John Gilbert head the topflight cast. Chaney plays a scientist whose baron benefactor steals both his discoveries and his wife. After Chaney is publicly humiliated when his patron slaps him, he becomes, of all things, a circus clown, whose hugely popular act involves being repeatedly slapped. (Amid all the melodrama, the film offers disturbing insights into masochism and the pleasure people take in the humiliation of others.) Gilbert and Shearer have a horse-riding act, and Chaney falls in love with Shearer. When

Mockery (1927), directed by Benjamin Christensen.

she is courted by the now-divorced baron, Chaney seizes an opportunity for revenge involving a circus lion. The film's combination of strangeness and pathos makes it one of Chaney's best.

Sjöström, who worked in Hollywood under the name Seastrom, went on to direct Garbo in *The Divine Woman* (1928) and Lillian Gish in two films, *The Scarlet Letter* (1927) and *The Wind* (1928). In the bravura *Wind*, Seastrom's Swedish themes are evoked once again as human passions play out against the violence of nature. Indeed, the wind is the title character. Gish's role is perfectly suited to her. She plays Letty, who moves out West to live with a cousin in a backwater, where the wind blows sand ceaselessly into every nook and cranny and face. Her cousin's wife becomes jealous and wants her out. She marries a ranch hand, Lige, played by Lars Hanson (another Swedish émigré), just to get out of the house. She is also pursued by a vile traveling salesman. The isolation and windswept desert drive her to the very edge of madness. It was — like the ending of *Greed* — shot in the Mohave Desert, with temperatures well over one hundred degrees. Eight airplane propellers were used to blow sand all over the set.

Seastrom returned to Sweden, where he continued to work as an actor. His last film role was as the aged professor in Bergman's 1957 *Wild Strawberries*.

Louis B. Mayer signed both Stiller and Garbo to MGM in 1925, but the studio was far more interested in the star than the director. Garbo's American debut, *The Torrent* (1926), was helmed by Monta Bell, and her second film, *The Temptress* (1926), was assigned to Stiller but taken away

Lillian Gish struggles against the unrelenting sand as the downtrodden Letty in Victor Seastrom's *The Wind* (1928).

from him after two weeks of shooting and given to Fred Niblo to direct. "I was broken to pieces," Garbo said.

While Garbo was on her way to becoming a superstar, Stiller moved to Paramount, where he made several films, including the stylish and compelling *Hotel Imperial* (1927), which starred Negri. Set during World War I, Negri plays a maid, Anna, whose hotel is commandeered by Russian soldiers. She protects a handsome Hungarian lieutenant, Almasy (James Hall), disguising him as a waiter, by flirting with a Russian general. When Almasy learns of plans to attack Hungarian forces, he kills a Russian spy, and Anna risks her life by making it appear a suicide.

Stiller returned to Sweden, in ill health, and died a few months later. "I have all my life wondered where I belong," he wrote shortly before his death, in 1928, at the age of forty-five.

After Benjamin Christensen's huge success in 1922 with the cult classic *Häxan*, he moved to Berlin, where he made three films and starred in Dreyer's *Chained* (1924), in which he plays a homosexual artist. In 1925, Hollywood beckoned. His two features for MGM, *The Devil's Circus* (1926), with Norma Shearer, and *Mockery* (1927), starring Lon Chaney, are lavish disappointments. Christensen moved to First National, where he directed four films, among them 1929's *Seven Footprints to Satan*, a haunted-house spoof, in the vein of Leni's *The Cat and the Canary*. He returned to Denmark, where after making several films, he became the manager of a movie theater in Copenhagen.

Lillian Gish as Hester Prynne in Seastrom's *The Scarlet Letter* (1927).

SOUND AND COLOR

TWO OF THE GREATEST MYTHS ABOUT THE SILENT ERA ARE THAT THE FILMS WERE INVARIABLY SILENT AND THAT THEY DEPICTED A WORLD SOLELY IN SHADES OF GRAY. A BETTER TERM FOR SILENT MOVIES — IF SOMEWHAT AWKWARD SOUNDING — WOULD BE NON-DIALOGUE FILMS, BECAUSE SO-CALLED SILENT FILMS NEARLY ALWAYS HAD SOME KIND OF MUSICAL ACCOMPANIMENT. WHETHER IT WAS A SIMPLE PIANO OR A FULL ORCHESTRA, IMPROVISED FAMILIAR TUNES OR A WRITTEN SCORE, MUSIC WAS A CRUCIAL PART OF THE MOVIEGOING EXPERIENCE BEFORE THE ARRIVAL OF TALKIES.

Additionally, most films of the silent era had some color. Even in their first decade, many films were in part or in whole beautifully hand colored. Scenes in feature films were tinted or toned. In the early twenties, some 80 percent of films used the coloring techniques of tinting and toning.

THE SOUNDS OF SILENTS

From the earliest days of moving pictures, films were rarely "silent." Usually some sort of narration accompanied the films. Soon even the humblest nickelodeon would typically have at least a piano and, perhaps, a drum set. Sometimes the music would be provided by self-playing pianos or organs. While the music was supposed to enhance the visual experience, at the very least it covered up the racket of noisy projection equipment.

Film companies began providing printed musical suggestions in late 1909, and over the next few years, they began creating cue sheets, which listed scenes and intertitles with suggested musical accompaniment. Conditions varied among theaters, and many musicians didn't have the time to prepare. They would have to wing it by improvising. The resulting performances varied tremendously.

Above: Directors often brought musicians along on film shoots to inspire their actors, as shown here in an issue of *Motion Picture Magazine*.

Left: Technicolor was used for this scene in Rupert Julian's *Phantom of the Opera* (1925).

French existentialist Jean-Paul Sartre, in his childhood memoir, *The Words*, describes just how large even a simple piano could loom in the cinematic experience: "Above all, I liked the incurable muteness of my heroes. But no, they weren't mute, since they knew how to make themselves understood. We communicated by means of music; it was the sound of their inner life. Persecuted innocence did better than merely show or speak of suffering: it permeated me with its pain by means of the melody that issued from it. I would read the conversations, but I heard the hope and the bitterness."

But often the musical experience was inappropriate or distracting. In the early nickelodeon days, when movies often changed every day, musicians sometimes just played ragtime regardless of what was on the screen.

Touring programs at higher-class houses, however, often had well-rehearsed players behind the screen. Music publishers sold classical and popular sheet music called for in cue sheets, and tonier theaters acquired huge libraries of sheet music; during the silent era, the Loews Theater chain's

Musicians and cast on the set of *One Night in Rome* (1924).

music library comprised fifty thousand scores. Several music anthologies were produced, such as the *Witmark Moving Picture Album* (1913). The most significant book of piano music was Erno Rapée's *Motion Picture Moods* (1924), which offered 370 works under different headings, such as "mother love" and "fire-fighting."

Growing out of the vaudeville tradition, slide shows with performers singing popular songs filled the gaps during reel changes. Illustrated song slides lasted well into the teens. With the rise of movie palaces, orchestras would perform full-fledged concerts in between film showings.

Competition forced theater owners to pay more attention to providing good music, both during the films and between them, while directors began to take a greater interest in the sound experience accompanying their films. Scores for films fell into two categories: compiled, which included classical and popular music as well as original music, and wholly original scores. Among the earliest original scores was Camille Saint-Saëns's work for the 1908 French film *The Assassination of the Duke of Guise.*

One director who took a great interest in music for his feature films was Griffith, who hired Joseph Carl Breil to write a score for *The Birth of a Nation.* It was a significant challenge: the score had 214 cues and called for a forty-piece orchestra and chorus. The compiled score drew on classical repertoire, such as Mozart, Mahler, and Wagner; Civil War songs; and folk tunes like "Turkey in the Straw." Breil also composed original music, producing what was probably the first hit tune from a movie: a love theme that became known as the "Perfect Song." After *Birth of a Nation*, large orchestras became de rigueur in movie palaces.

According to Lillian Gish, the director and composer often argued. "If I ever kill anyone," Griffith said, "it won't be an actor, but a musician." But the score was powerfully affecting, and Griffith and Breil collaborated again on *Intolerance.*

Other important film composers of the silent era include Gottfried Huppertz, who scored Lang's *Die Nibelungen* and *Metropolis*, and Mortimer Wilson, who wrote the music for *The Black Pirate* and *The Thief of Bagdad*, both starring Douglas Fairbanks.

Important as film music was to Griffith, he didn't use music on the set, a common practice beginning around 1918 to put actors in the mood for their performances. Directors as varied as Gance, von Sternberg, and DeMille did, however, use on-set musicians.

Because the scores and cue sheets were not directly attached to the films, they were frequently ignored. For instance, Griffith took his features on road shows where they played at prestige theaters

Sheet music for the Italian production of *Antony and Cleopatra* (1913), distributed in the United States by George Kleine.

under his careful supervision. *The Birth of a Nation* played at New York City's Liberty theater for forty-eight weeks before it went into general release around the country. At the Liberty, the film's synchronized score was carefully followed. But once *Birth* and other feature films went into general release, directors had little or no say over what music accompanied a film. Frequently, directors didn't bother themselves with the music at all, which became the concern of producers and theater music directors. By 1921, cue sheets were the most common guide.

The lack of direct ties between film and sound makes it difficult for film restorationists to determine what music was intended to be played with which movies. A surprising number of composers have, over the past several years, stepped in to fill this void, making a sort of cottage industry of producing scores (and DVD soundtracks) for these films.

Bessie Love, star of the first movie musical, *Broadway Melody* (1929), listening to her own voice on a talkie set.

Some have taken the approach of music historians. Musicologist-detective Gillian Anderson, author of *Music for Silent Films 1894–1929: A Guide*, has reconstructed and conducted scores for dozens of films (such as *Nosferatu*) based on archival research. Composers Timothy Brock (*The Last Laugh*) and Carl Davis (*The Crowd*) have likewise taken great care in matching their music to period styles.

Anderson, in an interview for the movie Web site aintitcoolnews.com, said: *Early filmgoing was a theatrical event, not like the screenings today. The original scores are what was intended, and the directors and composers made their choices very carefully. The music is an integral part of these films, even if it isn't physically attached. Restoring just the image makes no sense. You don't save half a building and call it a restoration. Obviously, we can't exactly re-create the experience of what it was like to see these films originally, because that experience varied. But if you're going to go to the trouble with this part of our cultural heritage, we can at least arrive at a close approximation — although it's always our best guess.*

Others, including Boston's Alloy Orchestra, are more cavalier, freely mixing styles and genres while rummaging through rock, jazz, and classical as well as period music. Some of the distinctly new scores are classics in their own right. The Alloy Orchestra's galvanic, percussive score for Vertov's *The Man with a Movie Camera*, and Richard Einhorn's mystical oratorio, *Voices of Light*, which accompanies Dreyer's *The Passion of Joan of Arc*, both stand up as great music on their own while enhancing the works that inspired them.

Part of what has produced the current spike of interest in silent film is live music accompaniment and new scores on DVD. Going to a silent movie, whether accompanied by a solo piano or organ or an orchestra, is more of an event than just another trip to the local multiplex. And scoring silent films provides an outlet for new music, often shut out of traditional venues such as classical concert halls.

Arranger and composer William Frederick Peters contributed music to a number of silent films, including Merian C. Cooper's *The Four Feathers* (1929) and D. W. Griffith's *Way Down East* (1920) and *Orphans of the Storm* (1921).

Top: Edison's experimental sound film, featuring William Kennedy-Laurie Dickson on violin, shot in 1894–95.

Bottom: Magazine advertisement for Vitaphone. Many early sound films, such as *Noah's Ark* (1929), produced by Warner Bros. were released simultaneously as silents to theaters that had not yet upgraded to talkie technology.

British composer and playwright Neil Brand (he scored the British Film Institute's restoration of E. A. Dupont's 1929 *Piccadilly*, starring Anna May Wong) is also a master of improvisational silent-film accompaniment, an art he has practiced for two decades. At a lecture at the Brooklyn Academy of Music a few years ago, he demonstrated the challenges of improvisation and offered some insights gathered over the years. He sees his role as silent-film accompanist as threefold: "As a communicator, I want to offer more than what you can see. As a translator, I don't try to reproduce scores of the period. I want to take into account all of the cinema music that's happened since. And as a commentator, you need to have an attitude. Silent film is that flexible. You can rescore films again and again as long as you follow the truth — the truth as you know it."

The idea of combining visual images with synchronized recorded sound was present at the birth of film. As we've seen, Edison conceived of moving pictures as an adjunct to his phonograph (he somewhat grandiosely imagined bringing operas into people's homes). He had his assistant Dickson combine his Kinetoscope and phonograph in the so-called Kineto-phonograph (a Kinetoscope with earphones). The synchronization was primitive, however, and only about forty-five of the devices were sold. Dickson claimed to have developed a Kineto-phonograph in 1889. Although the sound cylinder recording is lost, Dickson made a film in which he raised his hat and said, "Good morning, Mr. Edison, glad to see you back. I hope you are satisfied with the Kineto-phonograph."

There does exist, however, a fifteen-second film, *Dickson Experimental Sound Film*, which was made sometime between late 1894 and early 1895. In it, Dickson is seen playing the violin into a phonograph funnel. He is playing an elegiac barcarole from a French light opera by Robert Planquette, *Les cloches de Corneville*, while two men dance slowly nearby. Still, amplification, necessary for a theater audience, remained elusive, and the synchronization of film and sound didn't always work.

Several individuals in the United States and Europe were working simultaneously on synchronized recorded sound for film, much like the development of moving pictures. Two technologies competed: sound on disk (like the Edison system) and sound on film, which itself was not a new idea, for in 1906, Eugène-Auguste Lauste patented a device that could record sound and images on film.

In the early twenties, engineers in Germany, Denmark, and the United States made great strides in synchronizing sound. The German team of Hans Vogt, Josef Engel, and Joseph Massolle developed their Tri-Ergon sound-on-film system and debuted it in Berlin in 1922. P. O. Pederson and Vlademar Poulsen also developed a sound-on-film system, which at first used separate reels for film and sound, in 1923.

The Jazz Singer (1927), directed by Alan Crosland. With "wait a minute, you ain't heard nothin' yet," Jolson's first lines of dialogue in a feature-length movie began a revolution in film. Silent movies lasted for only a few more years.

Left: *Broadway Melody* (1929), the first all-talking musical, was an absolute sensation on its release, leading box-office sales in 1929 and winning Best Picture at the second annual Academy Awards.

Right: Advertisement for *St. Louis Blues* (1929), an early sound musical short based on W. C. Handy's classic song, which includes the only screen appearance of blues singer Bessie Smith.

In the United States, Lee de Forest and Theodore Case debuted their sound-on-film Phonofilm system the same year. Case produced a number of experimental sound shorts in the mid twenties, among them the bizarre *Gus Visser and His Singing Duck*, which features Gus and his duck performing a duet of "Ma (He's Making Eyes at Me)." This vaudeville act would not be out of place in a modern-day fringe arts festival and would have been a good film to show investors interested in bankrolling the new technology. All of these systems entailed the optical recording of sound on the celluloid strip. Progress in radio technology resolved the problem of amplification.

Although sound-on-film systems would prevail, the sound-on-disk system got there first. Western Electric had a sound-on-disk system ready by 1926 and persuaded the then-small studio Warner Bros. to buy its system, called Vitaphone. The system had its feature debut in John Barrymore's costume drama *Don Juan*, which opened on August 6, 1926, with a score played by the New York Philharmonic Orchestra. *Life* magazine film critic Robert Sherwood, in his review of *Don Juan*, wrote of the Vitaphone accompaniment that "it will be possible in the future to dispense with orchestras and organists in movie theatres. Well, I for one will shed no tears. I'm tired of hearing 'Hearts and Flowers' during the views of the United States Cavalry riding to the rescue, and 'Horses — Horses — Horses' during the tender love scenes."

Don Juan was not a talkie, however. Warner's second Vitaphone feature, *The Jazz Singer*, released in 1927, was — although its use of dialogue was spartan. Fox moved to compete by buying the rights to the Phonofilm system from Case, who had split with de Forest, and renaming it Movietone.

Initially, the bigger American studios Paramount and MGM resisted synchronized sound. But the success of talking pictures guaranteed the American industry's wholesale conversion to sound by 1929 (synchronized sound came to European films later).

The consequences were far-reaching, of course. It has been estimated that some ten thousand musicians lost their jobs between 1928 and 1930 and that approximately half of those worked in movie theaters. During the Depression, it was an economic catastrophe for them. On the other hand, while theaters were wiring for sound, the layoffs saved money for studios and theaters. Some actors, because of their accents or poor voices, failed to make the transition to talkies, but the number has been exaggerated.

An advertisement for FBO's *Gang War* (1929) in *Motion Picture News* tells patrons "don't be panicked by sound."

The sound-on-disk projection machine bought by Warner Bros. was called Vitaphone.

The transition was neither simple nor immediate. Films were sometimes released both as silents and with synchronized sound. Adding a few words of spoken dialogue allowed studios to trumpet the film as a "talkie." And some films, shot originally as silents, were reshot as talkies. (An example of this is depicted in Martin Scorsese's Howard Hughes biopic, *The Aviator*, in which Hughes, played by Leonardo DiCaprio, reshoots his silent film *Hell's Angels* with dialogue at phenomenal expense.)

Because translating intertitles was relatively simple, English sound dialogue briefly imperiled Hollywood's cinematic imperialism. Smaller European nations began producing their own native-language films, and quota systems were established to protect their cinemas. Hollywood responded first by making films in different languages, but within a couple of years, a reliable system of dubbing was developed, and American films quickly regained their dominance.

Not surprisingly, some resisted sound. *Photoplay* editor James Quirk opined eloquently: *The value of silence in art is its stimulation to the imagination, and the imaginative quality is art's highest appeal. The really excellent motion picture, the really great photoplay, are never mere photography. Continually, they cause the beholder to hear things which they suggest — the murmurs of a summer night, the pounding of the surf, the sigh of the wind in the trees, the babel of crowded streets, the whisperings of love. The "talking picture" will be made practical, but it will never supersede the motion picture without sound. It will lack the subtlety and suggestion of vision, that vision which, deprived of voice to ears of flesh, intones undisturbed the symphonies of the soul.*

Of course, one could make the same argument for literature being superior to film — it compels one to use one's imagination even more. With all advances in the arts come benefits and losses.

COLOR

As already noted, some of the earliest silent films used color, in which the celluloid was hand painted. Edison's 1895 *Serpentine Dances* offers Annabelle Moore's flowing multihued veils in imitation of colored stage lights. Méliès's twenty-minute 1904 epic *The Impossible Voyage* is meticulously hand colored frame by frame with brushes.

But precise registration was difficult. Pathé patented a stencil method of hand coloring, called *au pochoir*, in 1906. Matrixes, with the areas to be colored cut out, were placed on positive prints, then painted or dyed with the appropriate color. Multiple matrixes could be used for up to half a dozen tonalities. The Pathécolor technique permitted mass production of Pathé films, already heralded for their beautiful color.

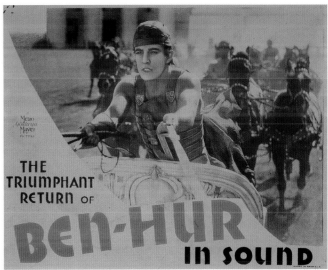

Some blockbusters from the silent era were dubbed by studios and rereleased as sound films, including *Phantom of the Opera* (1925, reissued 1929) and *Ben-Hur* (1925, reissued 1931).

Top: Filming of the Anna Case short, *La Fiesta* (1926), which was shown as a prelude to the first Vitaphone feature, *Don Juan* (1926). At right is the soundproof booth that housed the camera.

Bottom: Lobby card for *The Black Pirate* (1926) starring Douglas Fairbanks. The film was shot entirely in two-strip Technicolor.

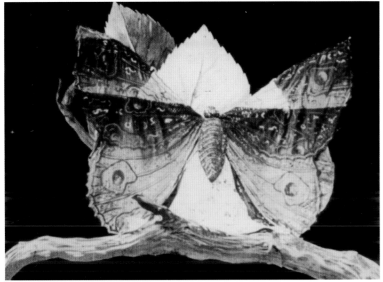

Examples of early hand tinting.

But even with stencils, hand coloring was a labor-intensive technique. More commonly, film stock would be uniformly colored. One of the earliest examples was in the 1901 British film *Fire!*, which used a red tint in a scene of a burning apartment building. Tinting involved dipping the film in colored dyes, which, according to the contemporary trade organization the Society of Motion Picture Engineers, caused "the whole picture to have a uniform veil of color on the screen." The practice of tinting films grew increasingly common, and by 1920, the society estimated that tinting was used in some 80 to 90 percent of films. In 1921, Eastman Kodak began releasing pretinted stock.

Another coloring technique, called toning, entailed replacing the silver salts in the film stock's emulsion with another colored metallic compound. In mordanting, similar to toning, the emulsion was mixed with insoluble silver salts that fixed a particular color.

The colors were used to indicate mood, location, or time of day, although there was no real systemic codification. Amber, for instance, was used for daylight, blue for night, and red for fire or passion. Sometimes a film would be shot entirely in amber, however, and smaller companies, with smaller budgets, would continue to make one- and two-reelers in black and white.

In 1906, Britain's G. A. Smith developed the first commercially successful natural-color process, Kinemacolor, with Charles Urban. It used a rotating filter with red and green sections, and the film was shot at thirty-two frames a second (twice the usual speed). When the film was projected, again at twice the normal speed, a colored image was produced. There were drawbacks, however. Each film had to be twice as long as it normally would have been to accommodate the alternating red and green frames, and producers were unhappy at the extra cost. The projector had to use a much stronger light source to penetrate the filters, and the high speed of projection stressed the filmstrip, which broke more frequently. Finally, the color range was limited, with blue and purple especially poorly rendered. Smith's three-color system was improved on in France by Gaumont in 1913 and in Germany by Agfa in 1915.

These systems are called additive synthesis — filters used for photographing and projecting films, with different colors superimposed — and required special arrangements for film showings.

The solution to "natural" color films would be subtractive synthesis, and the system that won out was two-strip Technicolor. In the mid teens, the Technicolor Motion Picture Corporation, founded by Herbert T. Kalmus, W. Burton Westcott, and Daniel Frost Comstock, developed a system of color using subtractive synthesis. It combined images from which the light of a particular

Magazine advertisement for *The Toll of the Sea* (1922), directed by Chester M. Franklin and
starring Anna May Wong, the first feature film to use two-strip Technicolor.

color had been filtered; when the images were recombined, color film resulted. This was still a two-color process, and the system went through several incarnations.

The 1922 feature *The Toll of the Sea*, directed by Chester M. Franklin and starring Anna May Wong, is the earliest surviving example of the two-color Technicolor system. A prism in the camera separated the red and green segments of the spectrum, which were recorded on alternate frames of the negative. Each print comprised two strips, dyed the correct colors and cemented together. Technically, the blue part of the color spectrum suffered, with sea and sky having a greenish cast, but the flesh colors were extraordinarily accurate for the time.

The Toll of the Sea is historically important, both for its use of color and for Wong's fine performance, the Chinese American actress's first starring role, at just seventeen. But the film itself, with a mediocre scenario by Frances Marion, is basically a retelling of *Madame Butterfly*, set in China. A *New York Times* review praised Wong's acting, noting that while remaining "completely unselfconscious of the camera . . . she makes the deserted little Lotus Flower a genuinely appealing, understandable figure." As for Marion, however, the *Times* quipped, "The only person, in fact, who seems to have anything against the picture is the title writer."

Certainly the most famous silent all-Technicolor feature was Douglas Fairbanks's swashbuckler *The Black Pirate* (1926). (Producers more frequently used Technicolor for specific scenes, as in Stroheim's 1928 *The Wedding March*, Rupert Julian's 1925 *The Phantom of the Opera*, and Niblo's 1925 *Ben-Hur.*) But two-strip Technicolor had significant problems. Exhibitors complained that the glued strips sometimes shrank, making it difficult to keep the film in focus.

Over the next few years, Technicolor developed a three-color process, which was first tested in Walt Disney's 1932 cartoon *Flowers and Trees*. The three-color process became the main color system in Hollywood features in the mid 1930s, although black and white remained predominant.

None of this, however, is intended to suggest the inherent superiority of color. Some of the most beautiful films of all time were filmed in black and white. The luminous clarity of Dreyer's sublime black-and-white feature *The Passion of Joan of Arc* will never fade from our cultural memory.

Top left: *The Viking* (1929), directed by R. William Neill, an all-color silent film.

Above: Night scenes, like this one from an unidentified Vitagraph film, were shot during the day and tinted blue.

EPILOGUE
FILM PRESERVATION AND RESTORATION

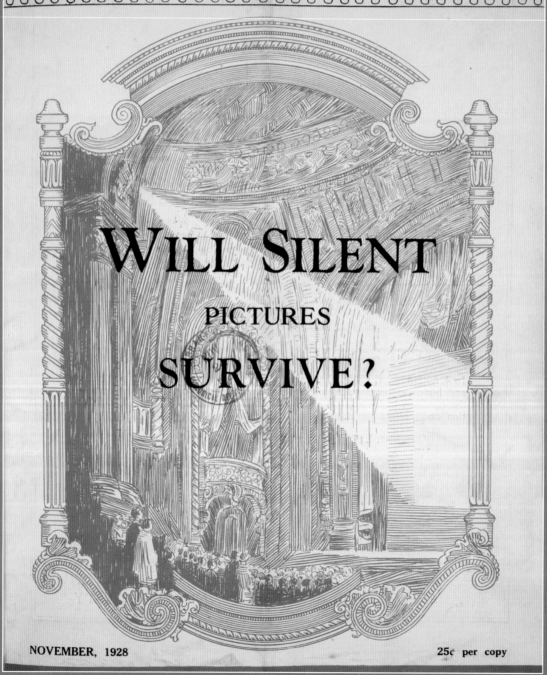

THE MOTION PICTURE

PROJECTIONIST

WILL SILENT

PICTURES

SURVIVE?

NOVEMBER, 1928

25¢ per copy

I N HIS SPOOKY, SURREALIST FILM *Decasia* (2002), BILL MORRISON USED A MONTAGE OF DECOMPOSING FILM FRAGMENTS. THE IMAGES — A WHIRLING DERVISH, CELLS DIVIDING, A CAMEL CARAVAN, A BOXER PUNCH-ING AT THE VOID — APPEAR AND DISAPPEAR INTO THE ETHER OF OBLIVION AS BUBBLES AND BLURS.

Although the nitrate cellulose filmstock fragments are mostly only fifty to sixty years old, *Decasia* has the feel of a silent film: it is in black and white, with no dialogue or voiceover, and has a modern score by Michael Gordon of the cutting-edge Bang on a Can ensemble. The film is truly gorgeous. Morrison follows in the footsteps of the Romantics, who in the early nineteenth century realized that there is a poignant beauty in decay.

But what *Decasia* represents, the gradual degradation and loss of thousands of films, is not a pretty picture. "Film is history," notes Academy Award–winning filmmaker Martin Scorsese. "With every foot of film that is lost, we lose a link to our culture, to the world around us, to each other, and to ourselves."

Film decay is rated by categories, ranging from one to five, with one and two showing some damage and three being unusable for restoration purposes. Five means the film has turned to powder. Kenneth Weissman, director of the Library of Congress Conservation Center, has seen *Decasia* and says that most of the film's shots are in category three. The fragments make an interesting film, but the restorationist's goal is to postpone films from becoming surreal blobs.

It is estimated that in world archives some thirty thousand prints of silent films survive. But because they have not been thoroughly catalogued, no one can say for certain how many are duplicates. Perhaps some 10 percent of films from the teens survive, while the survival rate of films from the twenties is probably 20 percent. Preserving what remains is crucial.

Unfortunately, preservation is also difficult. The film stock used in the silent era was cellulose nitrate, a close chemical relative of nitroglycerine that is explosive and highly flammable. Once ignited, nitrate film releases its own oxygen, increasing its combustibility. In early days, not just films were vulnerable but human lives were too. On May 4, 1897, at the Paris Charity Bazaar, 187 people were killed when a film caught fire in a Lumière projector. In 1937, an enormous explosion and fire in Little Ferry, New Jersey, destroyed most of Fox's silent films. Cellulose nitrate is also chemically unstable, and it begins — inevitably, ineluctably — to decay from the moment it is created. Controlled temperature and humidity conditions can slow its degradation, but not prevent it.

But the instability of the medium is not the only reason silent-era films have been lost. For

Above: The decaying set of *Intolerance*, 1917.

Left: The cover of the *Motion Picture Projectionist*, November 1928.

Top: A reel of damaged paper prints.

Bottom: Decomposed nitrate film.

decades the film industry saw its productions as having limited value: after their initial release, they were soon forgotten, or even destroyed for the few cents' worth of silver in the filmstrips' emulsion. Once dialogue films came along, silent films seemed irrelevant — except to be remade as sound films.

It took a long time for people to realize the importance of preserving "old" films, for all the reasons Scorsese cites above. As early as 1906, however, the trade publication *Views and Film Index* published an editorial calling for film preservation. "Are the manufacturers aware that they are making history?" it asked. Apparently not.

The situation today is greatly changed. In the United States, several institutions, among them the Library of Congress, the George Eastman House, the American Film Institute, the Museum of Modern Art, and the UCLA Film and Television Archive, are actively working to preserve our film heritage. In fact, archives such as the Svenska Filminstitutet, the British Film Institute, and the Archives du Film du Centre National de la Cinématographie strive to collect and preserve film heritage worldwide.

The Library of Congress's nitrate film collection currently is housed at the Motion Picture Conservation Center in Dayton, Ohio, which is located at the Wright-Patterson Air Force Base. The military, which had its own film-production facility, built the fireproof film vaults to hold its own collection, but allowed the Library to use them. The Library is consolidating its film holdings in a new facility in Culpepper, Virginia, and the transfer of its nitrate films is expected to be completed in 2007.

Weissman says that the Library's mandate is threefold: conservation, preservation, and restoration. The Library holds more than 100 million feet of nitrate film, from the 1890s to 1950, and they are kept under the strictest conservation conditions, at a temperature between 52 and 55 degrees Fahrenheit and at a relative humidity between 35 and 40 percent.

Preservation entails checking the nitrate film regularly for deterioration. Weissman says film cans are opened and checked for rust (decaying film gives off nitric acid, which causes rust) and smell (decomposing film gives off a "locker room" smell). If a film is deteriorating, a copy is made to safety stock. About half of the nitrate films have been copied. This is done at the center's film laboratory, whose equipment has been modified to properly copy aging and shrunken film. Wetgate, or full immersion, printers are used to help conceal the scratches and blots on old films.

Film restoration is not just hard work — it is expensive, too. Simply creating a new viewing print of a typical, black-and-white silent feature can cost more than $30,000 (it can cost far more if special restoration work is needed). Often, the restoration of a major work requires that it have significant commercial appeal to recoup the costs involved. Studios, too, have become much more conscious of the worth of their films and are more careful about preserving them.

Films kept in cans under carefully controlled climatic conditions are in a state of suspended animation, but restoration brings them back to life. It is a time-consuming process, frequently involving extensive research. Different versions, or even merely fragments, of a film may exist, parts of which may have decayed too much to be usable. Sometimes scripts, contemporary reviews, or a director's notes can be consulted.

Significant restorations in recent years have included Gance's *Napoléon*, Stroheim's *Greed*, and Lang's *Metropolis*. *Napoléon* has been restored in successively longer versions by Kevin Brownlow (whose lifelong obsession with the film began when he was fifteen). After decades of research and piecing together scenes from versions in archives around the globe, he debuted his first restoration, with Gance present, at the Telluride Film Festival in Colorado in 1979. It clocked in at about five hours. The following year, it was staged at London's Empire Theatre with a live orchestra playing Carl Davis's massive, impressive score. (In 1981, a three-and-a-half-hour version of the restoration was taken on a road show by Francis Ford Coppola's Zoetrope, scored by Coppola's father, Carmine, who also scored *The Godfather*). But if the American version was shorter, Brownlow's version became even longer. After the American Bambi Ballard discovered new footage in Corsica, Brownlow unveiled a five-and-a-half-hour version in London in 2000. Scenes are still missing and may yet be discovered. Brownlow once shrugged off his obsession by telling Elliott Stein of the *Village Voice*: "You just need a few lifetimes."

Rick Schmidlin's reconstruction of Stroheim's *Greed* debuted in 1999, using more than 650 rephotographed stills, dialogue from a continuity screenplay, new color tinting, and a new score. It is about a hundred minutes longer than the 140-minute version released in 1924 (after being cut by many hands). Schmidlin's version restores subplots entirely missing from the released version and offers a look, if through a glass darkly, at what Stroheim might have intended. The cut footage, however, is probably irretrievably lost, which is why Schmidlin modestly calls his work a reconstruction.

When Lang's science fiction epic *Metropolis* premiered in Berlin in 1927, it ran for more than two and a half hours. It was cut by 40 minutes, and then cut yet again and drastically reedited by Paramount for its U.S. release. Several versions have surfaced since then, including the ludicrous 1984 rock version scored by Giorgio Moroder, but the 2001 restoration, overseen by German film preservationist Martin Koerber, is likely to be the closest to Lang's vision for some time to come. (In the world of film restoration, it is always best to avoid the word *definitive*.)

Koerber's restoration is based on the Paramount version, a negative of which was stored in a German archive. He pieced together as much usable footage as possible, reedited the film according to the original script, and filled in still-missing sequences with written summaries. Dust and scratches were digitally removed and the original score by Gottfried Huppertz was restored. This

Unidentified film strips before (left) and after (right) restoration.

visionary spectacle can be appreciated in something very close to its former glory. It runs just over two hours.

While the Library has restored major films, such as *Mr. Smith Goes to Washington* and *The Maltese Falcon*, it also has a mission to preserve and restore so-called "orphan films" — documentaries, ethnic films, newsreels, and even home movies, often without copyright protection, that fall outside the scope of commercial preservation programs. These films can have significance because they broaden our understanding of our cultural history in important ways.

The preservation and restoration that the Library of Congress and other institutions are doing are important for several reasons. Silent films, as Scorsese says so eloquently, are part of history. Films such as *President Roosevelt's Inauguration* (1905), with scenes showing the march down Constitution Avenue in Washington, D. C., and Roosevelt being sworn in on the Capitol steps, and *Panorama of East Galveston* (1900), which depicts the devastation of the category 4 Great Galveston Hurricane just days after the storm hit, bring us as close to those events as we can possibly get.

Often, the history is unintentional, as when we see a real Tibetan Buddhist ritual in the middle of *Storm Over Asia*, or simply part of the "realism" of a fictional film (King Vidor put a camera in a fruit cart and had it pushed around the busy streets of New York for *The Crowd*). Even purely fictional films offer insights into fashions, fads, social mores, and contemporary stereotypes in a very vivid manner.

Over the three decades of silent film, we see the medium born, grow in fits and starts, and achieve an often remarkable maturity. In following film's progress — seeing various techniques discovered, used, discarded, or improved — we can gain insights into the films of today or those we grew up watching in theaters. This aesthetic knowledge makes us better able to appreciate all movies. Ingmar Bergman was influenced by Swedish silents, and viewing some of them makes us see Bergman's work in a new light. One can glimpse Soviet filmmakers' use of montage reflected in Francis Ford Coppola's *Apocalypse Now* and *The Godfather*, and knowing this expands our understanding of the American director's work. Woody Allen readily acknowledges his debt to Chaplin and Keaton.

Finally, silent films can be immensely entertaining and artistically challenging. For some, they are an acquired taste. But once one gets over the lack of spoken dialogue, silents begin to seem just like foreign films with subtitles. When one begins to explore this world, it becomes hard to imagine the film canon without the epic grandeur of *Intolerance* and *Napoléon* or the indelible comedy of *The General* and *The Gold Rush*. Of course, many of the films, just as today, were worthless, but no one knows what treasures may still be hidden in an archive somewhere. Because so much of what has survived is so extraordinary, preserving these fragile works of the past is vital.

WILLIAM FOX presents

"THE BLUE EAGLE"

A Fighting Drama of Adventure, Courage, Loyalty and Strength on the High Seas

WITH

GEORGE O'BRIEN

JANET GAYNOR · MARGARET LIVINGSTON · ROBERT EDESON · WILLIAM RUSSELL
DAVID BUTLER · RALPH SIPPERLY and "JERRY THE GIANT"
from the Story "The Lord's Referee" by Gerald Beaumont ... scenario by L.G. Rigby

JOHN FORD PRODUCTION

John Ford's *The Blue Eagle* (1926), beneficiary of the Library of Congress's restoration efforts.

Dorothy Devore in *Hold Your Breath* (1924).

ACKNOWLEDGMENTS

I would like to thank the many people at the Library of Congress who graciously permitted me to use its remarkable resources and whose hard work made this book possible. First, let me thank W. Ralph Eubanks, director of publishing, who planted the seed of this book. I am also grateful to Michael Mashon, head of the Moving Image Section of the Motion Picture, Broadcast, and Recorded Sound (MBRS) Division, who took me on my maiden voyage through the labyrinth of the Moving Image Section's collection; Patrick G. Loughney, former head of the Moving Image Section of MBRS (now curator of the Motion Picture Department at the George Eastman House), whose sage advice helped shape this book; Elena G. Millie, retired curator of Posters in the Prints and Photographs Division, who provided so many of the extraordinary images of this work; Kenneth Weissman, director of the Library's Conservation Center, who clarified the promise and difficulty of film preservation; and Charles Silver, associate curator, Department of Film and Media at the Museum of Modern Art, who made films available for viewing during the difficult period of the Museum's renovation.

Because this is such a strongly visual book, thanks go to Blaine Marshall, picture editor, who helped conceive the visual arc of the book; Brian Taves, cataloguer and film historian, whose knowledge of the Library's nooks and crannies conjured many of the images; and Christel Schmidt, writer/editor, whose creativity, knowledge, and love of silents added new depth and dimensions to the book. Writer/editor Aimee Hess was invaluable at writing and polishing text, corrections and handling style matters with aplomb. Wilson McBee, editorial assistant, shouldered a full share of text and research, tackling a new topic with energy and intelligence.

I also want to thank the indefatigable MBRS reference librarians Zoran Sinobad, Rosemary Hanes, and Josie Walters-Johnston, who called in countless requests and made it possible for me to spend many hours in the darkness of the Library's viewing room, as well as offering generous reference assistance on the most arcane of topics. Lee Ewing photographed with care and skill, and Sam Serafy did prodigious picture research. Pat Padua scanned images with alacrity and precision. Barbara Hall and Janet Lorenz at AMPAS assisted with last-minute requests for images. Film historian and biographer Robert Bichard, generous with his assistance, helped identify and confirm individual actors. The race sidebar was enriched by the guidance of Stephen Gong, Pearl Bowser, and Arthur Dong.

This book owes much to my editor at Little, Brown, Karyn Gerhard, and her extraordinary enthusiasm for silent cinema. Her careful editing of the book much improved it. Thanks and admiration also go to Little, Brown copyeditor Peggy Freudenthal. The book's designer, Roger Gorman of Reiner Design, added style to a project of scope. My agent, Martha Kaplan, worked indefatigably in support of the work. I would also like to thank Margaret Agnew for her close readings and comments.

Finally, I would like to thank Kevin Brownlow, whose perceptive insights and suggestions were exceptionally helpful.

Charlie Chaplin in *A Night in the Show* (1915).

AFTERWORD

For more than a century, motion pictures have documented American life and culture. The Library of Congress has been actively involved in preserving the history of cinema since October 6, 1893, when William Kennedy-Laurie Dickson, assistant to Thomas Edison and inventor of the Kinetoscope, recorded the first copyright registration for a commercially distributed movie. Dickson's claim marked the beginning of the film industry in America and predated by more than two years the Lumière brothers' projection of a film before a paying audience in Paris on December 24, 1895.

When Dickson filed his copyright claim, owners of motion pictures who wished to be protected from illegal duplication printed frames of their films onto paper stock and submitted the paper rolls as photographs to be copyrighted. Ever since, the Library has maintained records on every film copyrighted in America. Today, the Library of Congress makes accessible to scholars and researchers the largest collection of films in the world.

The Library of Congress leads the film archive movement in the United States and, since 1969, has undertaken more than half of all the 35mm film preservation completed in the United States. Still, there is much work to be done in the area of film preservation. In a 1993 report on the state of film preservation, I alerted the U.S. Congress that motion pictures were disintegrating faster than American archives could save them. Now, with the establishment by Congress of the National Film Preservation Foundation, the Library can continue its work to promote and ensure the preservation and public accessibility to the nation's film heritage.

Visibility of the Library's film collection goes hand in hand with our film preservation efforts. This book, *Silent Movies: The Birth of Film and the Triumph of Movie Culture*, is only one way the Library is working to increase the visibility of its film collections to the public. In addition to the film treasures introduced to you in the pages of this book, you can also visit our Motion Picture, Broadcasting, and Recorded Sound reading room on Capitol Hill to explore them in greater depth or view some of our preserved film collections at http://www.loc.gov/rr/mopic. However you visit and explore our motion picture collections, I hope you will come to value this priceless legacy as much as I do.

James H. Billington
The Librarian of Congress

Pitfalls of a Big City (1919).

BIBLIOGRAPHY

Abel, Richard. *French Cinema: The First Wave, 1915–1929*. Princeton, NJ: Princeton University Press, 1984.

Anderson, Gillian B. *Music for Silent Films 1894–1929: A Guide*. Washington: Library of Congress, 1988.

Anger, Kenneth. *Hollywood Babylon*. New York: Dell, 1975.

Auster, Paul. *The Book of Illusions*. New York: Henry Holt, 2002.

Baldwin, Neil. *Edison: Inventing the Century*. New York: Hyperion, 1995.

Barsacq, Léon. *Caligari's Cabinet and Other Grand Illusions: A History of Set Design*. Boston: New York Graphic Society, 1976.

Barson, Richard Meran. *Nonfiction Film: A Critical History*. New York: E. P. Dutton, 1973.

Baxter, John. *King Vidor*. New York: Monarch Press, 1976.

Bitzer, Billy. *Billy Bitzer: His Story*. New York: Farrar, Straus and Giroux, 1973.

Bordwell, David, and Kristin Thompson. *Film Art*. New York: Knopf, 1979.

Bowser, Eileen. *History of the American Cinema. Volume 2, The Transformation of Cinema: 1907–1915*, Berkeley: University of California Press, 1990.

Bowser, Pearl, and Louise Spence. *Writing Himself into History: Oscar Micheaux, His Silent Films, and His Audience*. New Brunswick, NJ: Rutgers University Press, 2000.

Broman, Sven. *Conversations with Greta Garbo*. New York: Viking, 1991.

Brown, Karl. *Adventures with D. W. Griffith*. New York: Farrar, Straus and Giroux, 1973.

Brownlow, Kevin. *Behind the Mask of Innocence*. New York: Knopf, 1990.

———. *Hollywood — The Pioneers*. New York: Knopf, 1979.

———. *Napoléon*. New York: Knopf, 1983.

———. *The Parade's Gone By...* New York: Knopf, 1968.

Card, James. *Seductive Cinema: The Art of Silent Film*. Minneapolis: University of Minnesota Press, 1999.

Clarens, Carlos. *An Illustrated History of Horror and Science-Fiction Films*. New York: Da Capo Press, 1997.

Dickson, William Kennedy-Laurie. *History of the Kinetograph, Kinetoscope, and Kinetophonograph*. New York: Arno Press, 1970.

Doctorow, E. L. *Ragtime*. New York: Random House, 1975.

Durgnat, Raymond, and Scott Simmon. *King Vidor, American*. Berkeley: University of California Press, 1988.

Eisner, Lotte H. *The Haunted Screen: Expressionism in the German Cinema and the Influence of Max Reinhardt*. Berkeley: University of Caifornia Press, 1973.

Engberg, Marguerite. *Asta Nielsen: Europe's First Film Star*. Berkeley: University of California Press, 1996.

Everson, William K. *American Silent Film*. New York: Da Capo Press, 1998.

———. *The Hollywood Western: 90 Years of Cowboys and Indians, Train Robbers, Sheriffs and Gunslingers, and Assorted Heroes and Desperados*. Secaucus, NJ: Carol Publishing Group, 1992.

Film Comment, special issue. "Designed for Film: The Hollywood Art Director," May/June 1978.

Fitzgerald, F. Scott. *The Jazz Age*. New York: New Directions Bibelot, 1996.

Gabler, Neal. *An Empire of Their Own: How the Jews Invented Hollywood*. New York: Anchor Books, 1988.

Grant, Barry Keith, ed. *Fritz Lang: Interviews*. Jackson: University Press of Mississippi, 2003.

Grieveson, Lee, and Peter Krämer, eds. *The Silent Cinema Reader*. London: Routledge, 2004.

Gunning, Tom. *The Films of Fritz Lang: Allegories of Vision and Modernity*. London: BFI Publishing, 2000.

Hendricks, Gordon. *The Edison Motion Picture Myth*. Berkeley: University of California Press, 1961.

Higham, Charles. *Cecil B. DeMille*. New York: Da Capo Press, 1980.

———. *Hollywood Cameramen: Sources of Light*. New York: Garland Publishing, 1986.

Kauffman, Stanley, ed. With Bruce Henstell. *American Film Criticism: From the Beginnings to Citizen Kane*. New York: Liveright, 1972.

Keaton, Buster, and Charles Samuels. *My Wonderful World of Slapstick*. New York: Da Capo Press, 1982.

Kerr, Walter. *The Silent Clowns*. New York: Knopf, 1975.

King, Emily. *A Century of Movie Posters: From Silent to Art House*. Hauppauge, NY: Barron's, 2003.

Klepper, Robert K. *Silent Films, 1877–1996: A Critical Guide to 646 Movies*. Jefferson, NC: McFarland, 1999.

Koszarski, Richard. *History of the American Cinema. Vol. 3, An Evening's Entertainment: The Age of the Silent Feature Picture 1915–1928*. Berkeley: University of California Press, 1990.

———. *The Man You Loved to Hate: Erich von Stroheim and Hollywood*. New York: Oxford University Press, 1983.

Kracauer, Siegfried. *From Caligari to Hitler: A Psychological History of the German Film*. Princeton, NJ: Princeton University Press, 1947.

Leyda, Jay. *Kino: A History of the Russian and Soviet Film*. London: Allen and Unwin, 1983.

MacCann, Richard Dyer, ed. *The Silent Comedians*. Metuchen, NJ: Scarecrow Press, 1993.

Mannoni, Laurent. *The Great Art of Light and Shadow: Archaeology of the Cinema*. Exeter, UK: University of Exeter Press, 2001.

McGillan, Patrick. *Fritz Lang: The Nature of the Beast*. New York: St. Martin's Press, 1997.

Miller, Nathan. *New World Coming: The 1920s and the Making of Modern America*. New York: Scribner, 2003.

Milton, Joyce. *Tramp: The Life of Charlie Chaplin*. New York: Harper Collins, 1996.

Moews, Daniel. *Keaton: The Silent Features Close Up*. Berkeley: University of California Press, 1979.

Musser, Charles. *History of the American Cinema. Vol. 1, The Emergence of Cinema: The American Screen to 1907*. Berkeley: University of California Press, 1990.

The National Film Preservation Foundation. Annette Melville, director. *The Film Preservation Guide: The Basics for Archives, Libraries, and Museums*. San Francisco, 2003.

Niver, Kemp R. *Early Motion Pictures: The Paper Print Collection in the Library of Congress*. Washington: Library of Congress, 1985.

Nowell-Smith, Geoffrey, ed. *The Oxford History of World Cinema*. New York: Oxford University Press, 1996.

Phillips, Ray. *Edison's Kinetoscope and Its Films: A History to 1896*. Westport, CT: Greenwood Press, 1997.

Pratt, George C. *Spellbound in Darkness: A History of Silent Film*. Greenwich, CT: New York Graphic Society, 1973.

Rainey, Buck. *The Strong, Silent Type: Over 100 Screen Cowboys, 1903–1930*. Jefferson, NC: McFarland, 2004.

Ramsaye, Terry. *A Million and One Nights: A History of the Motion Picture Through 1925*. New York: Simon & Schuster, 1926.

Rebello, Stephen, and Richard Allen. *Reel Art: Great Posters from the Golden Age of the Silver Screen*. New York: Abbeville Press, 1989.

Robinson, David. *From Peep Show to Palace: The Birth of American Film*. New York: Columbia University Press, 1996.

Rotha, Paul. *The Film Till Now: A Survey of World Cinema*. New York: Funk & Wagnalls, [1949].

Schapiro, Steve, and David Chierichetti. *The Movie Poster Book*. New York: Dutton, 1979.

Schickel, Richard. *D. W. Griffith: An American Life*. New York: Simon & Schuster, 1984.

Sklar, Robert. *Film: An International History of the Medium*. New York: Abrams, 1993.

Slide, Anthony. *Early American Cinema*. Metuchen, NJ: Scarecrow Press, 1994.

———. *Lois Weber: The Director Who Lost Her Way in History*. Westport, CT: Greenwood Press, 1996.

———. *Nitrate Won't Wait: A History of Film Preservation in the United States*. Jefferson, NC: McFarland, 2000.

———. *Silent Players*. Lexington: University Press of Kentucky, 2002.

Solnit, Rebecca. *River of Shadows: Eadweard Muybridge and the Technological Wild West*. New York: Viking Penguin, 2003.

Thompson, David. *The New Biographical Dictionary of Film*. New York: Knopf, 2003.

Usai, Paolo Cherchi. *Silent Cinema: An Introduction*. London: British Film Institute, 2000.

Wagenknecht, Edward. *The Movies in the Age of Innocence*. New York: Ballantine Books, 1971.

VIDEO

Brownlow, Kevin, and David Gill, directors and producers. Michael Winterbottom, writer. *Cinema Europe: The Other Hollywood*. Image Entertainment, 1999.

Feldman, Gene, and Suzette Winter, writers and producers. *Hollywood's Children*. Brighton Video, 1982.

Koszarski, Richard, writer, Patrick Montgomery, director. *The Man You Loved to Hate*, documentary. Killiam Films, 1979. Kino Video.

INDEX

PHOTO CREDITS AND PERMISSIONS

The following list provides the reproduction numbers for color and black-and-white copies of the objects reproduced in this book. Each entry contains page number, location on page (if necessary), Library of Congress custodial division, and reproduction number(s). Color transparencies are indicated by the prefix LC-USZC4 or LC-USZC2; all other reproduction numbers (e.g., LC-USZ62-XXXX, LC-DIG-ggbain-XXXX) indicate black-and-white negatives. Copies of color transparencies and black-and-white prints can be ordered directly from the Library of Congress Photoduplication Service, 101 Independence Avenue SE, Washington, DC 20540-4570 (tel. 202-707-5640). If a reproduction number is not listed, the division or institution cited should be contacted for further instructions on how to obtain a copy. The Library's general telephone number is 202-707-5000.

Abbreviations for Library of Congress Custodial Divisions

P&P   Prints and Photographs Division
MBRS   Motion Picture, Broadcasting & Recorded Sound Division
LC   General Collections
NP   Newspapers & Current Periodicals

Abbreviations for Other Institutions

NYPL   New York Public Library
LAPL   Los Angeles Public Library
AMPAS   Academy of Motion Picture Arts and Sciences
BAM/PFA   University of California, Berkeley Art Museum & Pacific Film Archive

Front Matter

Front spread: P&P, PPMSC-03510. Table of contents: MBRS. Dedication: MBRS. Foreword: MBRS. Introduction: MBRS.

Chapter 1: From Magic Lantern to Moving Pictures

xvi: P&P, LC-USZC4-1102. 1-4: MBRS. 5: P&P, LC-USZ62-103043. 6: P&P, LC-USZ62-73528. 7: MBRS. 8: MBRS. 9: P&P. 10-11: MBRS.

Chapter 2: The Early Years 1893-1914

12: MBRS. 13: top P&P, LC-USZ62-44602; bottom MBRS. 14: top P&P, LC-USZ62-102696; bottom P&P, LC-DIG-ppmsca-05119. 15-16: MBRS. 17: top P&P, LC-USZ61-707; bottom P&P, LC-USZ61-725. 18: MBRS. 19: top MBRS; bottom P&P, LC-USZ62-64311. 20-21: MBRS. 22: P&P, LC-USZ62-77875. 23: P&P, LC-USZ62-87447. 24: MBRS. 25: top MBRS; bottom P&P, LC-USZC4-13516, LC-USZC4-13517, LC-USZC4-13518. 26: top left P&P,

LC-USZC4-1376; top right LC-USZC4-1593; bottom right LC-USZC4-13515. 27: top left P&P, LC-USZC4-13506; top right P&P, LC-USZC4-13511; bottom left P&P, LC-USZC4-13514; bottom right LC-USZC4-13508. 28-30: MBRS. 31: P&P, LC-DIG-ppmsc-03704. 32: MBRS. 33: P&P, PPMSC-03509. 34-37: MBRS.

Chapter 3: The Business of Film

38-39: top MBRS; bottom P&P, LC-USZ62-65711. 40: top MBRS; bottom P&P, LC-DIG-ppmsca-05539. 41: MBRS. 42: top MBRS; bottom MBRS. 43: top MBRS; bottom MBRS. 44: top MBRS; bottom MBRS. 45: MBRS. 46: P&P. 47: MBRS. 48: left MBRS; right MBRS. 49: top MBRS; bottom P&P, LC-USZ62-63393. 50-53: MBRS.

Chapter 4: Genres

54-56: MBRS. 57: P&P LC-USZC4-6636. 58: MBRS. 59: MBRS. 60: top left MBRS; top right MBRS; bottom MBRS. 61: MBRS. 62: top left MBRS; bottom left P&P LC-DIG-ggbain-23327; bottom right, above MBRS; bottom right, below MBRS. 63: top left MBRS; bottom left MBRS; top right MBRS; middle right MBRS; bottom right MBRS. 64: P&P, LC-USZC4-2730. 65: P&P LC-USZ62-66512. 66: MBRS. 67: top P&P. 68-72: MBRS. 73: top left P&P, LC-USZ62-104085; top right MBRS; bottom MBRS. 75: MBRS. 76: top MBRS; bottom left MBRS; bottom right AMPAS. 77-84: MBRS. 85: top P&P, LC-DIG-ppmsc-02839; bottom left MBRS; bottom right MBRS. 86-91: MBRS.

Chapter 5: The Art of Film

92: P&P, LC-USZ62-60081. 93-94: MBRS. 95: P&P, LC-USZ62-99386. 96: P&P, LC-DIG-ppmsc-03692. 97-99: MBRS. 100: top P&P; bottom MBRS. 101-6: MBRS. 107: top MBRS; bottom P&P, LC-DIG-ppmsca-02979. 108: BAM/PFA. 109: MBRS.

Chapter 6: The Stars

110: MBRS. 111: P&P, LC-USZ62-113150. 112-16: MBRS. 117: top P&P, LC-USZC4-13370; bottom MBRS. 118-21: MBRS. 122: top P&P, LC-USZC4-13370; bottom MBRS. 123-28: MBRS. 129: P&P, LC-USZC4-13380. 130-35: MBRS. 136: P&P, LC-DIG-ggbain-31073. 137: top MBRS; bottom P&P, LC-G432-1989. 138: top P&P, LC-USZ62-58028; bottom P&P, LC-USZC4-8145. 139: P&P, LC-DIG-ggbain-38047. 140-43: MBRS. 144: top P&P, LC-DIG-ggbain-32041; bottom MBRS. 145-49: MBRS.

Chapter 7: Promotion and the Press

150: P&P, LC-USZC4-6807. 151-55: MBRS. 156: top left P&P, LC-USZC4-13382; top right P&P, LC-USZC4-13387;

bottom MBRS. 157: P&P, LC-USZC4-13504. 158: P&P, LC-USZC4-13509. 159: top left P&P, LC-USZC4-3067; top right LC-USZC4-13519, LC-USZC4-13520; bottom left P&P, LC-USZC4-6614; bottom right P&P, LC-USZC4-9406. 160: P&P, LC-USZC4-13503. 161: P&P, LC-USZC4-1684. 162-77: MBRS.

Chapter 8: The Directors

178: P&P, LC-USZ62-115719. 179-84: MBRS. 186: P&P, LC-USZ62-98062. 187: LC. 188: left P&P, LC-USZC4-1946; top right MBRS; center NYPL; bottom MBRS. 189: top left MBRS; center left LAPL; bottom left MBRS. 190: top MBRS; bottom NP. 191: NP. 192: MBRS. 193: P&P, LC-USZC4-13379. 194-202: MBRS. 203: P&P, LC-USZC4-13507. 204-9: MBRS. 210: AMPAS.

Chapter 10: Sound and Color

258-64: MBRS. 265: P&P, LC-USZC4-13513. 266-68: MBRS. 269: top MBRS; bottom P&P, LC-USZC4-13383. 270: top MBRS; bottom P&P, LC-USZC4-9471. 271-73: MBRS.

Epilogue: Film Preservation and Restoration

274-78: MBRS. 279: P&P, LC-USZC4-7234. 281: MBRS.

Back Matter

All MBRS.

Special Credits/Permissions

Every good-faith effort has been made to contact the copyright holders for the films and photographs in this book.

63: bottom left courtesy Hallmark Entertainment/RHI Entertainment.

68: top right © courtesy Paramount Pictures.

71: bottom © courtesy AB Svensk Filmindustri.

73: bottom © Turner Entertainment Co. A Warner Bros. Entertainment Company. All Rights Reserved.

76: bottom right courtesy of the Academy of Motion Picture Arts and Sciences; top right © Turner Entertainment Co. A Warner Bros. Entertainment Company. All Rights Reserved.

82: bottom left *Les vampires,* a film by Louis Feuillade. Production Gaumont. 1915; bottom right *Fantômas,* a film by Louis Feuillade. Production Gaumont 1913.

83: top *Tih-Minh,* a film by Louis Feuillade. Production Gaumont. 1918.

85: bottom left courtesy Walter Calmette, Felix the Cat Creations, Inc.

86: courtesy Modern Sound Pictures.

87: © Turner Entertainment Co. A Warner Bros. Entertainment Company. All Rights Reserved.

88: © Turner Entertainment Co. and Warner Bros. Entertainment Inc. All Rights Reserved.

90: bottom courtesy ADAGP—Paris.

91: bottom courtesy ADAGP—Paris; top courtesy Jean-Michel Mareau.

92: courtesy Marie-Hélène Méliès.

101: © courtesy Paramount Pictures.

102: bottom © courtesy Paramount Pictures.

104: bottom © Turner Entertainment Co. A Warner Bros. Entertainment Company. All Rights Reserved.

105: bottom left © Turner Entertainment Co. A Warner Bros. Entertainment Company. All Rights Reserved.

106: © courtesy Paramount Pictures.

108: courtesy University of California, Berkeley, and Pacific Film Archive.

109: courtesy Twentieth Century Fox Film Corporation.

117: top © Turner Entertainment Co. and Warner Bros. Entertainment Inc. All Rights Reserved.

118: bottom © courtesy Paramount Pictures.

121: top © courtesy Paramount Pictures; bottom courtesy Twentieth Century Fox Film Corporation.

125: © Turner Entertainment Co. A Warner Bros. Entertainment Company. All Rights Reserved.

126: top courtesy Twentieth Century Fox Film Corporation.

127: bottom left © Turner Entertainment Co. A Warner Bros. Entertainment Company. All Rights Reserved; bottom right © Turner Entertainment Co. A Warner Bros. Entertainment Company. All Rights Reserved.

133: top © Turner Entertainment Co. A Warner Bros. Entertainment Company. All Rights Reserved; bottom © Turner Entertainment Co. and Warner Bros. Entertainment Inc. All Rights Reserved.

134: courtesy Pathe.

135: bottom © courtesy Paramount Pictures.

141: top © Turner Entertainment Co. and Warner Bros. Entertainment Inc. All Rights Reserved.

142: © courtesy Paramount Pictures.

143: top courtesy The Douris Corporation—Raymond Rohauer Film Collection.

147: bottom courtesy The Douris Corporation—Raymond Rohauer Film Collection.

148: courtesy Universal Studios.

163: bottom right © Turner Entertainment Co. and Warner Bros. Entertainment Inc. All Rights Reserved.

168: bottom left © Turner Entertainment Co. A Warner Bros. Entertainment Company. All Rights Reserved.

173: © Turner Entertainment Co. A Warner Bros. Entertainment Company. All Rights Reserved.

174: bottom left, bottom right © courtesy Paramount Pictures.

175: top © Turner Entertainment Co. and Warner Bros. Entertainment Inc. All Rights Reserved.

176: top left © Turner Entertainment Co. and Warner Bros. Entertainment Inc. All Rights Reserved; bottom right © Turner Entertainment Co. A Warner Bros. Entertainment Company. All Rights Reserved; bottom left courtesy Universal Studios.

177: © Turner Entertainment Co. A Warner Bros. Entertainment Company. All Rights Reserved.

188: right center courtesy New York Public Library.

189: top right courtesy Arthur Dong's *Hollywood Chinese* documentary; center left *Herald Examiner* Collection, Los Angeles Public Library. Courtesy Arthur Dong's *Hollywood Chinese* documentary.

205: top © Turner Entertainment Co. A Warner Bros. Entertainment Company. All Rights Reserved; bottom © Turner Entertainment Co. A Warner Bros. Entertainment Company. All Rights Reserved.

206: top © courtesy Paramount Pictures.

207: © courtesy Paramount Pictures.

208: © Turner Entertainment Co. A Warner Bros. Entertainment Company. All Rights Reserved.

209: © Turner Entertainment Co. A Warner Bros. Entertainment Company. All Rights Reserved.

210: courtesy the Academy of Motion Picture Arts and Sciences; © Turner Entertainment Co. A Warner Bros. Entertainment Company. All Rights Reserved.

211: © Turner Entertainment Co. A Warner Bros. Entertainment Company. All Rights Reserved.

214: © courtesy AB Svensk Filmindustri.

215: © courtesy Paramount Pictures.

216: © courtesy AB Svensk Filmindustri.

217: top *La passion de Jeanne d'Arc,* a film by Carl Theodor Dreyer. Production Gaumont. 1928; bottom courtesy Nordisk Film International.

233: *Salammbo,* a film by Pierre Marodon. Production Gaumont. 1925.

234: courtesy Pathe.

235: courtesy Pathe.

236: courtesy Pathe.

238: courtesy Pathe.

250: © Turner Entertainment Co. and Warner Bros. Entertainment Inc. All Rights Reserved.

251: © courtesy Paramount Pictures.

252: © Turner Entertainment Co. and Warner Bros. Entertainment Inc. All Rights Reserved.

254: © Turner Entertainment Co. A Warner Bros. Entertainment Company. All Rights Reserved.

255: © Turner Entertainment Co. A Warner Bros. Entertainment Company. All Rights Reserved.

256: © Turner Entertainment Co. A Warner Bros. Entertainment Company. All Rights Reserved.

257: © Turner Entertainment Co. A Warner Bros. Entertainment Company. All Rights Reserved.

260: © Turner Entertainment Co. A Warner Bros. Entertainment Company. All Rights Reserved.

265: © Turner Entertainment Co. and Warner Bros. Entertainment Inc. All Rights Reserved.

266: left © Turner Entertainment Co. A Warner Bros. Entertainment Company. All Rights Reserved; right © Turner Entertainment Co. A Warner Bros. Entertainment Company. All Rights Reserved.

269: bottom © Turner Entertainment Co. A Warner Bros. Entertainment Company. All Rights Reserved.

270: top © Turner Entertainment Co. and Warner Bros. Entertainment Inc. All Rights Reserved.

273: left © Turner Entertainment Co. A Warner Bros. Entertainment Company. All Rights Reserved.

Little, Brown and Company
Hachette Book Group
237 Park Avenue, New York, NY 10017
Visit our Web site at www.HachetteBookGroup.com

First Edition: November 2007

Little, Brown and Company is a division of Hachette Book Group, Inc. The Little, Brown name and logo are trademarks of Hachette Book Group, Inc.

For the Library of Congress:
W. Ralph Eubanks, Director of Publishing; Blaine Marshall, picture editor; additional picture editing by Christel Schmidt; Lee Ewing, photographer; editorial assistance by Aimee Hess and Wilson McBee

Library of Congress Cataloging-in-Publication Data

Kobel, Peter.
  Silent movies : the birth of film and the triumph of movie culture / Peter Kobel ; foreword by Martin Scorsese ; introduction by Kevin Brownlow. – 1st ed.
      p. cm.
  Includes bibliographical references and index.
  0-316-11791-9/978-0-316-11791-3
  1. Silent films–History and criticism. I. Title.
  PN1995.75.K63 2006
  791.4309–dc22   2006027367

10 9 8 7 6 5 4 3 2

Design by Roger Gorman, Reiner Design NYC

Printed in China